The Charitable
Tax Exemption

The Charitable
Tax Exemption

John D. Colombo
and Mark A. Hall

Westview Press
BOULDER • SAN FRANCISCO • OXFORD

Copyright © 1995 by Westview Press, Inc.

Published in 1995 in the United States of America by Westview Press, Inc., 5500 Central Avenue, Boulder, Colorado 80301-2877, and in the United Kingdom by Westview Press, 12 Hid's Copse Road, Cumnor Hill, Oxford OX2 9JJ

A CIP catalog record is available for this book from the Library of Congress.
ISBN 0-8133-1832-7

Printed and bound in the United States of America

The paper used in this publication meets the requirements of the American National Standard for Permanence of Paper for Printed Library Materials Z39.48-1984.

10   9   8   7   6   5   4   3   2   1

For Dad, who devoted his life to making the tax system work a little better

J.D.C.

For my mother, whose charitable spirit inspires me

M.A.H.

Contents

Preface

For over 400 years, western societies have exempted nonprofit entities from taxation because of their "charitable" status. In the United States, this exempt sector of the economy is vast and growing rapidly. Over one-tenth of all private organizations in the United States (and up to one-third in some locations) pay no federal or state income, property and sales taxes, resulting in federal, state and local governments foregoing tens of billions of dollars of revenue each year. Despite the size and significance of the charitable tax exemption, modern scholars, legislators and regulators have no comprehensive and convincing explanation of what purpose the exemption serves or even of what constitutes a "charity." Accordingly, this book attempts to answer the twin questions, "why are charities tax-exempt?" and "what is a charity for this purpose?"

We explore these interrelated questions through a systematic legal, economic and public policy critique of the existing theories for exempting charitable organizations from taxation. In the first chapter, we sketch the history and scope of the charitable exemption and the tax-exempt sector of the economy, and we specify the four criteria that we employ in our analysis of the exemption. In the next chapter, after outlining the legal framework for exemption, we examine the fundamental theoretical dispute over whether exemption is in effect an indirect government subsidy to the exempt entity. In the following chapters we turn to a detailed critique of the traditional explanations of the charitable exemption: (1) that certain categories of activity are per se exempt based on the law of charitable trusts; (2) that the exemption serves as a quid pro quo for providing free services to the poor or relieving other government burdens; and (3) that the exemption is in exchange for the benefits that nonprofit institutions provide to the community at large. Chapter 6 then addresses two additional theories for the exemption advanced by academics: Professor Hansmann's capital subsidy theory, which demonstrates why it is defensible to use the exemption to help certain nonprofit firms to overcome their comparative disadvantage in accessing capital markets; and Professor Atkinson's implicit altruism theory, which argues that the mere formation of a nonprofit enterprise is a socially valued decision.

Finding these explanations deficient under our four criteria for evaluation, we develop in Chapters 7 through 11 the donative theory of the charitable exemption. We begin in Chapter 7 by articulating the classic economic and political explanation for the existence of donations and why this explanation supports a social subsidy that amplifies the effect of private philanthropy. We then apply this explanation in Chapter 8 to variant cases that do not meet the theoretical paradigm, demonstrating that this descriptive and normative theory can be broadly generalized to virtually any act of giving, however motivated. We also clarify what counts as a true gift and why the mere formation of a nonprofit institution is not an altruistic act deserving of a social subsidy. We complete our theoretical development of the donative theory by critiquing it in Chapter 9 under various systems of moral theory and then by evaluating it in Chapter 10 under the same criteria we apply to other theories.

In Chapter 11 we provide a detailed explanation of how the donative theory should be implemented in real world settings. We explain how the proper donative threshold should be set, how donations should be measured, and how to correct for fundraising abuse and for excess political activity. In the final chapter, we examine a number of classic types of charitable institutions to illustrate how the donative theory would affect each. Our aim is to offer a fully articulated account of what institutions are charities and why they deserve a tax subsidy in terms that are capable of easy administration and immediate implementation, at either the state or federal levels.

We began this work five years ago with an inquiry into the rationale for hospital tax exemption, thinking that we would find the general justification for charitable exemption to be well established and that our primary task would be to apply this settled theory to the situation existing in the health care sector. We were surprised and challenged to discover early on that the very foundations of charitable status were much in question and that the pending challenges to hospital tax exemption were symptomatic of difficulties facing virtually all types of charitable institutions. This realization inspired us to focus our attention on the foundational issues in order to solve the intellectual and public policy issues confronting hospitals. This early work, which forms the basis for most of Chapters 3 through 6, was published as Mark A. Hall & John D. Colombo, *The Charitable Status of Nonprofit Hospitals: Toward a Donative Theory of Tax Exemption*, 66 WASH. L. REV. 307 (1991). A second article examining the theoretical aspects of the exemption was published as Mark A. Hall & John D.

Colombo, *The Donative Theory of the Charitable Tax Exemption*, 52 OHIO ST. L.J. 1379 (1991). The portion of Chapter 12 dealing with educational institutions is drawn from John D. Colombo, *Why Is Harvard Tax Exempt? (And Other Mysteries of Tax Exemption for Private Educational Institutions)*, 35 ARIZ. L. REV. 841 (1993). We appreciate these journals for granting permission to incorporate these works in this fuller treatment.

Our odyssey into the land of tax exemption would not have been nearly so enjoyable and thorough if it had not been for the support and encouragement of numerous individuals, most notably, Professor Harvey Dale at New York University. Although we were at the time young academics and completely new to the field, he lent his astute ear to our interests, provided valuable resources and contacts and, most importantly, gave us a sense of our intended audience. For all of this, we are eternally grateful. We also owe a large debt of gratitude to our colleagues Rob Atkinson, Steve Bainbridge, Ira Ellman, Mark Gergen, Jeff Murphy, Jim Pfander, Steve Ross, Tom Ulen and the Arizona State University Moral, Political and Economic Theory Workshop members for their insightful guidance, demanding critiques and stimulating conversations about these issues. We are also grateful to the Vermont Law School for its hospitality over several summers. Last (but far from least), we thank Tina Colombo for taking time away from chasing after two young children to serve as our copy editor and "test lay person" and Christine McKimson and Julie Simpson for their tireless, prompt and thorough research assistance.

John D. Colombo
Mark A. Hall

PART ONE

Conventional Theories of Exemption

1

The Charitable Tax Exemption: An Introduction

The Structure and Significance of Exempt Status

The History and Rationale of the Charitable Exemption

Exempting charities from various forms of taxation is a practice that appears as old as western civilization itself. In the words of one scholar, "real property taxation, and exemption therefrom, seems to be about as old as history. . . . One historian reports that the 'economic equilibrium of the state was endangered' by the fact that the tax exempt temples owned fifteen percent of the cultivable land and vast amounts of slaves and other personal property during the reign of Ramses III about 1200 B.C."[1] Ezra 7:24 commands that "it shall not be lawful to impose toll, tribute, or custom upon . . . priests . . . or ministers of the house of God," and Genesis 47:24 declares that "Joseph made it a law over the land of Egypt unto this day, that Pharaoh should have the fifth part; except the land of the priests only, which became not Pharaoh's." England has had a charitable exemption in its income tax law since it was enacted in 1799 and reintroduced in 1842.[2] In the United States, federal tax law has relieved charitable organizations from income tax since the law's inception in 1894.[3] And, in both countries, charities have enjoyed exemption from state and local property taxes for centuries longer.[4]

The universal character of the charitable exemption extends internationally. A survey of ten other countries, both eastern and western (Austria, Belgium, Hungary, Israel, Italy, Spain, Taiwan, Thailand, United Kingdom, and West Germany) found that all conferred an exemption from corporate income tax and from some form of ad valorem taxation on nonprofit entities that we would classify as charitable, although the particular listings and descriptions varied.[5]

The long history of the charitable exemption has made it a virtually immutable part of the tax laws—so much so that the thought of taxing charitable organizations on the same basis as profit-making enterprises seems contrary to nature. As early as the nineteenth century, the custom of exempting education, religion, and care of the poor was "so grounded in the nature of our Government as to represent a practically irrevocable law."[6] Even those most critical of the exemption suggest its repeal in only the most tentative tones, preferring a reformulation instead.[7]

Given this universal status and ancient lineage, it is extraordinary that no generally accepted rationale exists for the charitable tax exemption. In searching for a coherent theoretical or public policy rationale in modern times, various commentators have conceded: "despite th[e] long history of the tax [laws], or perhaps because of this long history, there is very little logic, or reason, or legislative history to support . . . the tax exemption";[8] "the statutory phrases 'exclusively used for charitable purposes' [and] 'purely public charity' seem to mean less than nothing";[9] "we do not have any careful and comprehensive rationale for the scope and operation of the tax exemption. We do not have any satisfactory theory, legal or economic, to apply in making judgments about it";[10] "a comprehensive review of the standards and the rationale for tax exemption has never been undertaken";[11] and "think[ing] more seriously about what is meant by the concept of charity [is] a task that is about four hundred years overdue."[12]

Scholars have a murky idea of the basis for the exemption in prior ages, but these historical rationales no longer remain relevant. In ancient Egypt, Greece and Rome, temples and other religious institutions were not taxed because it was thought they were owned by the gods themselves and were thus beyond the reach of mortal taxing authorities. In medieval England, churches, monasteries and the like were not taxed, at first because in feudal times there was no centralized government capable of imposing such a tax; indeed, the churches themselves were a sort of taxing authority, collecting tithes from feudal lords. This power distribution changed dramatically later in England's history when churches were not only taxed but confiscated as part of the suppression of clerical power during the Reformation. The charitable exemption survived during this time by expanding its reach to secular charities as a way of further undermining the church's influence.

In the American colonies, the initial pattern was much more haphazard. Systems of taxation were inconsistent and incomplete because these new-formed governments lacked uniform methods for identifying taxable property or even an annual tax collection system.[13] Exemptions arose simply by virtue of these incomplete systems of taxation and therefore carried no rationale. As taxation become more systematized, exemptions typically were incorporated in corporate charters on an ad hoc basis, as a matter of legislative grace. The primary example of a uniform exemption in colonial America was for orthodox churches, which were not taxed because the colonies were established as theocracies and no government taxes itself. The religious exemption continued in the states even after the constitutional adoption of the separation principle, largely for reasons of historical Anglo-American tradition. Thus, it was expanded to cover education and other secular charitable purposes in early state statutes and often in state constitutions, because that was the pattern that prevailed in England at the time. The present form of charitable exemption in state property law is essentially unchanged from this time, when its political rationales disappeared.[14]

At the federal level, tax exemption was simply not an issue until the passage of the first income tax act in 1894. Prior to this, federal revenues came mostly from import duties and excise taxes, which did not affect the charitable organizations of that time. The first federal income tax law adopted in 1894, however, contained a broad exemption for "corporations, companies or associations organized and conducted solely for charitable, religious or educational purposes."[15] The legislative history is largely silent regarding the origins of this provision. It appears to have been completely uncontroversial, and not debated. As a result, most commentators have concluded that the federal exemption merely recognized the universality of the exemption at the state and local level, as well as the fact that a tax on profits should not include "nonprofit" organizations.[16] This recognition was then incorporated into subsequent tax acts: while the 1894 law was declared unconstitutional in 1895, every subsequent federal income tax law has contained a similar exemption.

In summary, the charitable exemption arose in earlier centuries as a consequence of the prevailing patterns of taxation. Classic charities such as churches were not taxed because they did not fit within the existing tax bases, not out of any sense of explicit social policy justification. As the structure of taxing systems evolved, however, the categories of non-taxed activities were retained, despite the change in rationale. As a consequence, we are left with a pattern of exemption defined largely by history and accident. The absence of a coherent rationale founded on the structure of our modern taxing systems gave rise to a subsidy theory of the exemption, one that generalizes the exemption as an attempt to help those entities that "do good" for society. This subsidy rationale differs sharply from the earlier tax-based theories in that it attempts a normative justification for excusing certain entities otherwise subject to tax from contributing their social share, whereas the earlier tax-base theories are a largely descriptive exercise of explaining why certain entities or activities do not fall within the prevailing system of taxation. In Chapter 2, we elaborate further on this distinction.

Turning briefly to the modern subsidy rationale, while our society superficially agrees that certain "good activities" are entitled to tax exemption, this superficial agreement masks considerable confusion over precisely what good activities qualify as charitable and why they are deserving of tax exemption. Part of the problem is the vast array of activities to which the exemption has been applied. While one intuitively thinks of classic charitable entities as those serving the poor or distressed, such as the Salvation Army or the Red Cross, in fact charitable exemption status extends to entities that have little to do with the poor—for example, symphony societies, opera houses, museums and any number of private schools and universities. Moreover, even those exempt entities that we might classify as unquestionably "doing good" are often replicated to a degree by nonexempt entities that perform the same functions. Health care, for example, is an area in which exempt and nonexempt institutions exist side-by-side in the same market in the form of nonprofit and for-profit hospitals, which provide virtually identical services to paying customers.[17] Likewise, while no one denies that the greatest research universities in the United States are nonprofit exempt organizations, there is certainly no lack of for-profit educational institutions, either.[18] The same is true in virtually all other sectors of exempt activity: while we know of no officially for-profit churches, certainly the music industry is dominated by for-profit record companies and recording groups existing alongside exempt opera companies and symphony societies; for-profit art galleries ply their wares amidst nonprofit museums, and exempt scientific organizations report on the research work done at Intel or Motorola.

This generality and nonspecificity of the modern subsidy theory, which society has adopted by default as a result of the disappearance of earlier political and tax-base rationales, forms the central problem of this book. In order for the charitable exemption to have a firm social and theoretical foundation, and in order to provide some guidance for its administration, it is necessary to search for the particular concept of "doing good" that makes sense of the actual universe of charitable activities that has been handed down through history, and that makes sense of why a subsidy should be administered through a tax exemption rather than more directly. To explain why this is an important undertaking, we next describe the vast scope of the exempt sector.

The Size of the Exempt Sector

Why should one care about the theory underlying exempt charitable organizations? The answer, in a word, is money. To that one, we might add power and influence, as well. The exempt sector as a whole (of which charitable organizations are a subset) is very large and growing rapidly. Burton Weisbrod notes that nonprofits "engage in hundreds of distinct activities; they are growing at the rate of thousands per year; they employ millions of workers; and they have hundreds of billions of dollars of annual revenues and assets."[19] The number of categories of federally exempt activities has grown from 90 to 260 since 1965.[20] Correspondingly, the number of federally exempt entities has nearly tripled over the last 25 years: at the end of 1993, there were 1,440,265 exempt organizations.[21] Alfred Balk summarizes without exaggeration that our society provides "cradle-to-grave" exemptions: "by careful planning, one now can live much of his life on tax-exempt property . . . [starting] with birth in a tax-exempt hospital, followed by baptism in an untaxed church and education in tax-immune public schools. . . . [H]e then could be interred in a tax-exempt cemetery beneath a gravestone that had been displayed in and engraved at a tax-exempt showroom."[22]

According to 1990 data, nonprofit organizations controlled property, cash and investments worth some *$850 billion*, not including churches and smaller nonprofit groups that do not have to report such holdings.[23] If one factors in churches, the figure likely exceeds $1 *trillion*. Recent estimates are that 10 percent of all private property in the United States is tax-exempt; if one includes government property, as much as one-third of all property in the country is exempt.[24] Revenues and expenditures are equally staggering. Nonprofits garnered some $400 billion in revenues in 1989, and expended some $327 billion.[25] In some local areas, the expenditures of charitable organizations actually exceed those of local government. Lester Salamon reports that one study of Baltimore, Maryland found that nonprofit expenditures in the Baltimore metropolitan area exceeded the total expenditures of the city of Baltimore and the five surrounding counties.[26]

Organizations exempt because of their *charitable* status constitute by far the largest component of the private exempt sector. Charitable organizations, numbering 540,000 as of December 1993, represent over one third of all federally exempt entities; in 1990, these entities (excluding churches, which do not report such data to the IRS) had revenues of $425 billion, assets of over $700 billion, and expenditures of over $390 billion.[27]

Exempting this vast array of property, sales, and income from taxation entails a considerable social cost. The value of the charitable exemption is impossible to measure exactly because tax assessors do not generally bother to value precisely exempt property. However, most commentators agree that "the tax benefits granted to charities and other exempt organizations by the United States are almost unique in their generosity."[28] As described in the next chapter, the exemption consists of federal and state components, it covers income, property, and sales tax, and it carries with it numerous ancillary benefits such as eligibility to receive tax-deductible donations, qualification to issue tax-exempt bonds, and reduced postage rates. It is possible to suggest the amount of money at stake by measuring some of these various components, both generally and by industry. For the charitable *deduction* alone, the federal budget estimates that for fiscal 1995, the government will lose $19 billion[29] of revenues, while the exemption from tax on interest paid on exempt bonds issued by charitable organizations will cost the federal government another $2 billion.[30] In the case of exempt hospitals, the figure that has the widest currency places the value of the exemption at $8.5 billion a year.[31] This number represents the sum of the following estimates: federal income tax, $1.6 billion; tax-exempt bonds, $1.7 billion; deductible charitable contributions, $1.2 billion (total federal, $4.5 billion); state and local income tax, $0.4 billion; property tax, $1.2 billion; sales tax, $2.4 billion (total state and local, $4.0 billion).[32]

Re-examining the Exemption

Given the dollars involved, it is not surprising that federal and state governments hard-pressed to balance strained budgets cast roving eyes at exempt organizations. Many communities have begun asking for voluntary payments to reimburse the community for lost tax revenues.[33] In addition, taxing authorities at both levels have become ever more aggressive in challenging the exempt status of a variety of organizations, including adoption agencies,[34] private schools,[35] arts organizations and nursing homes.[37]

Recent challenges to hospitals' tax exemption provide the most visible manifestation of these issues in recent years. The Utah Supreme Court shook the voluntary hospital sector to its core in 1985 by becoming the first court in modern times to revoke a hospital's exemption for its failure to provide a sufficient level of charity care.[38] Since then, local taxing authorities in at least four other states have challenged hospitals' exempt status,[39] and legislative re-examinations are pending or have occurred recently in over a dozen others.[40] Most recently, Congress has considered legislation that would entirely revamp the justification for the federal income tax exemption enjoyed by hospitals.[41] Given this legal and political foment, it is particularly timely to revisit from the ground up the foundation for exempting all charitable organizations. The erosion of the social and political rationale for the exemption has left a conceptual construct that is weak enough to topple under only modest pressure.

The rationale for charitable tax exemption also holds considerable intellectual challenge. The academic field of nonprofit enterprise has flowered during the past decade and a half as researchers from various disciplines began to recognize that this "third sector" of the economy (distinct from proprietary markets and government) has been neglected as a separate topic of serious inquiry. These pathbreaking scholars have made impressive progress toward explaining why nonprofit organizations exist, what their central characteristics are, and how they should be regulated.[42] These studies, however, have not satisfactorily explained why federal, state, and local governments exempt these organizations from paying various taxes.

This book undertakes to fill this analytical void by re-examining the theoretical reasons for tax exemption. In this undertaking, we will apply four explicit evaluative criteria to each existing theory of exemption. In our view, a successful theory of exemption should (1) identify activities deserving social subsidy, which entails a determination of both worth and need; (2) distribute the subsidy in rough proportion to the degree of deservedness; (3) explain both the income tax and the property tax exemption, and, ideally, explain the related charitable deduction as well as the various operational constraints that attach to charitable status; and (4) align generally with an intuitive concept of what constitutes a charity and the major historical categories of exempt entities.[43] We do not naively assert that each of these criteria must be fully satisfied before a theory of the exemption can be considered valid. Rather, we posit these as ideals against which to measure competing theories, in order to judge which is superior.[44]

Deservedness

Following the prevailing view that the charitable exemption constitutes an implicit government subsidy of the activities it covers (a point that is made more thoroughly in Chapter 2), the exemption is justified only where there is a convincing showing that the activity in question deserves such a subsidy. There are two elements to deservedness: *worth* and *need*. At a minimum, exemption requires some reliable indication of which activities out of the vast array of human endeavors are socially worthy of government subsidization. But worth alone is not sufficient without need. An organization may be willing to continue its meritorious pursuits absent a subsidy. If so, a subsidy is a waste of scarce government resources that could be devoted to other, more productive causes. Even if the level of service provided by the nonprofit sector would diminish without the exemption, the exemption is not necessary unless neither the proprietary sector nor the government is capable of providing the same social benefits as efficiently. Ideally, therefore, the definition of charity should identify activities whose social benefits would be irreplaceably reduced absent the subsidy.

Proportionality

In addition to guarding against subsidization of activities that are unworthy or that simply do not need support, an ideal concept of charity in the tax exemption arena should guard against oversubsidizing (or under-subsidizing) those activities that are deserving. In other words, a proper concept of charity should at least roughly match the level of support to the level of deservedness. In fact, most theories for the exemption bestow tax relief in such an arbitrary manner that "it would be sheer coincidence if the value of the tax exemption were to match the . . . actual needs for the service,"[45] or, more perversely, in a fashion that gives the greatest tax break to the least deserving.

Another way to capture the substance of the proportionality criterion is to ask whether it makes sense to administer a deserving subsidy implicitly through a tax exemption rather than through direct funding mechanisms. It is not enough to demonstrate that charitable institutions deserve government support; it is necessary to show that a particular *tax* subsidy represents the most sensible vehicle for support, that some form of direct grant might not more accurately approximate the optimal level of support, or that direct government provision of the same service is not preferable.

A political cynic might contend that it is hopeless to formulate such a theory of charitable exemption because this perfect proportionality criterion is too demanding of the flawed legislative process. Instead, legislators should be free to apply "charity" as nothing more than an empty label on whatever activity they desire to subsidize, for reasons of political expediency, through the tax system rather than through direct appropriations. One might also take issue with this criterion less cynically by maintaining that the exemption is frequently the only way that deserving organizations can obtain government support because legislators fear the voter approbation that attends direct funding. These arguments are unconvincing for the following reasons.

First, the fact that political expediency might describe political reality at some level should not deter the formulation of a more principled application of the exemption. Idealism aside, such cynical characterizations of the charitable exemption are largely inaccurate. Legislators rarely determine charitable status; the decision generally rests with taxing authorities. Even if politicians were to make this choice, they might choose to fund the worthwhile activity in a direct fashion if a coherent theory of the exemption foreclosed a tax subsidy as an option. Where the legislature declines to subsidize the activity, and an unprincipled application of the exemption is the only available option, perhaps the activity does not deserve support. A tax subsidy is considered politically expedient precisely because it disguises a spending decision from the legislators' political constituency.[46] If an informed constituency objects to the expenditure, then the propriety of any form of subsidy is questionable. Witness, for instance, the pork barrel politics that transpired during the Tax Reform Act of 1986.[47] Finally, we repeat that we do not impose these evaluation criteria in any absolute sense but only as comparative guides to test the relative performance of competing theories of exemption. Therefore, although we might agree that the politically pragmatic use of the charitable exemption is permissible, we also maintain that it is preferrable to search for an explanation of the charitable concept that is more principled.

Universality

The criterion of universality derives from the fact that the charitable exemption is structured as a unitary, coordinated system composed of a host of benefits and burdens that flow automatically from the determination of charitable status. Charitable organizations at once qualify for exemptions from both local property taxes and federal corporate income tax; these "501(c)(3) organizations" under federal law are also eligible under Code § 170 to receive contributions that are deductible in computing the donor's personal income tax. Charitable status usually results in exemption from state and local income and sales tax as well. On the burden side of the equation, the charitable exemption imposes certain limitations on an organization's structure and on its scope of operation. It must be truly nonprofit, so that no earnings inure to the benefit of a private individual, and it may not engage in substantial political lobbying or in any political campaigning.[48] Moreover, the exemption does not extend to earnings derived from activities unrelated to its exempt purpose, even if those earnings ultimately support the exempt purpose.[49] A coherent concept of charity or theory of exemption should offer a coordinated explanation for as many of these tax benefits and operational burdens as is possible.

Professor Harvey Dale disagrees with this universality criterion. Quoting the aphoristic wisdom of H.L. Mencken that "[f]or every complex problem, there is a solution which is simple, elegant, . . . and wrong," he maintains that the exemption is a creature of history, not logic, and advocates a case-by-case approach to applying the exemption that allows it to grow haphazardly like a coral reef.[50] Therefore, he opines "no single rationale can or should be expected to explain or justify tax-exempt status. The not-for-profit sector of our society is complex and varied; its lineage is ancient. It would be unreasonably simplistic to expect to capture its essence or justification within the compass of any theory."[51]

This theoretical agnosticism may be convincing in assessing the universe of exempt organizations, as legislators award peripheral exemptions for a variety of reasons unrelated to the charitable concept (for example, to attract new industrial growth or to enforce some social policy, such as exempting pension funds so that the earnings can compound tax-free, providing additional retirement income that will be taxed at retirement). Dale's perspective, however, cannot suffice for the core *charitable* exemption. This nucleus of the exempt sector employs a structure purporting to define the scope of its benefits through the single concept of charity. Therefore, it demands a coherent, organizing rationale. This is not the case, necessarily, for the myriad other types of exemption given to non-charitable entities. Under the federal income tax exemption paradigm, these would be entities exempt under parts of § 501 of the I.R.C. other than § 501(c)(3), such as business leagues, clubs, fraternal organizations, homeowners' associations, pension funds and others. We largely agree with Professor Dale that these other categories of exemption arise from disparate and unrelated considerations. We do not argue that extending the exemption in this fashion is wrong; only that, when exemptions are granted for other or ad hoc reasons, they cannot be thought of or justified as belonging to the core of "charitable" exemptions. Similarly, it is possible that each limitation connected with the charitable exemption, such as the prohibition on lobbying, can be sustained as a side constraint on the exemption, one whose justification is independent of its core rationale. However, all these limitations are generally thought to derive from the general concept of charity as that term has been developed through centuries of judicial decisions in the field of charitable trusts.

Denying that the charitable concept has any definitional content means that "charitable" is applied as a completely open-textured term to activities that are considered deserving of an exemption for a multitude of undisclosed policy reasons. In order to avoid this unprincipled state of affairs, we must search for a cohesive concept of what constitutes a charity and why it should be exempt. If no such unifying rationale for the charitable exemption exists, it should be abandoned and replaced by a structure that forthrightly acknowledges whatever the charitable label is masking.

Historical Consistency

A satisfactory theory of the charitable exemption should also be historically consistent with the major categories of exempt activities. It is not our naive ambition either to repudiate the charitable exemption or to reformulate it to fit some overly fine sense of intellectual aesthetics. Because the concept of charity explicitly refers to over 400 years of legal precedent, it would constitute an abandonment, not an explanation, of the charitable exemption to construct a theory that is oblivious to this history. Therefore, a successful explanation should encompass the major historical categories of religion, education, and social welfare. Ideally, it should also comport with at least a general, unstudied sense of why the exemption exists and what it attempts to do. In short, the theory should be intuitively convincing.

We do not maintain that these exact four criteria are either essential to or exhaustive of an informed analysis of the charitable exemption. Rather, we articulate them as our chosen criteria so that we can be as clear as possible at the outset about our normative framework—both for our critique of conventional and academic theories of the exemption and for our construction and refinement of the donative theory. Before undertaking this analysis, however, it is necessary in the next chapter to lay some additional groundwork by outlining the sources of law that define charitable status and by justifying our selection of a subsidy theory over a tax-base theory.

Notes

1. Carroll H. Sierk, *State Tax Exemptions of Non-Profit Organizations,* 19 CLEV. ST. L. REV. 281, 282 (1970).

2. MICHAEL R. CHESTERMAN, CHARITIES, TRUSTS AND SOCIAL WELFARE 58–59 (1979). Interestingly, however, English law does not totally exempt charities from taxes. Charities are required to pay local property taxes, albeit at reduced rates.

3. The Revenue Act of 1894, ch. 349, § 32, 28 Stat. 556 (1894). The complete history of the federal charitable exemption is traced in many sources, including Kenneth Liles & Cynthia Blum, *Development of the Federal Tax Treatment of*

Charities, 39 LAW & CONTEMP. PROBS. 6 (AUTUMN 1975); William R. Ginsberg, *The Real Property Tax Exemption of Nonprofit Organizations: A Perspective,* 53 TEMPLE L.Q. 291 (1980); John P. Persons et al., *Criteria for Exemption Under Section 501(c)(3),* 1909, 1924–25 (4 U.S. DEPT. OF TREASURY, RESEARCH PAPERS SPONSORED BY THE COMMISSION ON PRIVATE PHILANTHROPY AND PUBLIC NEEDS 1977) [hereinafter FILER COMMISSION PAPERS].

4. *See generally* JENS JENSEN, PROPERTY TAXATION IN THE UNITED STATES (1931); Chauncey Belknap, *The Federal Income Tax Exemption of Charitable Organizations: Its History and Underlying Policy,* in FILER COMMISSION PAPERS *supra* note 3 at 2028–29 (1977); Ginsberg, supra note 3, at 291; Persons et al., *supra* note 3, at 1923; Carroll H. Sierk, *State Tax Exemptions of Non-Profit Organizations,* 19 CLEVE. ST. L. REV. 281, 282 (1970); Alvin G. Warren, et al., *Property Tax Exemptions for Charitable, Educational, Religious and Governmental Institutions in Connecticut,* 4 CONN. L. REV. 181, 184–89 (1970).

5. BURTON A. WEISBROD, TAX POLICY TOWARD NONPROFIT ORGANIZATIONS: AN ELEVEN COUNTRY SURVEY (Aug. 1990).

6. Belknap, *supra* note 4, at 2029–30.

7. ALFRED BALK, THE FREE LIST 128 (1970). Only a few scholars have advocated or suggested the outright repeal of the exemption. *See* Robert T. Bennett, *Real Property Tax Exemptions of Non-Profit Organizations,* 16 CLEV.-MAR. L. REV. 150, 166 (1967) ("[A] solution would appear to be the abolition of all non-governmental property tax exemptions, completely."); Robert C. Clark, *Does the Nonprofit Form Fit the Hospital Industry,* 93 HARV. L. REV. 1417, 1476 (1980) (suggesting repealing property tax exemption for hospitals); Claude W. Stimson, The *Exemption of Property from Taxation in the United States,* 18 MINN. L. REV. 411, 416-18 (1934).

8. *Unrelated Business Income Tax: Hearings Before the Subcomm. on Oversight of the House Comm. on Ways and Means.,* 100th Cong., 1st Sess. 11 (1987) [hereinafter *UBIT Hearings*] (statement of O. Donaldson Chapoton, Deputy Assistant Secretary, U.S. Department of the Treasury).

9. Comment, *Judicial Restoration of the General Property Tax Base,* 44 YALE L.J. 1075, 1087 (1935).

10. *See UBIT Hearings, supra* note 8, at 1864–65 (statement of Prof. Harvey P. Dale, N.Y.U. School of Law).

11. *Id.* at 37 (Statement of Deputy Assistant Secretary of the Treasury O. Donaldson Chapoton).

12. Henry B. Hansmann, *The Two Independent Sectors, A Paper Presented at the Independent Sector Spring Research Forum* 5 (Mar. 17, 1988) (on file with the authors).

13. *See generally,* Stephen Diamond, *Of Budgets and Benevolence: Philanthropic Tax Exemptions in Nineteenth Century America* 7–9, in RATIONALES FOR FEDERAL INCOME TAX EXEMPTION (collection of papers for the 1991 NYU Conference on Philanthropy and the Law); Persons et al., *supra* note 3, at 1924; Kenneth Liles & Cynthia Blum, *Development of the Federal Tax Treatment of*

Charities, 39 LAW & CONTEMP. PROBS. 6 (Autumn 1975).

14. *See generally* BALK, *supra* note 7, at 23–27; Belknap, *supra* note 4, at 2027–28; Persons et al., *supra* note 3, at 1914, 1923; Stimson, *supra* note 7, at 416–18.

15. Revenue Act of 1894, ch. 349, §32, 28 Stat. 556 (1894).

16. Belknap, *supra* note 4, at 2031; Persons et al., *supra* note 3, at 1924.

17. *See* Mark A. Hall & John D. Colombo, *The Charitable Status of Nonprofit Hospitals: Toward a Donative Theory of Tax Exemption*, 66 WASH. L. REV. 307, 374–377 (1990) (extensive discussion of empirical studies of for-profit vs. nonprofit hospitals).

18. John D. Colombo, *Why Is Harvard Tax Exempt? (And Other Mysteries of Tax Exemption for Private Educational Institutions)*, 35 ARIZ. L. REV. 841, 863 (1993).

19. WEISBROD, *supra* note 5, at 62.

20. U.S. GENERAL ACCOUNTING OFFICE, TAX POLICY: COMPETITION BETWEEN TAXABLE BUSINESSES AND TAX-EXEMPT ORGANIZATIONS, BRIEFING REPORT TO THE JOINT COMM. ON TAXATION 14 (Feb. 1987) [hereinafter GAO, TAX POLICY].

21. REFORMS TO IMPROVE THE TAX RULES GOVERNING PUBLIC CHARITIES, A REPORT BY THE SUBCOMMITTEE ON OVERSIGHT OF THE HOUSE COMMITTEE ON WAYS AND MEANS, (May 5, 1994), *reprinted in* 9 EXEMPT ORG. TAX REV. 1219, 1220 (1994) (hereafter, PUBLIC CHARITIES REPORT).

22. BALK, *supra* note 7, at 5–6.

23. GILBERT M. GAUL & NEILL A. BOROWSKI, FREE RIDE: THE TAX-EXEMPT ECONOMY 3 (1993).

24. BALK, *supra* note 7, at 11–12; L. Richard Gabler & John F. Shannon, *The Exemption of Religious, Educational and Charitable Institutions from Property Taxation*, in FILER COMMISSION PAPERS, *supra* note 3, at 2535.

25. VIRGINIA A. HODGKINSON ET AL., NONPROFIT ALMANAC 1992–1993, Table 4.2 at page 147 (1992).

26. LESTER M. SALAMON, AMERICA'S NONPROFIT SECTOR: A PRIMER 25 (1992).

27. HODGKINSON ET AL., *supra* note 25, at 145, Table 4.1.

28. Steven Stone, *Federal Tax Support of Charities and Other Exempt Organizations: The Need for a National Policy*, 20 U.S. CAL. L. CENTER TAX INST. 27, 30–31 n.11 (1968).

29. BUDGET OF THE UNITED STATES GOVERNMENT, ANALYTICAL PERSPECTIVES, Fiscal Year 1995, 77.

30. *Id.* at 66. (This figure is the sum of the cost of the exclusion of interest on state and local debt for private nonprofit educational facilities and the exclusion of interest on state and local debt for private nonprofit health facilities.)

31. John Copeland & Gabriel Rudney, *Federal Tax Subsidies for Not-For-Profit Hospitals*, MARCH 1990 TAX NOTES 1559, 1565.

32. *See also* David Falcone & David Warren, *The Shadow Price of Pluralism: The Use of Tax Expenditures to Subsidize Hospital Care in the United States*, 13 J. HEALTH POL., POL'Y & L. 735, 740–52 (1988) (by a rough, liberal estimate, the

hospital exemption costs $3 billion a year in income and property tax, $1.8 billion of this in federal income tax); Bernard S. Friedman et al., *Tax Exemption and Community Benefits of Not-For-Profit Hospitals,* in 11 ADVANCES IN HEALTH ECONOMICS AND HEALTH SERVICES RESEARCH (1990) 131, 136–38 (value of exemption in 1983–1985 estimated between $4.7 and $7.3 billion).

33. *See infra,* Chapter 2, n.35.

34. *E.g.,* Easter House v. United States, 12 Cl. Ct. 476 (1987).

35. *E.g.,* Prince Edward School Foundation v. Comm'r, 478 F.Supp. 107 (1979).

36. *E.g.,* James Conley, *Tax Court: Arts Groups Are Not 'Literary and Charitable Institutions,'* 9 EXEMPT ORG. TAX REV. 962 (detailing Oregon tax court decision holding that organization sponsoring live theater is not charitable).

37. *E.g.,* St. Margaret Seneca Place v. Board of Property Assessment, 145 Pa.Cmwlth. 615, 604 A.2d 1119 (1992); Intercare Health Systems, Inc. v. Cedar Grove Tp., 11 N.J. Tax 423 (Tax Ct. 1990). The New Jersey decision recently was overruled by new legislation granting exemption in New Jersey to nonprofit nursing homes. Charles M. Costenbader, *Nonprofit Nursing Homes Exempt From Property Taxes,* 8 EXEMPT ORG. TAX REV. 826 (1993).

38. Utah County v. Intermountain Health Care, Inc., 709 P.2d 265 (Utah 1985).

39. However, the courts reversed in each instance. Callaway Community Hosp. Ass'n v. Craighead, 759 S.W.2d 253 (Mo. App. 1988); St. Luke's Hosp. v. Board of Assessment Appeals, No. 88-C-2691 (Pa. C.P., Lehigh Co., Apr. 19, 1990); Downtown Hosp. Ass'n v. Tennessee State Bd. of Equalization, 760 S.W.2d 954 (Tenn. App. 1988); Medical Center Hosp. v. City of Burlington, 152 Vt. 611, 566 A.2d 1352 (1989).

40. *See generally* Therese Hudson, *Not-For-Profit Hospitals Fight Tax-Exempt Challenges,* HOSPITALS, Oct. 20, 1990, at 32–37; Howard Larkin, *Financial Success May Invite Local Tax Scrutiny,* HOSPITALS, Oct. 5, 1988, at 30 (discussing challenges pending in at least 20 state courts or legislatures); Shannon Pear, *Tax Exemptions of Nonprofit Hospitals Scrutinized,* N.Y. TIMES, Dec. 18, 1990, at A1, col. 2, B17, col. 5 ("Local officials have tried to revoke tax exemptions from nonprofit hospitals in at least 12 states."); Michele Robinson, *Via Donation or Tax, Cities Want More Revenues,* HOSPITALS, Mar. 20, 1989, at 55 (same); the Pennsylvania Independent Regulatory Commission approved a regulation that codified the Pennsylvania Supreme Court's opinion in Hospital Utilizing Project v. Commonwealth 507 Pa. 1, 487 A.2d 1306 (1985) which defined the criteria for charitable exemption, 23 Pa. Bull. 5989 (December 18, 1993).

41. In 1990-91, two bills were introduced in the House of Representatives that would have revamped exemption standards for hospitals. H.R. 709, 102d Cong., 1st Sess. (1991) (bill introduced by Rep. Edward R. Roybal); H.R. 1374, 102d Cong., 1st. Sess. (1991) (bill introduced by Rep. Brian Donnelly). Neither bill was enacted, and both sponsors retired at the end of their terms. Adam Clymer, *Citing Rise in Frustration, Dozens of Lawmakers Quit,* N.Y. TIMES, April 5, 1992 at 1. In 1994, the issue of tax exemption for hospitals and other health care providers again bubbled to the forefront of politics as part of the health care reform debate. *See* John

D. Colombo, *Health Care Reform and Federal Tax Exemption: Rethinking the Issues,* 29 WAKE FOR. L. REV. 215, 264–71 (1994) (discussing and critiquing the tax exemption provisions of President Clinton's health care reform proposals, H.R. 3600, 103d Cong., 1st Sess. (1993)). See also, Philip S. Neal and Suzanne M. Papiewski, *Taxation of HMOs Now and Under Health Care Reform - Separating Fact From Fiction,* 9 EXEMPT ORG. TAX REV. 577 (1994) (criticizing the provisions of President Clinton's health care reform bill relating to tax exempt status for HMO's).

42. The leading discussions include JAMES DOUGLAS, WHY CHARITY? THE CASE FOR A THIRD SECTOR (1983); THE ECONOMICS OF NONPROFIT INSTITUTIONS (Susan Rose-Ackerman ed., 1986); WEISBROD, *supra* note 5; Ira Mark Ellman, *Another Theory of Nonprofit Corporations,* 80 MICH. L. REV. 999 (1982); Henry B. Hansmann, *The Role of Nonprofit Enterprise,* 89 YALE L.J. 835 (1980). *See generally* RICHARD GASSLER, THE ECONOMICS OF NONPROFIT ENTERPRISE (1986); ESTELLE JAMES & SUSAN ROSE-ACKERMAN, THE NONPROFIT ENTERPRISE IN MARKET ECONOMICS (1986); THE NONPROFIT SECTOR: A RESEARCH HANDBOOK (Walter Powell ed., 1987); William Yoder, *Economic Theories of For-Profit and Not-for-Profit Organizations,* in INSTITUTE OF MEDICINE, FOR PROFIT ENTERPRISE IN HEALTH CARE 19 (Bradford H. Gray ed., 1986).

43. Some of these criteria have been suggested previously in JENSEN, *supra* note 4, at 148 and STANLEY S. SURREY & PAUL R. MCDANIEL, TAX EXPENDITURES 72–83 (1985).

44. We have been criticized in the past for the arbitrariness of this listing. Why four? Why not five or three? Why these four and not others? These criticism are misdirected. What we are attempting to do here is concisely categorize all the criteria that might be considered relevant or significant in critiquing an explanation for the exemption. If some of these criteria are irrelevant, or if there are others we have left out that do not fit within our terminological framework, our critics should point out these flaws and we will then be pleased to alter our comparative analysis. The point of this exercise, then, is not to sell exactly these four criteria, but to engage in some comparative evaluation of competing theories of the exemption, and to be explicit about what criteria one uses to compare them and why.

45. L. Richard Gabler & John F. Shannon, *The Exemption of Religious, Educational, and Charitable Institution from Property Taxation,* in FILER COMMISSION PAPERS, *supra* note 3, at 2535, 2544.

46. SURREY & MCDANIEL, *supra* note 43, at 104. Not all commentators agree, of course. *See, e.g.,* our discussion of Professor Zelinsky's views in Chapter 2.

47. JEFFREY H. BIRNBAUM & ALAN S. MURRAY, SHOWDOWN AT GUCCI GULCH 146–47 (1987).

48. For a discussion of the general limitations on exempt status, see Chapter 2.

49. I.R.C. § 511–14 (1988) (the unrelated business income tax, or UBIT). For a further discussion of the UBIT, see Chapter 8.

50. *UBIT Hearings, supra* note 8, at 1860, 1864 (statement of Harvey P. Dale, Professor of Law and Director, Study on Law and Philanthropy, N.Y.U. School of Law).

51. Harvey P. Dale, *Rationales for Tax Exemption* 1 (Feb. 1, 1988) (unpublished manuscript available through author).

2

The Legal and Theoretical Foundations
of Charitable Tax Exemption

Legal Foundations

Sources of Law

The most visible source of law for the charitable exemption is § 501(c)(3) of the Internal Revenue Code (I.R.C. or Code), which exempts from income taxes nonprofit "[c]orporations . . . organized and operated exclusively for religious, charitable, scientific, . . . literary, or educational purposes."[1] Despite what seems a fairly specific list, this language in fact encompasses a vast array of nonprofit activities. Specific items in the list are broadly interpreted: "educational" activities, for example, include not just traditional schools, but also museums, zoos, planetariums, symphony orchestras, wild bird sanctuaries, jazz festivals, counseling groups, discussion forums and even professional seminars for bankers and lawyers.[2]

Perhaps more important, however, is that courts and commentators generally agree that this statutory language is a nonexclusive listing of common activities that are considered charitable.[3] Thus, "charitable" organizations are not distinct from "religious, scientific, literary, or educational" ones, nor are they limited to these categories. The specifically enumerated activities are presumptively eligible for exemption (as long as they meet certain organizational and operational requirements) by virtue of this legislative declaration of their charitable status, but the exemption also extends to other, nonenumerated organizations such as hospitals that pursue purposes the law considers charitable. By combining these various activities into a unified concept of exemption, this statutory formulation conveniently allows us to examine the universe of § 501(c)(3) organizations under the single term "charitable," which we will do throughout this text.

While § 501(c)(3) is be the dominant source of law, it may be less important in terms of practical impact than various state exemption laws. Federal *income tax* exemption does not greatly affect many charities because they often lack any net income to tax; but virtually all charities own property subject to state property taxation. States control exemption through separate state statutes and constitutional provisions that apply to three different main taxing systems of their own: the income tax, the property tax and the sales tax. These state statutes and constitutional provisions tend to follow a pattern nearly identical to I.R.C. § 501(c)(3). Many states, for example, automatically confer income tax exemption on any organization that carries a federal § 501(c)(3) exemption, or they use language that is virtually identical.[4] Property tax exemptions exist by virtue of independent state law provisions,[5] but these too are worded in a strikingly similar fashion to § 501(c)(3): the predominant pattern confers the exemption on religious, educational and charitable organizations.[6] Similarly, most states exempt religious, educational and charitable organizations from paying sales taxes on their purchases, although states generally do not exempt such organizations from collecting sales taxes on their retail sales.[7]

Another reason for the importance of the § 501(c)(3) definition is the fact that this same language is used in other areas of the Code to confer additional tax benefits on charitable organizations. By far the most prominent of these is I.R.C. § 170, which defines that group of entities eligible to receive tax-deductible donations with almost exactly the same language as used in § 501(c)(3).[8] In addition, the exemption test under § 501(c)(3) defines what entities are entitled to issue tax-exempt bonds under I.R.C. § 145, and similar language controls what entities are entitled to the special reduced postal rates for exempt organizations.[9] Thus the charitable concept controls not only all categories of exempt activites, but also all dimensions of exempt benefits, for a broad array of exempt organizations.

Nevertheless, there are important components of the exempt universe that § 501(c)(3) fails to capture. Related to, but distinct from, this provision is § 501(c)(4), which exempts "social welfare organizations." These entities have quasi-charitable status; they engage in public service but they fail to qualify under one of the limitations discussed below. Therefore, they are denied some of the ancillary benefits of charitable exemption, such as eligibility to receive tax-deductible donations and to issue tax-exempt bond financing.

I.R.C. § 501 also lists a whole host of organizations that are exempt for reasons entirely unrelated to charitable status. Examples include governmental entities, which are not taxed under the theory that it makes no sense for governments to tax themselves nor, reciprocally, for one government to tax another. Another example is mutual benefit organizations such as fraternities and clubs, which are exempt from federal income taxation (although usually not from state property taxation), not because they are charitable, but because the pooling of members' dues does not constitute the generation of new income but only the shared use of wealth already taxed. In addition, governments often grant exemptions to for-profit entities on a purely ad hoc basis in order to attract new jobs and promote economic development. In general, we will not discuss the theoretical grounds for exempting these organizations. As explained in Chapter 1, our goal is to understand the core of the exempt universe contained in § 501(c)(3) and its related state law—that is, those entities that are exempt because they are considered *charitable*.

Limitations on Charitable Status

In addition to defining the kinds of activities eligible for charitable exemption, § 501(c)(3) also creates a set of limitations on charitable status. After listing the exempt categories, the statute cautions that these entities are exempt only if "no part of the net earnings of which inures to the benefit of any private shareholder or individual, no substantial part of the activities of which is carrying on propaganda, or otherwise attempting, to influence legislation . . . and which does not participate in, or intervene in . . . any political campaign on behalf of (or in opposition to) any candidate for public office." Thus this statutory language contains two main limitations on exempt status. First, a charitable entity must be true to its nonprofit status and so must not be guilty of "private inurement," which generally refers to siphoning off the economic benefits of exemption to "insiders" such as managers or directors. Second, the entity may not engage in certain kinds of political activity.

In addition to these limitations listed in § 501(c)(3), the common law of charities generally has imposed a third limitation: a charitable organization may not engage in activities contrary to a clearly established public policy. The U.S. Supreme Court, for example, has used this latter limitation to uphold the IRS's revocation of exempt status for racially discriminatory schools.[10] Finally, since 1950 federal income tax law has created a fourth limitation in the form of the Unrelated Business Income Tax (UBIT), which imposes income tax on trade or business activities of exempt organizations that are "unrelated" to their charitable purposes.[11]

Once again, states generally follow the federal scheme, although the limits are more often expressed in judicial opinions than in statutes. Thus state common law generally adopts the view that an entity is not charitable if it engages in private inurement, excess political activity, or violates established public policy.[12] States may have their own statutory form of UBIT for income tax purposes, and in the property tax arena a sort of UBIT concept arises in the requirements of many states that only property used "primarily" for charitable purposes is exempt.[13]

Although these basic sources of law show remarkable congruence on the scope of the charitable exemption, they create two difficulties in comprehending the theoretical and public policy basis for the exemption. The first is the need to explain why such a diverse array of activities and organizations deserve such numerous and overlapping benefits (the federal and state exemptions from income, property and sales taxes, plus eligibility to receive tax deductible donations and to issue tax-exempt bonds, and lower postage rates to boot) all on account of their charitable status. The second difficulty is the desire to reconcile these sweeping benefits with the several limitations, all under a single concept of charitable. This is the task we set for ourselves. We will begin by surveying historical explanations for the charitable exemption, and then proceed to review a basic theoretical dispute regarding the nature of exemption.

Theoretical Foundations:
Tax-Base vs. Subsidy Rationales

Historical Tax-Base Justifications for Exemption

In general, there are two competing sets of explanations for charitable tax exemption: tax-base theories and subsidy theories. According to the first, exemption exists for entities that simply do not have any of what the particular tax system attempts to tax: e.g., no net disposable income or no real property. The subsidy theory, in contrast, assumes that the entity does fit within the ordinary tax base but views the entity as deserving of an implicit government subsidy, which is administered by foregoing the imposition of taxes.[14] The tax-base theory is like a direct defense in the law, whereas the subsidy theory is like an affirmative defense. The first argues that the tax does not apply at all, while the second argues that, even though the tax applies, extraordinary reasons exist to excuse the entity from paying.

Historically, tax-base justifications underlay the exemption of charitable entities from taxation. As noted above, churches originally were not exempt because it was thought that it was beyond the power (or at least the jurisdiction) of governments to tax the property of God. Later, the property of orthodox churces was not taxed if it was used directly to advance the state-supported religion, but otherwise churches were subject to taxation. After Disestablishment, the prevailing rationale for exempting charitable organizations from property taxes was that the property had been donated to nonproductive, noncommercial use. Similarly, the original rationale for federal tax exemption of charities probably was that these organizations earned no income (although we are not sure since the issue was not debated).

Each of these historic rationales for exemption of charitable entities is seriously flawed as an explanation for the modern scope of the exemption. Churches are no longer quasi-state property. Property taxes are not aimed at only productive or commercial real estate: they reach residential homes and vacant lots, as well. Many nonprofit organizations in fact earn substantial income (private nonprofit hospitals and educational institutions are examples); in fact, this is why the phrase "not-for-profit" more accurately describes these organizations by elliptically acknowledging that these organizations may make a profit (in the sense of having a net surplus of earnings over expenses) but that profit is not their primary purpose.

Bittker and Rahdert's Modern Tax-Base Theory

Despite these obvious differences between the historic reasons for exemption and its modern scope, scholars continue to debate the tax-base versus subsidy rationales for exemption. The most thorough exposition of the tax-base theory is contained in Boris Bittker and George Rahdert's landmark 1976 article on the nature of federal income tax exemption.[15] Those authors argue that nonprofits are exempt from federal income tax because of the inherent difficulty in measuring their income and assessing the incidence of tax. For example, donations to charitable entities would not appear to be income, but rather gifts exempt from income taxation under I.R.C. § 102. Expenditures by these entities on their beneficiaries might not be classified as deductible business expenses, because an entity that does not seek profit generally is not considered engaged in a "trade or business" for purposes of I.R.C. §162, governing business expense deductions. Moreover, selecting an appropriate tax rate for charitable entities is difficult. If one conceives of a charitable organization as a kind of trust doling out assistance to its beneficiaries on a need basis, the proper tax rate would be the rate applicable to the beneficiaries. The breadth of most charitable classes, however, makes such "imputation" rates incalculable. Substituting an entity tax for a beneficiary tax would be possible, but would run the risk of overtaxing because most beneficiaries of charitable institutions likely would be taxed at very low rates, if at all.

While it is undoubtedly true that many charitable institutions have no *net* income in the accounting sense,[16] Bittker and Rahdert's theory has serious problems as an explanation of the entire scope of charitable exemption. First, they do not even attempt to explain state property tax exemption. They also do not address why charitable status carries with it the affiliated benefits of eligibility for receipt of deductible donations, favorable postage rates, and tax-exempt bond financing.[17]

Perhaps the biggest problem with the theory, however, is that it simply is wrong with respect to a number of charitable organizations. As Henry Hansmann has observed, many "charitable" organizations in fact derive nearly all their income from sales of goods or services they produce, and measuring income for such "commercial" nonprofits is no more difficult than for any other business.[18] Hospitals are one notable example, deriving virtually all their income from service fees.[19] Educational institutions are another: tuition (fees for educational services rendered) falls squarely within the definition of income in I.R.C. § 61[20] and constitutes over half the revenues for four-year private colleges and universities.[21] One has the sneaking suspicion that Harvard could come up with a taxable income number if pressed to do so. Even classic charities fit the taxable income model with little difficulty. Professor Atkinson, for example, has commented, "Tiffany's net income available for distribution to its stockholders is arguably different from the Red Cross's distributions of donations to flood victims, but the two could be made subject to tax with roughly equal convenience."[22] Another commentator has noted that more charities are operating in a "businesslike" fashion, generating surplus receipts, hiring professional managers, creating reserves for operations and so on.[23]

As for the rate-setting difficulties, our taxing system does not generally look toward an entity's customers in determining the tax rate for business enterprises.[24] In fact, the issue regarding the incidence of entity-level taxation (i.e., whether the tax ultimately is paid by the entity's owners, customers, employees, or someone else) is one that economists have debated for decades for ordinary commercial enterprises.[25] The exemption, moreover, is completely blind to the actual ability to pay of the entity's beneficiaries. In many instances (symphony orchestras, art museums, and Harvard all come to mind), the majority of patrons come from high income classes.

This theory is equally unsatisfying when applied to state property tax exemption. While it may be difficult to measure income for some charitable institutions, they most certainly own property, and their property is no more difficult to value than property owned by Microsoft or the corner grocery store.[26] Whatever the rationale was for the original exemptions from property tax, it cannot have been that charitable entities lacked property to tax. Nevertheless, even here some commentators have used the "incidence of tax" prong of Bittker & Rahdert's argument to construct a tax-base theory of state property tax exemption. Peter Swords, for example, argues that the incidence of property tax must fall either on the exempt entity's beneficiaries or donors.[27] (He apparently does not consider that the tax could result in reduced wages for employees, a possibility raised by economists). Swords notes that many beneficiaries of charitable enterprises will be poor, and thus should not be subject to the incidence of property tax under the "ability to pay" criterion of assessing tax. This argument, of course, suffers the same problems as in the income tax arena: our taxation systems generally do not set property rates based upon the ability of the entity's customers to pay; moreover, charitable exemption is not limited to organizations that serve the poor and many patrons of charitable organizations in fact do have the ability to pay.

Swords does acknowledge this latter point (as do Bittker and Rahdert) but nevertheless justifies exemption as a method to keep prices of exempt goods or services low, which encourages wider distribution. The problem here is that there is no necessary connection between exemption and lower prices or wider distribution of goods and services. The economic benefits of exemption might just as easily be used to pay managers or employees higher salaries. In fact, most economists who have examined the issue of pricing by exempt organizations have concluded that exempt organizations are not likely to use the economic benefits of exemption to lower the prices of their goods.[28]

Swords' alternative argument is that the tax burden would land on contributors to charities, thereby subjecting them to unfair "double taxation" since they have already paid their own property and income taxes on the donated assets. The result might be fewer contributions. However, the same is true for property or income used in commercial transactions. It too is taxed both to the spender and to the recipient.

We do not deny that there is a core element of truth to these tax-base explanations. Indeed, they are undoubtedly correct when applied to certain noncharitable exemptions such as those for governmental entities and mutual benefit societies.[29] For the charitable exemption, tax-base theories are strongest when applied to institutions that rely heavily on donations, which are precisely the institutions that our own theory would exempt. Our differences are over the theoretical basis for reaching this conclusion, which is critical to accepting the argument and understanding how far it carries. The tax-base theories are an unsatisfying explanation for the charitable exemption both at a descriptive and at a normative level. They fail to accurately describe which entities are in fact exempt, and, most importantly, they provide little basis for determining which entities *should* be exempt. Entities truly without income can be exempted from income tax simply by requiring them to submit an income tax return showing zero income. Accomplishing this result by categorically exempting a class of nonprofit activities is both overbroad and underinclusive, since this class will include many entities that in fact earn substantial income and will exclude many that do not. Moreover, this formulation of the exemption does nothing to explain what charitable means. It makes no sense to say that all organizations without income are charitable, and it is not true that all charitable organizations have no income. Since the charitable concept is thought to be coterminous with the rationale for the exemption, this is a critical failure. For these reasons, the tax-base theories fare poorly under both the universality and historical consistency criteria set out in Chapter 1.[30]

The generic fallback to the failure of a tax-base theory is a subsidy theory: that the exemption exists simply as a means to subsidize certain worthy activities in the amount of the taxes foregone. This is the view of most commentators[31] and it is also the dominant view expressed by courts interpreting the scope of exemption. In 1983, the U.S. Supreme Court stated in *Regan v. Taxation Without Representation*, "Both [federal income] tax exemptions and tax deductibility are a form of subsidy that is administered through the tax system."[32] The Court reiterated this view in 1989 in the context of a state sales tax exemption on religious publications, opining that "Every tax exemption constitutes a subsidy that affects nonqualifying taxpayers, forcing them to become 'indirect and vicarious "donors." ' "[33] State supreme courts also have adopted the subsidy view.[34]

These observations do not mean that either the colonial legislatures that enacted property tax exemptions for charitable institutions or Congress in 1894 explicitly viewed the exemption as the equivalent of a subsidy. In fact, as noted above, both the federal income and state property tax exemptions stemmed from a more general, vague notion that such entities simply should not be taxed. Not being aware of a specific rationale for exemption at the time of enactment, however, does not render inappropriate the view that at least today exemption in fact is equivalent to the government forgiving the tax that otherwise would be due from the exempt entity. For example, most local communities that play host to exempt universities are acutely aware of the economic benefit conferred by property tax exemption, and have begun asking exempt entities for payments in lieu of taxes to offset some of the lost tax revenue.[35] Exempt entities also are aware of the economic consequences of losing exemption,[36] and even legislatures now assess exemption issues from the subsidy viewpoint.[37]

For these reasons, we adopt the subsidy view of tax exemption for charitable entities. Although a tax-base theory may have been historically correct at a time when different tax bases prevailed, the comprehensive nature of taxing systems in the modern world renders this history anachronistic. Subsidy theories do a better job of attempting to justify the contemporary scope of the charitable exemption in all of its dimensions. Accordingly, we will assume in the remainder of this book that the charitable exemption is an attempt to designate certain activities as good for society and to devise a method for indirect support. The debate then shifts to what about these activities is worthy and how the subsidy should be administered in order to best match the exemption with its purpose. This is where most of the modern debate has focused: on various explanations for why charitable organizations deserve a subsidy, and what this tells us about what constitutes a charity.

Notes

1. I.R.C. § 501(c)(3) (1993). The statute also lists as charitable testing for public safety, fostering amateur sports competition, and the prevention of cruelty to children or animals.

2. Treas. Reg. 1.501(c)(3)-1(d)(3); Rev. Rul. 70-640, 1970-2 C.B. 117 (marriage counseling); Rev. Rul. 69-441, 1969-2 C.B. 115 (personal financial counseling); Rev. Rul. 68-504, 1968-2 C.B. 211 (update seminars for banking); Rev. Rul. 65-271, 1965-2 C.B. 161 (jazz festival); I.T. 2134, 4-1 C.B. 214 (1925) (wild bird sanctuaries). *See* Kentucky Bar Found. v. Comm'r, 78 T.C. 921, 924 (1982) (IRS conceded continuing legal education was an educational activity entitled to exemption). Even the IRS, however, has its limits: a dog obedience school was held not exempt since it neither trains individuals nor educates the public. Rev. Rul. 71-421, 1971-2 C.B. 229.

3. Bob Jones Univ. v. United States, 461 U.S. 574, 586 (1983); *see* Treas. Reg. § 1.501(c)(3)-1(d)(2) (1959) ("The term 'charitable' is . . . not to be construed as limited by the separate enumeration in section 501(c)(3) of other tax–exempt purposes which may fall within the broad outlines of 'charity' as developed by judicial decisions."); PAUL E. TREUSCH, TAX-EXEMPT CHARITABLE ORGANIZATIONS 118 (3d ed. 1988) ("'[C]haritable' purpose was a catch-all category for most of the more specific purposes that were later added.").

4. Mark A. Hall & John D. Colombo, *The Charitable Status of Nonprofit Hospitals: Toward a Donative Theory of Tax Exemption*, 66 WASH. L. REV. 307, 323 n. 53 (1991).

5. William R. Ginsberg, *The Real Property Tax Exemption of Nonprofit Organizations: A Perspective*, 53 TEMPLE L. Q. 291, 292 (1980) (every state has a statute on the subject and all but seven have a constitutional provision).

6. *See* W. HARRISON WELLFORD & JANNE G. GALLAGHER, UNFAIR COMPETITION? THE CHALLENGE TO TAX EXEMPTION app. A (1988) (50-state survey of the laws of charitable property tax exemption).

7. Janne G. Gallagher, *Sales Tax Exemptions for Charitable, Educational, and Religious Nonprofit Organizations*, 7 EXEMPT ORG. TAX REV. 429 (1993).

8. I.R.C. § 170(c)(2)(B) (1993) defines a charitable contribution as a contribution to "A corporation . . . organized and operated exclusively for religious, charitable, scientific, literary, or educational purposes . . . ."

9. 39 C.F.R. § 200.0212 (1994) (defining nonprofit entity eligible for second class postage rates).

10. Bob Jones University v. United States, 461 U.S. 574 (1983).

11. I.R.C. §§ 511-514 (1993).

12. State exemption statutes which follow the language of I.R.C. § 501(c)(3) (1993) incorporate similar standards by implication. Other state property and income tax exemption statutes explicitly contain the inurement prohibition. *See, e.g.*, GA. CODE ANN. § 91A-1102(a)(5) (Harrison 1989); HAW. REV. STAT. § 246-32(e) (1985); WIS. STAT. ANN. § 70-11(4m) (West 1989). Even where the language is less precise, as in most state property tax exemption provisions, lack of private inurement is generally considered essential to "charitable" status. *See, e.g., In re* Claim of Assembly Homes v. Yellow Medicine County, 273 Minn. 197, 203–04, 140 N.W.2d 336, 340 n.41 (1966) (construing the words "purely public charity" as incorporating a prohibition against private inurement). The same is true for the restriction on political activity. *See, e.g.*, Pennsylvania v. American Anti-Vivisection Soc'y, 32 Pa. Commw. 70, 377 A.2d 1378 (1977) (since primary activity of organization was political lobbying, organization was not a charity). As for the public policy limitation, it arose from the common law of charitable trusts and hence is a part of the general common law of charities. IVA. SCOTT ON TRUSTS 76-107, §§362-362.2 (1993).

13. *See, e.g.*, Hattiesburg Area Senior Services, Inc. v. Lamar County, 1994 Miss. LEXIS 38, 633 So.2d 440 (1994) (residential property owned by Hattiesburg Area Senior Services and used for senior citizen housing not exempt because not used solely for activities of exempt entity, violating Mississippi "exclusive use" requirement); Women's Club of Topeka Kansas, v. Shawnee County, 253 Kan. 175, 853 P.2d 1157 (1993) (property owned by women's club used for club gatherings and luncheons in addition to being rented to churches fails exclusive use requirement; not exempt); St. Mary's Medical Center of Evansville, Inc. v. Indiana Bd. of Tax Commissioners, 534 N.E. 2d 277 (Ind. Tax Ct. 1989) (property rented by exempt hospital to physicians for private practice of medicine not exempt because

not used exclusively for charitable purposes).

14. *See generally*, John G. Simon, *The Tax Treatment of Nonprofit Organizations: A Review of Federal and State Policies, in* THE NONPROFIT SECTOR: A RESEARCH HANDBOOK 67, 69, 73–82 (Walter W. Powell, ed., 1987); Boris I. Bittker & George F. Rahdert, *The Exemption of Nonprofit Organizations from Federal Income Taxation*, 85 YALE L.J. 299, 304 (1976); Rob Atkinson, *Altruism in Nonprofit Organizations*, 31, B.C.L. REV. 501 605–613 (1990); Henry B. Hansmann, *The Rationale for Exempting Nonprofit Organizations from Corporate Income Taxation*, 91 YALE L.J. 54, 58–59, 66 (1981); Mark A. Hall & John D. Colombo, *The Charitable Status of Nonprofit Hospitals: Toward A Donative Theory of Tax Exemption*, 66 WASH. L. REV. 307, 313 (1991); *Developments in the Law: Nonprofit Corporations*, 105 HARV. L. REV. 1578, 1620 (1992); Note, *Alternatives to the University Property Tax Exemption*, 83 YALE L.J. 181, 183 (1979).

15. Boris I. Bittker & George F. Rahdert, *The Exemption of Nonprofit Organizations from Federal Income Taxation*, 85 YALE L.J. 299, 304 (1976). One should note that Bittker and Rahdert's article does not limit its discussion to charitable organizations. Rather, it considers all types of tax exemption, including exemption for "mutual benefit" organizations such as fraternities, chambers of commerce and the like exempt under other subsections of I.R.C. § 501. The text focuses on only that part of the article dealing with exemption of traditional charitable institutions, which Bittker and Rahdert refer to as "public service" organizations.

16. That is, no surplus of revenues over expenses. *See* Simon, *supra* note 14, at 81 (income tax exemption provides little in the way of support for most nonprofits).

17. To be fair, however, Professor Bittker did address the existence of the charitable donation deduction in I.R.C. § 170 on tax-base grounds in another article. Boris I. Bittker, *Charitable Contributions: Tax Deductions or Matching Grants?*, 28 TAX L. REV. 37 (1972). As far as we know, however, neither Professor Bittker or any other scholar has attempted to explain tax-exempt bond financing and reduced postal rates on tax-base grounds.

18. Hansmann, *supra* note 14, at 59.

19. *See* Hall & Colombo, *supra* note 14, at 405–408.

20. *See* I.R.C. § 61(a)(1) (1993) (gross income includes "compensation for services, including fees . . . .").

21. SAMUEL F. BARBETT, ET AL., STATE HIGHER EDUCATION PROFILES 17, table 5 (4th ed. 1992). This data is summarized in John D. Colombo, *Why is Harvard Tax Exempt? (And Other Mysteries of Tax Exemption for Private Educational Institutions)*, 35 ARIZ. L. REV. 841, 881 (1993).

22. Rob Atkinson, *Rationales for Federal Income Tax Exemption* 27 in RATIONALES FOR FEDERAL INCOME TAX EXEMPTION (1991) (collection of papers prepared for the 1991 NYU Conference on Philanthropy and the Law).

23. BRUCE R. HOPKINS, THE LAW OF TAX-EXEMPT ORGANIZATIONS 191 (6th ed. 1992).

24. Hansmann, *supra* note 14, at 65; Simon, *supra* note 14, at 75 (noting that the incidence of taxation argument rests on the notion that the charitable entity is a conduit for its beneficiaries, a theory that has not been accepted in most of tax law).

25. A good overall summary of the debate is contained in DOUGLAS BRADFORD, UNTANGLING THE INCOME TAX 133–47 (1986). *See also*, George F. Break, *The Incidence and Economic Effects of Taxation*, in THE ECONOMICS OF PUBLIC FINANCE (Brookings 1974).

26. Some states, in fact, actually list exempt property on the tax rolls along with a valuation. *See* Simon, *supra* note 14, at 81; JoAnn Moody, *Tax Policy: Some Issues for Higher Education*, in FINANCING HIGHER EDUCATION: THE PUBLIC INVESTMENT 125, 129 (John C. Hoy and Melvin Bernstein, eds. 1982) (listing exempt property valuations done by the Massachusetts Department of Revenue). Simon does note that state and local officials have every incentive to undervalue exempt property in making such estimates; hence the listed valuations probably are unreliable. Simon, *supra* note 14, at 81.

27. PETER L. SWORDS, CHARITABLE PROPERTY TAX EXEMPTIONS IN NEW YORK STATE, 191–209 (1981).

28. Most of these discussions have come in the context of the Unrelated Business Income Tax, I.R.C. §§ 511–514, passed by Congress in 1950 to allay concerns that exempt organizations had an unfair competitive advantage over for-profit firms competing in the same market. *See* Harvey P. Dale, *About the UBIT . . .*, 18TH CONF. ON TAX PLANNING FOR 501(C)(3) ORGANIZATIONS §9.02 at 9-5 (1990). Economists who have studied the behavior of exempt firms have noted, however, that they are no more likely to engage in predatory pricing (e.g., using the economic benefits of exemption to underprice their competitors). *See* Henry B. Hansmann, *Unfair Competition and the Unrelated Business Income Tax*, 75 VA. L. REV. 605, 610–11 (1989); Richard L. Kaplan, *Intercollegiate Athletics and the Unrelated Busines Income Tax*, 80 COLUMB. L. REV. 1430, 1465–66 (1980); William A. Klein, *Income Taxation and Legal Entities*, 20 UCLA L. REV. 13, 65–66 (1972); Susan Rose-Ackerman, *Unfair Competition and Corporate Income Taxation*, 34 STAN. L. REV. 1017, 1021 (1982).

29. See text *supra* pp. 20-21.

30. Tax-base theories fail even to invoke the deservedness and proportionality criteria, since these are premised on a subsidy theory.

31. Hansmann, *supra* note 14, at 66 ("A rather common view of the exemption is that it is a means of subsidizing particular services . . . ."); Atkinson, *supra* note 22, at 12 & n. 18 (subsidy view is "widely expressed"; citing several authorities); Simon, *supra* note 14, at 75 (noting "limited popularity" of tax-base approaches); Charles T. Clofelter, *Federal Tax Policy and Charitable Giving*, in PHILANTHROPIC GIVING 105 (Richard Magat, ed. 1989) ("The United States is distinctive in the degree to which it subsidizes the nonprofit sector through its tax system.").

32. Regan v. Taxation Without Representation, 461 U.S. 540, 544 (1983).

33. Texas Monthly, Inc. v. Bullock, 489 U.S. 1, 14 (1989).

34. Mutual Life Insurance Company of New York v. City of Los Angeles, 50 Cal.3d 402, 787 P.2d 996, 267 Cal. Rptr.589 (1990); Hearst Corporation v. Iowa Department of Revenue and Finance, 461 N.W.2d 295 (1990); Department of Revenue v. Magazine Publishers of America , Inc. 586 So.2d 1304 (Fla. 1990); Mathias v. Department of Revenue, 312 Or. 50, 817 P.2d 272 (Or. 1991); Gallagher v. Commissioner of Revenue Services, 221 Conn. 166, 602 A.2d 996 (1992).

35. The City of Urbana, for example, recently complained about the exempt status of the University of Illinois' married student housing, ostensibly because Urbana was incurring costs of educating such students' children, but the University was not contributing to such costs through property taxes. CHAMPAIGN-URBANA NEWS GAZETTE, Mar. 25, 1993 at A-1. The city of Evanston, Illinois, voiced similar complaints about Northwestern University. *Evanston Sizes Up Tax On Tuition for NU, Other Schools*, CHICAGO TRIBUNE, May 23, 1990, page 1. Even Boston sought legislative approval for a "public safety excise tax" on exempt educational institutions. Tom Moccia, *Boston Legislators Seek Local Option Property Tax on Exempt Educational Institutions*, 7 EXEMPT ORG. TAX REV. 877 (1993). In late 1993, Providence, Rhode Island, requested that its six private hospitals and four private colleges voluntarily pay between $10 and $12 million to the city. Janne G. Gallagher, *Capitol Seeks Payments in Lieu of Property Taxes from Hospitals, Colleges*, 8 EXEMPT ORG. TAX REV. 1142 (1993). *See* also, Yale Note, *supra* note 9, at 185 (other universities already make "payments in lieu of taxes" to their host communities).

36. Otherwise, there would be little in the way of hue and cry when exemption was revoked. J. David Seay, for example, has eloquently defended the tax-exempt status of nonprofit hospitals by arguing that they promote community service and are (or to be exempt, should be) more responsive to community needs. J. David Seay, *Tax Exemption for Hospitals: Towards an Understanding of Community Benefit*, 2 HEALTH MATRIX 35, 45–48 (1992). Implicit in this defense, however, presumably is a recognition that without the economic benefits of exemption, many nonprofit hospitals would cease to exist. If this were not the case, exempt status would be irrelevant, because the lack of exemption certainly would not prohibit hospitals from pursuing the lofty goals articulated by Seay. Put another way, Seay must view exemption as providing a necessary economic benefit that permits nonprofit hospitals to pursue their community service.

37. A bill recently introduced in New Hampshire, for example, would require all exempt organizations to pay municipalities a "core service charge" based upon the value of their property. Janne G. Gallagher, *Report Recommends Changes in Property Tax Exemption Laws*, 9 EXEMPT ORG. TAX REV. 716 (1994). Legislation introduced in Pennsylvania in 1993 would permit local communities to collect payments in lieu of taxes on all charitable property. Janne G. Gallagher, *Hospitals Introduce Exemption Legislation, Agree to Municipal Service Charges*, 8 EXEMPT ORG. TAX REV. 628 (1993). Texas enacted legislation in 1993 tying exempt status for hospitals to specific levels of charity care as a sort of quid pro quo for exemption. Janne G. Gallagher, *Legislation Sets Standards for Hospital Charity*

Care, 8 EXEMPT ORG. TAX REV. 629 (1993). The subsidy view has also surfaced at the federal level. In his statement opening the hearings before the House Select Committee on Aging on a bill that would have revamped exemption standards for hospitals, Rep. Edward R. Roybal stated "[U]ntil this Nation commits itself to a national health policy protecting all Americans, [we] cannot afford to lose the $8 billion in [foregone tax revenues] that tax-exempt status potentially offers." *Hospital Charity Care and Tax-Exempt Status: Restoring the Commitment and Fairness, Hearings Before the Select Committee on Aging,* at 2 (1990). Similar sentiments were express by Rep. Brian Donnelly in hearings on another bill introduced in 1991 regarding tax-exempt status for hospitals, "Mr. Speaker, the fundamental basis under which Congress exempts organizations from taxation is the belief that those organizations will relieve a governmental burden . . . . My legislation, consequently, imposes some realistic requirements on hospitals if they wish to enjoy the generous benefits which the Government provides." 137 CONG. REC. E896 (1991). Neither bill passed and both representatives subsequently retired from Congress.

3

Charitable Trust Law

The most common source of precedent in searching for the meaning of the *tax* law's concept of the charity is the law of charitable *trusts*. Trusts are ancient legal instruments that accomplish a variety of purposes, the primary of which is to separate the ownership and control of assets from their beneficial use. *Charitable* trusts are those whose assets are used for especially worthy purposes. They receive special, favorable treatment in the law, and a four-century body of precedent has developed concerning which particular purposes qualify as charitable.

Various legal sources have recognized that the definition of a charitable entity in I.R.C. § 501(c)(3) and its state law counterparts begins with the common law of charitable trusts. In the celebrated case of *Commissioners v. Pemsel*,[1] the House of Lords in 1891 declared that the law of charitable trusts governed the charitable tax exemption in England.[2] Just three years later, the U.S. Congress apparently patterned the exemption in the original income tax after the existing English model.[3] IRS regulations published in 1959 state that charitable is to be understood according to its "generally accepted legal sense . . . as developed by judicial decisions,"[4] and in a famous 1969 ruling regarding the charitable status of nonprofit hospitals, the IRS began its analysis by noting that the promotion of health for the benefit of the community as a whole had long been considered charitable under the common law of charitable trusts.[5] Similarly, the Supreme Court reiterated in 1983 that "underlying all relevant parts of the Code . . . [are] certain common-law standards of charity" and "the origins of [the] exemptions lie in the special privileges that have long been extended to charitable trusts."[6]

The Statute of Charitable Uses

Charitable trust law came into prominence in 1601 with the Elizabethan Statute of Charitable Uses, which strengthened the mechanisms for preventing the misuse of assets given to charitable purposes. The statute's preamble catalogued the various purposes for which charitable trusts had until then been established. Despite its haphazard content, this listing has become a virtual oracle of charitable trust law, achieving an "immortality of definition" through centuries of decisions that looked to it to determine which trusts qualified for protection.[7]

The statute's preamble reads:

> WHEREAS lands, tenements, rents, annuities, profits, hereditaments, goods, chattels, money and flocks of money have been heretofore given, limited, appointed and affirmed, as well by the Queen's most excellent majesty, and her most noble progenitors, as by sundry other well-disposed persons; *some for relief of aged, impotent and poor people, some for maintenance of sick and maimed soldiers and mariners, schools of learning, free schools, and scholars in universities, some for repair of bridges, ports, havens, causeways, churches, sea-banks and highways, some for education and preferment of orphans, some for or towards relief, stock or maintenance for houses of correction, some for marriages of poor maids, some for supportation, aid and help of young tradesmen, handicraftsmen and persons decayed, and others for relief or redemption of prisoners or captives, and for aid or ease of any poor inhabitants concerning payments of fifteens, setting out of soldiers and other taxes;* which lands, tenements, rents, annuities, profits, hereditaments, goods, chattels, money and stocks of money, nevertheless have not been employed according to the charitable intent of the givers and founders thereof, by reason of frauds, breaches of trust, and negligence in those that should pay, deliver and employ the same . . . .[8]

This extensive listing, and the centuries of caselaw interpreting it, appear to make the task of applying the charitable exemption a simple one. In theory, all that tax administrators need do is consult this body of law to determine if the applicant organization engages in one of these categories of historically charitable enterprise or its modern equivalent. If so, it is presumptively eligible for charitable status, subject to satisfying other organizational and operations criteria (such as maintaining a nonprofit form, not engaging in prohibited political activity, and avoiding private inurement, as discussed in Chapters 2 and 10). We refer to this as the per se, categorical theory of exemption. The only threshold inquiry one needs to make is whether the core activity falls within one of the categories recognized as per se charitable by this established body of trust law precedent.

Deficiencies in Transplanting
the Charitable Trust Definition

Despite unanimity of authority that the tax law concept of charity was drawn from charitable trust law, considerable theoretical difficulties exist in extending this per se approach to tax exemption. The primary deficiency is encountered under the deservedness criterion. Simply put, because charitable trust law serves a wholly different purpose than the charitable exemption, the trust definition of charity does not properly identify activities that deserve an implicit government subsidy.

The Purpose of Charitable Trust Law

The primary purpose of charitable trust law is to protect assets which founders choose to devote to worthy causes. Trust law provides this assistance by creating rigorous enforcement mechanisms to police abuses of these socially worthy trusts (such as authorizing attorneys general to bring enforcement actions) and by exempting such trusts from some of the technical requirements that apply to ordinary trusts. Early English law developed a somewhat hostile attitude toward trusts (originally called "uses" as a consequence of their conveyance of legal title to a nominal owner "for the use of" another), because they originated in feudal times as devices for hiding land from creditors and the exactions of land lords (an early form of property tax). The fraud and confusion caused by these unrecorded separations of legal title from equitable title led to the 1535 Statute of Uses, which sought to abolish this device altogether, but courts continued to allow uses in assets other than land, and uses upon uses (in other words, a transfer of title to X for the use of Y, who holds for the use of Z). The term "trust" arose as a means for distinguishing these still-enforceable uses from those outlawed by the Statute of Uses. Nevertheless, courts did impose numerous legal and technical restrictions on enforceable trusts such as requirements that they have identifiable beneficiaries and that they last only for a certain time period (the Rule Against Perpetuities).[9]

Charitable trusts, however, received some relief from these technicalities as a result of the special treatment that ecclesiastical courts accorded devises for religious purposes. The Chancery courts carried on this tradition after the Reformation.[10] Hence, unlike ordinary trusts, charitable trusts need not have definite, identifiable beneficiaries, they may exist in perpetuity, and, through the *cy pres* doctrine, courts will substitute a new, similar purpose to prevent them from failing when their stated purpose becomes impossible to achieve.[11]

The result of this history is that while trusts in general faced both statutory and judicial hostility, charitable trusts were treated favorably. Thus for two centuries after the Statute of Uses, charitable status for a trust was a desirable characteristic, and courts were fairly lenient in granting charitable status. In 1736, however, Parliament completely reversed the desirability of the charitable label with the Mortmain Act, which responded to concerns at the time that the Church was pressuring individuals to leave unduly large bequests to it at the expense of their disinherited families.

This legislation invalidated charitable bequests of land that were not executed through rigid formalities more than one year prior to death.[12] To avoid these restrictions, "objects which were in danger of being stigmatized as charitable often sought to divest themselves of this unwelcome status."[13] Affected legatees maintained that challenged gifts were not "charitable," and courts, often struggling to uphold such gifts, began to draw unprincipled distinctions regarding what properly should be deemed charitable. This shift in the statutory context threw the meaning of charity into complete confusion, resulting in sporadically restrictive holdings such as the absurd decision that a trust for "benevolent" purposes does not fall within the Statute of Charitable Uses.[14]

The Scope of Charity Under Charitable Trust Law

The stream of irreconcilable holdings emanating from this historical confusion typifies the kind of law that gives attorneys a bad name. Through it all, judges claimed to be able to divine, but not define, the "spirit and intendment" of the Statute of Charitable Uses that constitutes the essence of the legal concept of charity. "The equity, or 'spirit' of the preamble, as it was called, was elevated into the Delphic oracle of legal charity."[15] George Keeton, a leading British authority, once characterized this body of law as "probably the worst exhibition of the operation of the technique of judicial precedent which can be found in the law reports."[16]

Anglo-American law took a large step toward sorting out this confusion in *Commissioners v. Pemsel,*[17] perhaps the most celebrated case in the history of charitable trusts. The distinguished jurist Lord McNaughten cut through centuries of mindless distinctions by observing that the Statute of Charitable Uses was never intended to define charity but was merely illustrative of the broad range of particular objects of charitable trusts that happened to be in vogue at the time. Accordingly, he encapsulated the legal concept of charity in the following, enduring formulation:

"Charity" in its legal sense comprises four principal divisions: trusts for the relief of poverty; trusts for the advancement of education; trusts for the advancement of religion; and trusts for other purposes beneficial to the community, not falling under any of the preceding heads.[18]

In 1960, England's Nathan Commission adopted the *Pemsel* precedent in the Charities Act of 1960, which finally repealed the Statute of Charitable Uses.[19] Similarly, in the United States, the Restatement of Trusts adopted essentially the *Pemsel* formulation, including the residual category of "other purposes the accomplishment of which is beneficial to the community."[20]

Freed of the historical constraints of the Mortmain Act, courts reverted to giving a broad interpretation to "charitable." For example, courts have sustained as charitable a bequest for purposes as trivial as "provid[ing] fishing facilities for the inhabitants of a town."[21] The law of charitable trusts is willing to take such a generous view of the subject matter it protects because all that is at stake is the societal cost of the procedural protection attending these trusts, such as the additional case burden on courts hearing trust enforcement actions. No societal resources are committed to funding the trust, in contrast to the effect of a tax exemption. Given these relatively low stakes, trust law is able to rely for subject-matter limitation simply on the decision of public-spirited founders to endow whatever purpose they desire. As one court explained:

> What is the tribunal which is to decide whether the object is a beneficent one? It cannot be the individual mind of a Judge . . . . On the other hand, it cannot be the vox populi, for charities have been upheld for the benefits of insignificant sects, and of peculiar people. It occurs to me that the answer must be—that the benefit must be one which the founder believes to be of public advantage, and his belief must be at least rational, and not contrary either to the general law of the land, or to the principles of morality. A gift of such a character, dictated by benevolence, believed to be beneficent, devoted to an appreciably important object, and neither contra bonos mores nor contra legem, will, in my opinion, be charitable in the eye of the law . . . .[22]

Most trust scholars would disagree with the assertion that the legal concept of charity has no specific boundaries,[23] but this misses the point. The limits that trust law imposes are largely organizational and operational, not substantive. Charitable status turns not so much on *what* is done but rather on *how* it is done. The guiding precept that emerges from centuries of abstruse case law is that charitable trusts must be created to provide public, not private, benefit. This limitation requires that charities benefit the public at large rather than the founder or the founder's family and friends. For instance, a trust to maintain a public graveyard is valid, but one to maintain a particular tomb is not.[24] Similarly, charities must be nonprofit entities, their earnings may not inure to the benefit of any private individual, they may not engage in self-dealing transactions, they must serve a large group, and they may not pursue purposes that contravene public policy.[25]

With these operational constraints satisfied, however, virtually any substantive purpose will suffice. Charity is "broad enough to include whatever will promote, in a legitimate way, the comfort, happiness and improvement of an indefinite number of persons."[26] As the Supreme Court declared over a century ago, charity includes "anything that tends to promote the well-doing and well-being of social man."[27] Students of the law of charity acknowledge that "[n]early everything produced by . . . private industry—ranging from buildings and food to books and music—contributes to our welfare."[28] "In a sense, all legitimate economic activities are affected with a public interest."[29]

This truth is one of the classic lessons taught by the fundamental turn in Constitutional jurisprudence that occurred earlier this century when, after over half a century of Supreme Court efforts to confine social and economic legislation to businesses "affected with the public interest,"[30] the Court abandoned substantive due process scrutiny with respect to such legislation, observing, "there is no closed class or category of businesses affected with a public interest . . . ."[31] Attempts to police the substantive limits of the exemption under the rubric of "public benefit" would be as flawed as the Supreme Court's abandoned attempt to police the substantive wisdom of economic and social legislation.

This is why virtually no one has succeeded in giving "charity" in trust law some definitional content.[32] Instead, courts and commentators find themselves repeatedly forced to rest on the unilluminating platitude that "charity is an evolving concept which must be allowed to change and expand in response to the needs of society."[33]

The Need for a Principle to Limit the Exemption

This completely open-textured approach to defining the term "charitable" may be appropriate in trust law where the concern is *procedural* protection of an *individual* donor's gift to society. But reliance on these trust law precedents in tax law defies logic where the policy stakes are entirely different. A proper concept of charity for tax exemption purposes must identify activities that deserve the *financial* support of *society*. This cannot be accomplished by relying on an expansive concept of charity that reaches all activities worthy of protection under trust law. If the trust concept is imported into tax law, essentially any legitimate nonprofit institution that serves the public at large is presumptively eligible for charitable tax exemption. This principle largely matches what has occurred in practice and thus meets at least the historical consistency criterion.

As Professor Hansmann has observed, "the exemptions have traditionally been read so broadly as to encompass nearly all nonprofits of any financial significance. . . . In general, the words 'nonprofit' and 'tax-exempt' have been coterminous."[34] However, a definition of charity that contains essentially no substantive limiting principle, and thus imposes minimal subject matter restrictions on which activities are exempt (i.e., restricts only how the activity is organized and carried out), must be rejected because such a definition contains no test to ascertain when the exemption is either deserved or proportionate to the benefit society receives. By classifying as "charitable" any activity which meets the inherent procedural restrictions of charitable trust law, this test potentially provides exempt status, and the accompanying tax subsidy, to activities that either might be provided just as well without a tax subsidy or to activities whose dollar value to the community is less than the amount of the foregone tax revenues.

Binding the law of tax exemption to precisely the same category of activities historically covered by charitable trust law is thus manifestly absurd. This is especially so because a trust law precedent established by the decision of a single donor would have the effect of exempting an entire industry from taxation. Suppose, for instance, that a successful veterinarian left her wealth in trust to promote the practice of veterinary medicine. Such a trust would be sustained as charitable.[35] Subsequently, any proprietor of an animal hospital who chose to organize as a legitimate nonprofit operation would qualify for exemption from federal income tax, local property tax, and possibly state income and sales taxes, as well as reduced postage rates and tax-exempt financing, even if the firm relied entirely on borrowed capital and charged full market rates to all of its customers.

Even absent an established precedent in trust law, tying the exemption to the charitable trust definition of charity would permit exemption in cases where merely theorizing that if a trust for the same purpose were established, it would provide sufficient public benefits to deserve protection from the Rule Against Perpetuities. For instance, in one case an exemption for a boy scout camp was upheld because "an institution is charitable when its property and funds are devoted to such purposes as would support the creation of a valid charitable trust." The court cited similar holdings for dining rooms, women's residences, and museums.[36] Even as early as the 1920s, the IRS concluded that the educational exemption can extend to activities as diverse as studying ruffled grouse, maintaining wild bird sanctuaries and forest land, and disseminating geographic knowledge.[37]

Such a potentially limitless extension of the exemption may at first seem like a small risk because adopting the nonprofit form requires the organizer to forego any share of the profits, a sacrifice that most persons would not care to make absent an overriding commitment to benefitting the public. However, businesses do exist from which organizers expect nothing more than full compensation for their labor; such organizers would benefit by adopting a genuinely nonprofit form of business that automatically ensures a substantial social subsidy, even if they are thereby denied any return on capital. Physician group practices are just such a business. Even in a proprietary form, the practice group essentially pays physician members the share of the group income attributable to their patients, a remuneration system that is not sacrificed by adopting the nonprofit form. Consequently, physician groups have a strong incentive to seek property tax exemption for their real estate holdings, and sales tax exemption for their purchase of equipment and supplies.[38]

The inadequacy of a concept of charity that mechanically refers to trust law precedents is acknowledged at least implicitly by the failure to follow it consistently, even by those who seemingly advocate this approach. A careful analysis of IRS decisions in the health care field, for example, reveals that the Service in fact imposes numerous substantive limitations on the exemption. Despite the fact that its leading ruling on the exempt status of hospitals relied on trust law to state that the promotion of health for the benefit of the general community constitutes a per se charitable purpose,[39] in a multitude of rulings the IRS has developed the position that only inpatient hospital services—not health care sevices per se—are exempt. The IRS consistently refuses to extend the exemption to physician groups,[40] and consistently imposes more exacting exemption requirements on health maintenance organizations (HMOs), nursing homes, and other nonhospital health care services.[41] The IRS also has ruled that a nonprofit pharmacy is disqualified from the charitable exemption even though supplying drugs is as intimately connected with health care as administering drugs, and even though pharmacy sales within a hospital are exempt.[42]

The precedents are equally confusing in other arenas of charitable activity. For example, in *Scripture Press Foundation v. United States*,[43] the Court of Claims held that an organization that published teaching materials for Bible classes operated in a manner similar to a commercial publisher and accordingly was not charitable. Two decades later, however, the Third Circuit held a similar publisher exempt, stating that "success in terms of audience reached and influence exerted, in and of itself, should not jeopardize the tax-exempt status" of the organization, and that large accumulations of cash should not be viewed suspiciously if reinvested in exempt activities.[44] Similarly, the Oregon Tax Court recently ruled that organizations that sponsored live theater were not exempt charitable organizations, despite a long history of exemption for these organizations in both Oregon and federal law and despite the fact that other literary organizations are exempt in Oregon.[45]

It is evident from these varied sources that courts, legislatures, and taxing authorities are searching for a limiting principle that will define which activities deserve the exemption and which do not. It is also evident that charitable trust law interpreted in this fashion does not provide that limiting principle. We will see later (in Chapters 10 and 12) how the charitable trust precedents are actually relevant, but it is not via categorical lists of per se qualifying activities. By paying lip service to the Statute of Charitable Uses and its expansive caselaw without really following it, tax exemption decisions are reasoned on bases that in some cases are unprincipled, in others inconsistent, and in others undiscernible. Thus, while the dominant instinct to constrain the boundaries of the exemption is correct, these decisions fail to isolate and articulate a workable limiting principle.

The scope and content of a proper limiting principle is the subject of the remainder of this book. At this point, we have only established that virtually everyone who has given thought to the matter recognizes that some substantial subject matter limits must be imposed on the charitable exemption.[46] As a consequence, the per se, categorical position drawn from charitable trust law—to which many decisions give passing reference—cannot be sustained, and in fact is not followed.

Notes

1. 1891 App. Cas. 531 (H.L.).

2. *See* LIONEL A. SHERIDAN & GEORGE W. KEETON, THE MODERN LAW OF CHARITIES 29, 299 (3d ed. 1983); Chauncey Belknap, *The Federal Income Tax Exemption of Charitable Organizations: Its History and Underlying Policy*, in RESEARCH PAPERS SPONSORED BY THE COMMISSION ON PRIVATE PHILANTHROPY AND PUBLIC NEEDS, 2025, 2031 (U.S. Dep't. of the Treasury, ed. 1977) [hereinafter, FILER COMMISSION PAPERS].

3. Bob Jones Univ. v. United States, 461 U.S. 574, 589 n. 13 ("[T]he list of exempt organizations appears to have been patterned upon English income tax statutes . . . . ").

4. Treas. Reg. § 1.501.(c)(3)-1(d)(2) (1959).

5. Rev. Rul. 69-585, 1969-2 C.B. 118.

6. Bob Jones Univ. v. United States, 461 U.S. 574, 586 (1983).

7. WILBUR K. JORDAN, PHILANTHROPY IN ENGLAND 1480-1660, at 112 (1959). Jordan's discussion is typical of the reverential tones that trust law scholars use to describe the preamble: he refers to it as "eloquent," with "almost casual but beautiful wording," that seeks "to state and to ennoble aspirations which had become and were to remain central to the structure of the liberal society." *Id.* at 112, 114.

8. An Act to Redress the Mis-Employment of Lands, Goods and Stocks of Money Heretofore Given to Certain Charitable Uses (Statute of Charitable Uses), 1601, 43 Eliz., ch. 4, *reprinted in* 7 STAT. AT LARGE 43 (Eng. 1763). This preamble is widely quoted, both in the Middle English and in modern prose, by a number of secondary sources addressing charitable trust and charitable exemption law. *E.g.*, Boris I. Bittker & George K. Rahdert, *The Exemption of Nonprofit Organizations from Federal Income Taxation*, 85 YALE L.J. 299, 331 n.81 (1976). This listing bears striking resemblance to a literary passage from William Langland's fourteenth-century poem *Vision of Piers Plowman*, which recites that in order to save their souls, wealthy merchants should devote their fortunes to "repair hospitals, help sick people, mend bad roads, build up bridges that had been broken down, help maidens to marry or to make them nuns, find food for prisoners and poor people, put scholars to school or to some other crafts, help religious orders, and ameliorate rents or taxes." John P. Persons, et al., *Criteria for Exemption Under Section 501(c)(3)*, in FILER COMMISSION PAPERS, *supra* note 2, at 1912, quoting the modern English version of the "B" text of the poem.

9. GEORGE G. BOGERT, THE LAW OF TRUSTS AND TRUSTEES §§ 7–13.

10. SHERIDAN & KEETON, *supra* note 2, at 1–2; Persons, *supra* note 8, at 1916–17.

11. RESTATEMENT (SECOND) OF TRUSTS §§ 209–10, 365, 399.

12. GEORGE JONES, HISTORY OF THE LAW OF CHARITY 1532–1827, at 109–10 (1969).

13. *Id.* at 128.

14. Morice v. Durham, 10 Ves. 521, 7 Rev. Rep. 232 (1804); *see* Austin W. Scott, *Trusts for Charitable and Benevolent Purposes*, 58 HARV. L. REV. 548 (1945).

15. JONES, *supra* note 12, at 133.

16. Persons, *supra* note 8, at 1915 (quoting older edition of Keeton's treatise).

17. 1891 App. Cas. 531 (H.L.).

18. *Id.* at 583.

19. Persons, *supra* note 8, at 1915–16.

20. RESTATEMENT (SECOND) OF TRUSTS § 368(f) (1959).

21. *Id.* § 374 comment c, comment f; *see also* WILLIAM F. FRATCHER, SCOTT ON TRUSTS § 374.2 (1989) (hereinafter SCOTT ON TRUSTS).

22. *In re* Cranston, [1897] 1 I.R. 431, 446–47 (Ir. H. Ct.), *quoted in* SCOTT ON TRUSTS, *supra* note 21, at § 374.7.

23. For example, Professor Thompson argues that the boundless nature of the exemption can be contained by reference to "the common law legal concept of charity." Tommy F. Thompson, *The Unadministrability of the Federal Charitable Tax Exemption: Causes, Effects and Remedies*, 5 VA. TAX REV. 1 (1985).

24. RESTATEMENT (SECOND) OF TRUSTS § 376 comment a. For further elaboration of this distinction, see P. Atiyah, *Public Benefit in Charities*, 21 MOD. L. REV. 138 (1958).

25. *See* SHERIDAN & KEETON, *supra* note 2, at 32–50. *See generally* MICHAEL CHESTERMAN, CHARITIES, TRUSTS AND SOCIAL WELFARE 316 (1959) (discussing the connection between these organizational limitations and the requirement of public benefit).

26. Harrington v. Pier, 105 Wis. 485, 520, 82 N.W. 345, 357 (1900).

27. Ould v. Washington Hosp. for Foundlings, 95 U.S. 303, 311 (1877).

28. Comment, *Collaboration Between Nonprofit Universities and Commercial Enterprises: The Rationale for Exempting Nonprofit Universities from Federal Income Taxation*, 95 YALE L.J. 1857, 1864 (1986).

29. JENS JENSEN, PROPERTY TAXATION IN THE UNITED STATES 148 (1931).

30. Munn v. Illinois, 94 U.S. 113, 126 (1877),

31. Nebbia v. New York, 291 U.S. 502, 536 (1934).

32. SCOTT ON TRUSTS, *supra* note 21, § 368 ("The truth of the matter is that it is impossible to frame a perfect definition of charitable purposes. There is no fixed standard to determine what purposes are charitable."); SHERIDAN & KEETON, *supra* note 2, at 26 ("Judges long ago abandoned the task of attempting to define what a charitable purpose is."). For a particularly tortured attempt to tease some meaning out of the public benefit concept, in the context of distinguishing between legitimate public interest law firms and those established to advance the interests of major commercial firms, *see generally* Oliver Houck, *With Charity for All*, 93 YALE L.J. 1415 (1984).

33. Persons, *supra* note 8, at 1909.

34. Henry B. Hansmann, *The Two Independent Sectors*, A Paper Presented at the Independent Sector Spring Research Forum 4 (Mar. 17, 1988) (unpublished manuscript on file with the authors).

35. *See* University of London v. Yarrow, 24 Eng. Rep. 649 (Ch. 1857) (upholding a trust to establish a veterinary institute).

36. *See* Alvin C. Warren et al., *Property Tax Exemptions for Charitable, Educational, Religious and Governmental Institutions in Connecticut*, 4 CONN. L. REV. 181, 238 & n.212 (1971).

37. I.T. 1475, 1-1 C.B. 184 (1922); I.T. 2134, 4-1 C.B. 214 (1925); I.T. 2282, 5-1 C.B. 80 (1926).

38. In most cases, an income tax exemption would not be relevant to a group of physicians because they usually organize in an entity, such as a partnership or S corporation, that is not subject to a separate income tax. Instead, group earnings are taxed only to the individuals on a pass-through basis. Using an exempt entity, however, may permit doctors a tax advantage on earnings reinvested in capital

equipment. Also, it may open up avenues for tax-exempt bond financing for equipment purchase and facility construction. Moreover, exemption may be important because structural limitations on the partnership or S corporation form of business may require a "regular" corporate entity.

39. Rev. Rul. 69-585, 1969-2 C.B. 118.

40. The IRS refuses to exempt physician groups because it views them as serving the private interests of doctors rather than the public's interest in health care; but this is transparently inconsistent. As long as physician groups are willing to accept anyone in the community able to pay and in need of care, there is no distinction between the public quality of services delivered by physician groups or hospitals. It is true that group practices pay doctors handsome salaries, but doctors also earn handsome incomes from hospitals. Remuneration for services rendered should not defeat nonprofit or charitable status unless the amount paid exceeds the fair market value of the services. *See* John D. Colombo, *Are Associations of Doctors Tax-Exempt? Analyzing Inconsistencies in the Tax Exemption of Health Care Providers*, 9 VA. TAX REV. 469, 492–98 (1990).

41. *See generally, id.* at 517–21; John D. Colombo, *Health Care Reform and Federal Tax Exemption, Rethinking the Issues*, 29 WAKE FOREST L. REV. 215, 216–228 (1994).

42. Federation Pharmacy Services v. Comm'r, 72 T.C. 687 (1979), *aff'd*, 625 F.2d 804 (8th Cir. 1980); *see also* Colombo, *supra* note 40, at 485–92, 512–21.

43. 285 F.2d 800 (Ct. Cl. 1961), *cert. denied*, 368 U.S. 985 (1962).

44. Presbyterian & Reformed Publishing Co. v. Comm'r, 743 F.2d 148 (3d Cir.1984).

45. James Conley, *Tax Court: Arts Groups Are Not 'Literary and Charitable Institutions '*, 9 EXEMPT ORG. TAX REV. 962 (1994).

46. Professor Atkinson stands as the leading exception, as his altruism theory would provide exemption for virtually any nonprofit entity. Rob Atkinson, *Altruism in Nonprofit Organizations*, 31 B.C.L. REV. 501 (1990). Even Professor Atkinson recognizes that some limits on exemption may be necessary, however. *See id.* at 636–37 (possible room for public policy limitation as an extraneous constraint). Professor Atkinson's theory is discussed in detail in Chapter 6.

4

Relief of Government Burden

Although courts and commentators recognize that tax exemption for charitable organizations has its roots in charitable trust law, charitable trust law has never been used as the sole rationale for exemption. Instead, the conventional explanation for exempt status has been that exempt entities relieve government from the burden of performing certain services or providing certain goods for the populace. The essence of this theory is that tax exemption exists as a quid pro quo for the private, nonprofit sector's costs of producing these goods and services that absent exemption would be borne by the government. In the words of Senator Hollis, a principal architect of the federal tax code, "[f]or every dollar" of taxes foregone "the public gets 100 percent" return in free services.[1] This "relief of government burden" or "quid pro quo" theory has been widely expressed by both courts and legislators. As recently as 1991, Representative Brian Donnelly prefaced his introduction of a bill to revise exemption standards for hospitals by noting "the fundamental basis under which Congress exempts organizations from taxation is the belief that those organizations will relieve a governmental burden . . . ."[2] Similarly, in *Bob Jones University v. United States*, the U.S. Supreme Court stated, "charitable exemptions are justified on the basis that the exempt entity confers a public benefit—a benefit which the society or the community may not itself choose or be able to provide, or which supplements and advances the work of public institutions already supported by tax revenues."[3] Another influential court opinion explains that "[t]he rationale for allowing the deduction of charitable contributions has historically been that by doing so, the Government relieves itself of the burden of meeting public needs which in the absence of charitable activity would fall on the shoulders of the Government."[4]

General Deficiencies in the Government Burden Theory

Historical Consistency and Universality

Despite its near-universal acceptance as a rationale for exemption, the relief of government burden theory fails on a number of fronts. First, the theory fails the historical consistency criterion because it does not explain exemption for a number of traditionally-exempt activities. Many classic charitable activities are not, technically speaking, government responsibilities, and the most prominent activity—religion—is one for which there is not only no governmental obligation but an outright prohibition on governmental involvement. The government burden theory might accommodate this anomaly as sui generis in our governmental structure, except that there are many other instances of traditionally exempt functions that cannot properly be said to constitute a governmental responsibility. Referring to the listing in § 501(c)(3) quoted in the second chapter (exempting religious, charitable, scientific, literary and educational institutions) only education clearly appears to fit the characterization of a traditional government responsibility, and even it is not a traditional function of the *federal* government, which confers income tax exemption.

A somewhat modified version of the government burden theory, known as the "relief-of-poverty" formulation, avoids some of the deficiencies of the strict version by encompassing any free service rendered to the poor. This version of the government burden theory recognizes the government has a strong interest in the relief of poverty even if the government is not affirmatively obliged to directly render the particular form of relief. Under this formulation, one need not show that the government would actually have chosen to or have been obliged to render the same service absent the exemption. One can presume that any services given to the poor are sufficiently needed that the government, and society generally, has an interest in supporting the service organization.

A theory of charitable exemption that is based on the relief of poverty in any manner is broadly consistent with the original purpose and context of the Statute of Charitable Uses, which, as discussed in the prior chapter, is the principal source of the common law's concept of charity. This statute was enacted in conjunction with the Elizabethan Poor Laws,[5] which sought to address the critical problems faced by the increasingly destitute populations in urban centers. The Poor Laws placed the responsibility on local towns to care for their indigent residents. At the same time the Statute of Charitable Uses sought to lessen this local governmental burden by strengthening the role of private philanthropy. The historical connection between these two statutes demonstrates that the original notion of charity was principally concerned with the relief of poverty. Michael Chesterman explains that, "according to the intentions of the Elizabethan legislature and the authoritative contemporary interpretation, the 1601 preamble's concept of 'charitable' contained a 'public benefit' requirement calling for benefit to the poor . . . . Without this, the Act's objective of lightening the burden of parish poor relief . . . would not be achieved."[6] Another influential historian elaborates:

> To prevent vagabondage and begging the state undertook [in the Poor Law] to maintain only the poor and impotent, the utterly helpless. Those in a position to pay have, therefore, no claim on state support. In housing such inmates an institution is in no way relieving the state of a burden which the latter has ever undertaken to bear.[7]

Care for the indigent is also at the core of the rationale for granting charities immunity from tort liability in some states when the doctrine of charitable immunity still existed.[8]

Nevertheless, a conception of charity limited to free services to the poor would radically alter the current scope of the exemption. The notion that the Statute of Charitable Uses was restricted to services for the poor prevailed for only a comparatively short time in British law. Instead, the law of charities has long since held that trusts need not serve the poor at all to be classified as charitable. In *Commissioners v. Pemsel,*[9] discussed in the previous chapter, Lord McNaughten recognized this fact and rejected relief of poverty as the sole ground for charitable trust classification.

Nor has the concept of poverty relief governed the law of charity in more modern times. The classic charitable purposes, religion and education, have always served the rich as well as the poor. Several of the classic instances of tax-exempt charitable organizations in modern times serve the rich almost exclusively—symphony orchestras, art museums and opera companies, for example. Some individual churches and schools serve the rich predominantly, if not exclusively. Likewise, hospitals, which were once considered exempt because of their historical role as "almshouses for the poor," were never exclusively devoted to the care of indigent patients. Instead, doctors were allowed to supplement their salaries with paying patients. Even as long ago as the 1930s, as many as 90 percent of hospital patients paid their own way;[10] today, nonprofit hospitals provide even less of their resources without compensation.[11]

The same observation is true for charities generally, which, after the 17th century in England and after the advent of the massive governmental welfare programs in the United States, have devoted only a small portion of their resources to social services for the poor. Professor Roberts documents that, in England after 1660, "payments under the Poor Law became almost everywhere the ordinary source of relief for indigence with private charity a supplementary source of varying importance, called on for great efforts only in times of extraordinary distress."[12] In contemporary America, "[p]rivate charity in the United States is approximately zero" in the sense of helping the poor; only 10 percent of philanthropic donations go to "social services" and only a fraction of that amount goes to the poor.[13]

One might attempt to rebut these historical authorities by observing that they establish only that charities need not *exclusively* serve the poor; none supports the much bolder proposition that an institution is charitable even it if provides *no* free care for the poor.[14] As just noted, however, several classes of traditionally exempt entities in fact cater almost exclusively to those who are well off. These mixed precedents can be reconciled through yet another variation of the government burden/quid-pro-quo theory, one that values any free services, regardless of whether they are given to the poor or to the community at large. This "gift-to-the-community" variant[15] sees the charity relieving government burden by returning to the community the value of the tax exemption through any service the government would be empowered to render if it so chose (absent a specific prohibition such as the Establishment Clause).

Because this looser gift-to-the-community variation counts any free services to the community as government relief, it encounters fewer obstacles in satisfying historical and modern precedents. Nevertheless, IRS and state tax rulings are wildly inconsistent on whether and to what extent various charities must render any free services in order to qualify for tax exemption. Hospitals need not provide any free care except in the emergency room, whereas nonprofit nursing homes may not discharge any of their patients for failure to pay. In order to be tax exempt, public interest law firms may receive compensation for only half the costs of their services, consumer credit counseling agencies must discount all their services, and grocers serving low-income customers may not charge anything.[16] Therefore, although this gift-to-the-community variation has broader compatibility with historical precedents, it still falls short of reconciling the quid pro quo theory with the modern scope of the exemption. Whether this is a failure of the modern administration of the exemption, or whether this is a failure of the theory itself, will be revealed by examining other criteria for evaluation.

Deservedness

The most essential inquiry for evaluating a particular theory of charitable tax exemption is whether it identifies a set of activities that are both worthy of and in need of the exemption. The first portion of this deservedness criterion appears to be easily met by the government burden theory since it requires the showing of a concrete quid pro quo. One might quibble, as the different variations do, over whether the return services must be explicit government obligations or traditional government services, whether only service to the poor counts, or whether any free service to the community is equally worthy. For instance, the South Dakota Supreme Court ruled that a health club that, among other activities, sponsors "Splashdash Parties," does not relieve a government burden.[17] Regardless of which version of the government burden is *most* compelling, however, in our view any of them establishes at least a plausible case for worth so long as services to the community are free.

Still, one might have qualms about using the exemption to support government functions from private sales in only a small portion of the economy. In order for nonprofit institutions to deliver free or heavily discounted services, they must raise their rates to paying customers if they do not receive substantial donations. This creates a form of redistribution through cross-subsidization that might be highly regressive, depending on the nature of the service, who is paying, and who is being subsidized. For example, in the case of hospitals, this cross-subsidization might be characterized as a tax on the sick to benefit the mostly middle class patients who are uninsured.[18] This regressive redistributive characterization is heightened by observing that the resulting increase in health insurance costs produces a tax benefit (due to the exclusion of employer-paid health insurance premiums under I.R.C. § 106) whose incidence falls more heavily on the rich. As a consequence, academic commentators have observed that internal hospital cross-subsidization "is a profoundly regressive way to finance care for the poor."[19]

On the other hand, this form of redistribution by voluntary private transaction, unlike government taxation, is not coerced. Moreover, if hospitals did not deliver some services for free, their pricing behavior for paying patients would not necessarily be any less irrational or exploitative. Hospitals would only make different use of the profits. Therefore, as long as nonprofit entities devote their revenue surplus to a use that relieves a government burden, the fact that the government might accomplish the same objective more efficiently or fairly is not a decisive blow to the worth of the free services that nonprofits in fact render.[20]

More troubling is whether charitable entities need the tax exemption in order to continue providing free services. In Chapter 1, we explain that the deservedness criterion entails this need component as well. To satisfy it under the government burden standard, nonprofit organizations must show that their free services would be irreplaceably compromised without the subsidy—that is, that in the absence of exemption, these services would not be provided by either themselves or by a for-profit entity.

As for nonprofits themselves, it is difficult to know for sure whether an exempt entity might continue the free service at the same level even without the exemption since no before-and-after studies are available. It is possible, however, to obtain a glimmer of insight by observing the variation in free services according to varying degrees of exemption benefits among similar entities, controlling for other factors. Doing so for hospitals, for instance, reveals a cloudy picture. Existing research shows some relationship between the size of the tax subsidy and the amount of free services, but not a large statistically significant one.[21]

It is easier to examine whether, in the absence of nonprofit provision, for-profits would pick up the slack. In several sectors of charitable activity, there is no competition between for-profit and nonprofit entities. The only alterative to nonprofits is government provision or going without. This is true for churches and social welfare agencies, for instance. However, most exempt sectors do contain for-profit versions of the same activity. Education, performing arts, day care facilities, and hospitals are classic examples. It is possible in these cases to determine whether exempt providers give away services that are not given away by similarly-situated for-profit providers, and hence would become the expense of government if exempt entities did not exist.

This comparison with for-profit competitors is necessary under the government burden theory because, without nonprofits, the full amount of the free care they provide would not fall on the government. Moreover, a certain portion of free care provided by nonprofits is not voluntarily given in the spirit of charity but merely reflects "a business decision that the cost of attempting to collect on a debt is greater than the potential gain."[22] Therefore, the bad debt component of free services represents an ordinary cost of doing business borne by nonprofits and for-profits alike. As observed by one judge who criticized a hospital for attempting to claim credit for bad debt amounts, "[t]hese 'uncompensated care' patients . . . are aggressively pursued by [the hospital] through every avenue of the collection process. [The hospital] has sued the very patients that it would now have this court deem objects of charity."[23]

For similar reasons, it is often necessary to discount or disqualify free services whose purpose is promotional, since these too are ordinary, revenue-enhancing business decisions. For instance, nonprofit hospitals often attempt to claim credit for free health screening and health promotion campaigns, which also serve the purpose of advertising their services and attracting paying customers. Again, the surest test for whether the service is not actually a gift to the community is whether for-profit competitors provide similar free services. When the U.S. Government Accounting Office studied these hospital community benefit programs, it found that, although nonprofit hospitals were somewhat more likely to offer them, for-profit hospitals also did so and were equally likely not to charge for them.[24]

The point of this analysis is that, properly applied, the government burden theory is fully capable of meeting both the worth and the need branches of the demanding deservedness criterion. Whether in fact particular nonprofit institutions actually measure up is a separate question, one that we defer until our case study of hospitals, later in this chapter. At this point, it is sufficient to conclude that, as an abstract theory, the government burden rationale establishes a strong case for deservedness.

Proportionality

On the other hand, the relief of government burden theory, in both its strict and its looser incarnations, suffers under the proportionality criterion because the financial benefit provided by exemption bears no predictable relation to the costs of providing the service that relieves the government burden. Moreover, to the extent there is a relation between costs and benefits, exemption has a perverse tendency to operate in a profoundly regressive fashion, awarding the largest subsidy to those organizations that least need it and deserve it, other things being equal. Students of tax expenditure analysis will recognize that a general tax exemption suffers from the same "upside down" effect as do many tax deductions:[25] those entities with the highest net revenues or the greatest value of otherwise-taxable property receive the greatest amount of subsidy, yet these are the entities that least need support. At a tax rate of 35%, for example (the current maximum corporate rate), an entity with net revenues of $1 million receives a tax subsidy of $350,000, while an entity with net revenues of $100,000 receives a subsidy of just $35,000. From the standpoint of equity among different tax-exempt entities, the result of the general tax exemption is that entities that are the "poorest" in either an income or property tax sense, and thus most in need of subsidization to perform the services that relieve government burdens, in fact receive the least government assistance.

Moreover, because services and goods provided by exempt entities constitute an expense item, those organizations with the most net revenues are more likely to have actually rendered the least free services, all other things being equal. Similarly, for the property tax exemption, those organizations that devote the most net surplus to capital expansion, rather than using surplus to support the poor, will enjoy the largest subsidy.[26] Suppose, for instance, an entity receives a charitable exemption for providing housing for the urban poor. If its net revenues were ten percent of its gross revenues because it uses almost all of its revenues to subsidize housing, the value of the income tax exemption would be small in comparison with an entity of the same financial size that retains ninety percent of its net income yet still pays no taxes. The entity that provides nine times more free services would receive an implicit tax subsidy worth only 1/9th as much as the other entity, all other things being equal. Put simply, because the financial benefits of exemption do not necessarily correspond in dollar amount to the costs of providing the free services, exemption can either oversubsidize (if the value of exemption is greater than costs of the services) or undersubsidize (if the value of the exemption is less than the costs of the services provided) the entity providing the services.

These problems might be ameliorated if the exemption were administered on a institution-specific, annual basis, requiring each organization to demonstrate yearly its delivery of free services in an increment sufficient to earn the subsidy. In such a system, an institution with sufficient property and net revenues would receive a tax benefit at least equal to the dollar value of its free services. This system, however, would not help those entities whose free services were sufficient only to *partially* justify a tax exemption. At the other extreme, this system would provide no benefit under an income tax exemption to an institution that gives away so many free services that its net revenues are zero. Hence, even this theoretical system would suffer proportionality problems. Such a system would also be more cumbersome to administer than the current system.

Another corrective technique would be to replace the exemption with a tax credit, guaranteeing proportionate support to each organization by allowing each to subtract the exact amount or a defined portion of its annual charity services from its tax liability. But a tax credit is not just a minor repair; it is a repudiation of the exemption, because it replaces the exemption with a system that is, in effect, simply another means for administering a direct subsidy. Moreover, unless the law contains a concept of a "refundable credit"—i.e., provides a cash refund to entities with no tax liability—the system would still suffer from proportionality problems.[27]

Another troubling aspect of the government burden theory under the proportionality criterion stems from the intergovernmental nature of the tax exemption subsidy and the multi-jurisdictional nature of many traditionally charitable services. Specifically, the burdens relieved are not necessarily those of the particular taxing authority that grants the exemption. Instead, one governmental unit may be enjoying the charitable services supported by another's subsidy. This phenomenon has been explored most comprehensively in the context of the property tax exemption for education, where, for instance, it is extremely difficult to maintain that Cambridge, Massachusetts receives a fair quid pro quo for Harvard University's exemption via the city's relief from the burden of operating a university of international stature.[28] Clearly, the government burden of operating such an institution would be borne at a state or perhaps national level absent the tax subsidy. Similarly, the connection between the federal *income tax* exemption and local primary education is equally remote, since primary education generally has been the responsibility of local and state, not federal government.

As noted in Chapter 1, one way to test proportionality is to consider whether the particular form of subsidy that the theory contemplates might be more rationally administered through a system of direct subsidies or direct provision. Direct funding is readily available for delivering many historically exempt services. Examples include government schools, hospitals, and welfare programs. Under the proportionality criterion, these are vastly superior to the exemption for their ability to accommodate widely varying needs over time and among different localities according to demographic factors. A direct subsidy is also just as easy or difficult to administer properly as a tax exemption. As Professors Surrey and McDaniel have observed, the degree of administrative complexity is not a function of the method of subsidy. Rather, the apparent simplicity of the tax subsidy is purchased at the price of a sacrifice in monitoring and accuracy, a trade-off that could be accomplished just as well in a direct subsidy system, if we so desired.[29]

Not everyone, of course, believes that direct expenditures are preferable to tax subsidies. Professor Edward Zelinsky has argued strongly that the tax and finance committees in Congress are subject to greater political and public oversight than are the more specialized subject matter committees that originate direct subsidy legislation. Because of the more focused interest group pressures that come to bear on these specialized committees, he contends that they are more subject to industry capture and therefore to compromise of the public interest. Accordingly, Zelinsky believes that "tax subsidies ought to be preferred to direct expenditures when there is a need for detached administration and oversight by decisionmakers less suscepti- ble to capture."[30] Zelinsky's arguments may carry some force when the questions concern specific subsidies for specific interest groups. Charitable tax exemption, however, covers a myriad of activities that stretch across every economic sector of the country. In this arena it is clear that neither Congress nor the IRS has been able to stop the inexorable growth of the exempt sector. Congress, for example, has not seriously reconsidered what entities should qualify for exemption since the 1969 tax reform hearings.[31] As for the IRS, in 1990 it approved 38,469 applications for exemption, while rejecting only 656; in fact, the rejection rate over the last decade has dropped from one in twenty-seven applications in 1980 to one in sixty applications in 1990.[32] If anything, the nonprofit sector has already coopted the legislative and administrative machinery of taxation; one can hardly imagine direct expenditure machinery that would produce more dramatic results. Moreover, concern about interest group pressures on direct subsidies should be lower in the nonprofit sector, which is precluded from excessive lobbying as a condition of charitable status.[33] Therefore, Zelin- sky's arguments, if valid at all, apply only to amendments that would create activity- or industry-specific tax exclusions rather than to the administration and interpretation of the generic charitable exemption.

In summary, neither the strict formulation of the relief of government burden theory nor the relief-of-poverty/gift-to-the-community variants are accurate as general explanations for the charitable tax exemption in anything like its current or historical scope. These theories also suffer under the proportionality criterion. These defects are not fatal, however. Rejecting relief of government burden as the only explanation for exemption does not necessarily preclude its serving as a sufficient standard. If the test is both properly formulated and met by a particular entity or sector, a strong case can be made for its deserving an implicit subsidy through the tax system, particularly where the quid pro quo is earned through free services to the poor. This deservedness showing is an exacting one, however, that has not yet been made by most parts of the nonprofit sector. It requires a demon- stration of free services greater than those provided by any for-profit competitors and greater by an amount that equals the value of all attributes of exempt status. We will use nonprofit hospitals as a specific case in point to explore whether actual exempt entities can meet this demanding test in real world settings.

Nonprofit Hospitals as a Case Study

Nonprofit hospitals claim that they easily meet the government burden test by giving away billions of dollars of services for free each year.[34] This argument contains a number of flaws, however. First, they count as free services not only true "charity" care, which is treatment for which the hospital never expects to receive payment, but also bad debts, which are accounts that were initially billed to the patients but not collected, due largely to the costs of collection and the poor likelihood of recovery. As discussed above, these bad debts should not count as a "gift to the community" since they are an ordinary business practice engaged in equally by for-profit hospitals. Moreover, some hospitals attempt to claim as free care the "contractual adjustments" that represent the difference between a hospital's normal charges and the amount the hospital agrees to accept from a third-party insurer. Once again, though, it is inappropriate to count these voluntary bulk discounting arrangements as "gifts," particularly when for-profit hospitals engage in the same activity.[35]

The difficulty with focusing on pure charity care, however, is that this designation rests on the subjective reasons for discounting services. This corporate "state of mind" test might allow hospitals to simply adjust their accounting practices to reflect more of their bad debts and contractual adjustments in their charity care ledgers. One simple solution to these measurement complexities is to deduct from nonprofits' total uncompensated care figures the proportion of free care rendered by for-profit hospitals. This is justifiable under the approximation that essentially all for-profit free care constitutes bad debt. It is also justified by the need component of our earlier evaluation, which holds that no relief of government burden exists to the extent that for-profit competitors stand to pick up the slack.

More troublesome is whether this increment should be measured in terms of charges or costs. Hospitals traditionally report uncompensated care in terms of foregone revenues measured by their normal charge structures. The difficulty is that, like the manufacturer's suggested retail price on consumer electronics, hospitals seldom collect their posted charges. Therefore, they can manipulate the level of reported charity care simply by posting price increases they never intend to collect. However, the attempt to substitute a measure of "true" costs for nominal charges encounters the difficulties of whether to measure only marginal costs rather than total average costs. A fair case can be made for crediting hospitals with only marginal costs, since the short-run costs of filling a few empty beds with nonpaying patients or taking a few additional X-rays with an already-purchased machine are rather slight. Nevertheless, because nonpaying patients are a permanent burden, these costs will eventually result in having to expand the facility somewhat more and replace worn equipment somewhat earlier. Therefore, total average costs are a fair measure. The simplest means of measurement is to deduct from posted charges an average cost-to-charge ratio that reflects the experience of the entire hospital.

Using these measures of free care, the existing empirical evidence is much more ambivalent about whether nonprofit hospitals provide sufficient relief of the government burden of delivering health care to pay back the full value of their exemption. From the fragmentary evidence available, it appears that nonprofit hospitals do not provide incremental free care services that match their foregone tax revenues. The only extensive study that directly measures the value of tax savings conservatively estimates that California nonprofit hospitals gave $82 million in charity care in 1984–1985 and saved $300 million in federal and state tax revenue.[36] One national study indicates that "most voluntary and proprietary hospitals [are] very similar in their willingness to treat patients freely. . . . [F]or the nation as a whole there appear to be only small differences between voluntary and proprietary hospitals in access to care."[37] The leading study found "no clear difference between for-profits and not-for-profits," the former supplying 3.7% of their care for free in 1983 and the latter 4.2%. By comparison, the figure for public hospitals is 11.5%. "Overall, the national data from AHA surveys provide weak support for the hypothesis that for-profit hospitals do less than not-for-profit hospitals to meet the needs of patients who are unable to pay."[38] On an aggregate dollar basis, nonprofit hospitals provided an increment of uncompensated care above that provided by for-profits, in the following amounts: 1982—$1.06 billion; 1981—$0.51 billion; 1980—$0.41 billion.[39] Even taking into account inflation, these amounts are dwarfed by the $8.5 billion recent estimate of the annual value of the exemption.[40]

A similar comparison consists of adding (1) the percentage of revenue for-profit hospitals typically lose to uncompensated care and (2) the percentage of revenue they pay in taxes, and then (3) comparing that sum to the percentage of revenues exempt hospitals report as uncompensated care. This formula assumes that nonprofits are relieved from approximately the same proportion of taxes as for-profits pay.[41] On a national level, this comparison does not justify providing a tax exemption to nonprofits. In

1983, for the four largest investor-owned multihospital companies (Hospital Corporation of America (HCA), Humana, National Medical Enterprises (NME), and American Medical International (AMI)), "the sum of income taxes and uncompensated care (5.6 % of gross revenues) exceeded the 4.1% of gross revenues that not-for-profit hospitals accounted for as uncompensated care."[42]

The scattered data on a local level are also equally unconvincing. For example, a study of eleven nonprofit hospitals and four for-profits in Utah found that in 1986 the nonprofits provided only one-third the amount of uncompensated care that for-profits incurred in free care plus taxes (3.2% versus 10.3% of net revenue).[43] Similarly, data reported for 1984 by the North Carolina Center for Public Policy Research revealed that nonprofit hospitals in Wake County reported 4% of their revenues as uncompensated care, while for-profits in the same area reported uncompensated care plus taxes of 14.1% of gross revenues—more than *three times* the nonprofit amount.[44] A selective sampling in Florida found that five of seven provided much less charity care than the value of their tax exemptions.[45] When measured at an individual-hospital level, however, some particular institutions, especially urban teaching hospitals, easily meet this standard.

Proponents of hospital exemption frequently attempt to circumvent these unsupportive or inconclusive statistics by positing a notion of deservedness that is not grounded on a strict quid pro quo formulation. This alternative theory requires only that tax-exempt hospitals maintain an "open door" policy, accepting every patient seeking admission regardless of ability to pay.[46] Hospitals contend that maintaining an open admissions policy meets their social responsibility because hospitals treat all indigent patients who actually seek care. Anything more would require hospitals unfairly to provide more free care than is demanded. This is a refrain that is likely to emerge even more strongly if national health care reform is enacted that provides universal coverage.

Even assuming that nonprofit hospitals practice an open door policy as fervently as they preach it,[47] this formulation of the government burden theory is flawed because it does not require a showing that hospitals actually relieve poverty. If the need for free care ever becomes so slight that hospitals are prevented from establishing that they render a quid pro quo for the exemption, then no significant government burden exists for hospitals to relieve. It may be unfortunate for them that they cease to meet this test, but the fact would remain that, under this criterion of deservedness, the need for an indirect subsidy has been displaced by increased direct government subsidies.

The difficulties that nonprofit hospitals face in satisfying a carefully-applied application of the government burden theory are likely to be encountered by entities in many other nonprofit sectors, particularly those like education and day care that have significant for-profit competition. Only the purely charitable arenas of social welfare and religion, where the tax benefits are fewer and the relief of government burden more obvious, are likely to be easy cases. But the number of such cases, although significant, are likely to be very small in proportion to the existing size of the nonprofit sector. Therefore, the relief of government burden rationale, while sufficient in theory, is inadequate as a general explanation for the actual, existing scope of the exemption.

Notes

1. 55 CONG. REC. S6728 (1917).
2. 137 CONG. REC. E896 (1991).
3. Bob Jones Univ. v. United States, 461 U.S. 574, 590–91 (1983).
4. McGlotten v. Connally, 338 F. Supp. 448, 456 (D.D.C. 1972). *See also* H.R. Rep. No. 1860, 75th Cong. 3d Sess. 19 (1938) ("The exemption from taxation of money or property devoted to charitable and other purposes is based upon the theory the Government is compensated for the loss of revenue by its relief from the financial burden which would otherwise have to be met by appropriations from other public funds . . ."); Rob Atkinson, *Rationales for Federal Income Tax Exemption* 12, n.18, *in* RATIONALES FOR FEDERAL INCOME TAX EXEMPTION (1991) (collection of papers prepared for the 1991 NYU Conference on Philanthropy and the Law); BRUCE R. HOPKINS, THE LAW OF TAX-EXEMPT ORGANIZATIONS 8–9 (6th ed. 1992) (exemption is "derivative of the concept that they perform functions which, in the organizations' absence, government would have to perform); *Report of the Filer Commission, in* RESEARCH PAPERS SPONSORED BY THE COMMISSION ON PRIVATE PHILANTHROPY AND PUBLIC NEEDS 103 (U.S. Dep't. of the Treasury ed., 1977) (hereafter FILER COMMISSION PAPERS) (relief of government burden theory "a frequently cited justification" for exemption).
5. An Act for the Relief of the Poor, 1601, 43 Eliz. 1, ch. 2., *reprinted in* 7 STAT. AT LARGE 30 (Eng. 1763).
6. MICHAEL R. CHESTERMAN, CHARITIES, TRUSTS AND SOCIAL WELFARE 56–57 (1979).
7. George J. Adler, *Historical Origin of the Exemption From Taxation of Charitable Institutions*, in WESTCHESTER COUNTY CHAMBER OF COMMERCE, TAX EXEMPTIONS OF REAL ESTATE: AN INCREASING MENACE 59, 80 (1922). *See also* GARETH JONES, HISTORY OF THE LAW OF CHARITY 22–23 (1969) (discussing the connection between the Elizabethan Poor Laws and the Statute of Charitable Uses); LIONEL A. SHERIDAN & GEORGE W. KEETON, THE MODERN LAW OF CHARITIES 8–9 (3d ed. 1983) (same).

8. *See* Morton v. Savannah Hosp., 148 Ga. 438, 96 S.E. 887, 887–88 (1918) (charitable immunity attaches only to treatment of nonpaying patients); Adams v. University Hosp., 122 Mo. App. 675, 99 S.W. 453, 454 (1907) (the purpose of the charitable immunity is to prevent funds from being "diverted from such kindly purposes" as "administering relief to those in need"). *But see* City of Richmond v. Richmond Memorial Hosp., 202 Va. 86, 116 S.E.2d 79, 83 (1960) ("[S]everal tort cases . . . establish that hospitals . . . are 'charitable' institutions despite the fact that they charge all who can afford to pay.").

9. 1891 App. Cas. 531 (H.L.).

10. DAVID ROSNER, A ONCE CHARITABLE ENTERPRISE: HOSPITALS AND HEALTH CARE IN BROOKLYN AND NEW YORK, 1885–1915, at 8–9, 36–61 (1982); PAUL STARR, THE SOCIAL TRANSFORMATION OF AMERICAN MEDICINE 146 (1982); Rosemary Stevens, *Voluntary and Governmental Activity*, HEALTH MATRIX, Spr. 1985, at 26, 28.

11. *See* Mark A. Hall & John D. Colombo, *The Charitable Status of Nonprofit Hospitals: Toward a Donative Theory of Tax Exemption*, 66 WASH. L. REV. 307, 346–48 (1990).

12. James Roberts, *A Positive Model of Private Charity and Public Transfers*, 92 J. POL. ECON. 136, 141 (1984).

13. *Id.* at 147 & n.47.

14. Note, *Hospitals, Tax Exemption, and the Poor*, 10 HARV. C.R.-C.L. L. REV. 653, 679 (1975).

15. *See* Utah County v. Intermountain Health Care, Inc., 709 P.2d 265, 269–70 (Utah 1985) (charity requires a "gift to the community" that "can be identified either by a substantial imbalance in the exchange between the charity and the recipient of its services *or* in the lessening of a government burden").

16. *See* John P. Persons, et al., *Criteria for Exemption Under Section 501(c)(3)*, *in* FILER COMMISSION PAPERS, *supra* note 4, at 1909, 1940–1949 (1977) (discussing various rulings and noting a "considerable degree of ad hoc line-drawing by the IRS . . . in this area"); John G. Simon, *The Tax Treatment of Nonprofit Organizations: A Review of Federal and State Policies*, *in* THE NONPROFIT SECTOR: A RESEARCH HANDBOOK 67, 85 (Walter W. Powell, ed., 1987).

17. Sioux Valley Hospital Association v. South Dakota State Board of Equalization, 513 N.W.2d 562 (S.D. 1994).

18. *See* PAUL FELDSTEIN, HEALTH CARE ECONOMICS 268–69 (1979) (criticizing hospital internal cross-subsidization); Robert Clark, *Does the Nonprofit Form Fit the Hospital Industry?*, 93 HARV. L. REV. 1417, 1438 n39, 1467 (1980) (describing as "elitist" the "minigovernment" model of hospital exemption which fosters redistribution of income through covert "taxation," effectively "disenfranchising" the public); Charles Phelps, *Cross-Subsidies and Charge-Shifting in American Hospitals*, *in* UNCOMPENSATED HOSPITAL CARE: RIGHTS AND RESPONSIBILITIES 108 (1986) (same); Richard Posner, *Taxation by Regulation*, 2 BELL J. ECON. & MGMT. SCI. 22 (1971) (seminal discussion of the economic effect of hidden taxation).

19. Robert A. Carolina & M. Gregg Bloche, *Paying for Undercompensated Hospital Care: The Regressive Profile of a "Hidden Tax,"* 2 HEALTH MATRIX 141, 147 (1992). *See also* Howard P. Tuckman & Cyril F. Chang, *Who Bears the Burden of Uncompensated Hospital Care?* 2 J. HEALTH & SOC. POL'Y 9 (1990).

20. *Accord*, Howell v. County Board of Cache County, 1994 WL 479554 (Utah 1994) ("Hospitals ease the community's burden by channeling funds, both donations and fees for services, to provide indigent care.").

21. Richard Frank & David Salkever, *The Supply of Charity Service by Non-Profit Hospitals: Motives and Market Structure*, 22 RAND J. ECO. 430 (1991); Kenneth Thorpe & C. Phelps, *The Social Role of Not-for-Profit Organizations: Hospital Provision of Charity Care*, 29 ECO. INQUIRY 472 (1991). Instead, these researchers find that hospitals are much more likely to be responsive to the level of charity care provided by their competitors in the same market..

22. James Simpson & Diane Lee, *Nonprofit Community Hospital Tax Exemption: Issues for Review* 10 n.14, *reprinted in Unrelated Business Income Tax, Hearings Before the Subcomm. on Oversight of the House Comm. on Ways and Means*, 100th Cong., 1st Sess. 778 (1987).

23. School Dist. v. Hamot Medical Center, No. 138-A-1989, slip op. at 14 (Pa. Ct. C.P., Erie Co., May 18, 1990).

24. U.S. GENERAL ACCOUNTING OFFICE, NONPROFIT HOSPITALS AND THE NEED FOR BETTER STANDARDS FOR TAX EXEMPTION, REP. NO. 90-84, at 4 (May 30, 1990) (hereafter GAO REPORT).

25. *See* STANLEY S. SURREY & PAUL R. MCDANIEL, TAX EXPENDITURES 71–72 (1985).

26. The first source to note this regressive effect was Note, *Exemption of Education, Philanthropic and Religious Institutions from State Real Property Taxes*, 64 HARV. L. REV. 288, 294 (1950); *see also*, Alvin C.Warren, Jr., et al., *Property Tax Exemptions for Charitable, Educational, Religious and Governmental Institutions in Connecticut*, 4 CONN. L. REV. 181, 300 (1971).

27. *See generally*, SURREY & MCDANIEL, *supra* note 24, at 108–11.

28. Chauncey Belknap, *The Federal Income Tax Exemption of Charitable Organizations: Its History and Underlying Policy, in* FILER COMMISSION PAPERS, *supra* note 4, at 2025, 2033.

29. SURREY & MCDANIEL, *supra* note 25, at 100–02.

30. Edward A. Zelinsky, *James Madison and Public Choice at Gucci Gulch: A Procedural Defense of Tax Expenditures and Tax Institutions*, 102 YALE L.J. 1165, 1190 (1993).

31. GILBERT M. GAUL & NEILL A. BOROWSKI, FREE RIDE: THE TAX EXEMPT ECONOMY 18 (1993).

32. *Id.*

33. See discussion in Chapter 2, *supra*.

34. U.S. PROSPECTIVE PAYMENT ASSESSMENT COMMISSION, THE TREND AND DISTRIBUTION OF HOSPITAL UNCOMPENSATED CARE COSTS (Oct. 1991).

35. The possible exception is for Medicaid shortfalls, since hospitals have little discretion to refuse Medicaid patients, and since the shortfalls are often much more substantial than under Medicare. *See In re* St. Margaret Seneca Place, 640 A.2d 380 (Pa. 1994) (nursing home entitled to exemption due to Medicaid shortfalls of one-third of treatment costs for half of patients).

36. Simpson & Lee, *supra* note 22, at 10 n.14.

37. J. ROGERS HOLLINGSWORTH & ELLEN J. HOLLINGSWORTH, CONTROVERSY ABOUT AMERICAN HOSPITALS: FUNDING, OWNERSHIP AND PERFORMANCE 106–07 (1987).

38. INSTITUTE OF MEDICINE, FOR PROFIT ENTERPRISE IN HEALTH CARE 102 (Bradford J. Gray ed., 1986). For 1988, these numbers were estimated to be 4.8% for nonprofits, 5.2% for for-profits. GAO REPORT, *supra* note 23, at 2. *See also* U.S. PROSPECTIVE PAYMENT COMMISSION, *supra* note 33; David Burda, *Charity Care: Are Hospitals Giving Their Fair Share?*, MODERN HEALTHCARE, June 15, 1992, at 33. These aggregate, national comparisons, however, are not representative of each location because for-profit hospitals are unevenly distributed across the country. In a study commissioned by the Volunteer Trustees of Not-For-Profit Hospitals Foundation, Lewin & Associates observed that for-profits are concentrated mostly in southern and western states that tend to have less generous Medicaid programs for the poor and, thus, a greater demand for indigent care by private hospitals. In contrast, nonprofit hospitals are more evenly dispersed across the fifty states, which means that their average national uncompensated care statistics are diluted by those states where there is much less need for private hospital charity. This study demonstrates that, in a selection of four states where for-profits compete with nonprofits, nonprofit hospitals outperform proprietary institutions at a level ample to meet the deservedness criterion at its threshold. Carl Lewin et al., *Setting the Record Straight: The Provision of Uncompensated Care by Not-For-Profit Hospitals*, 318 N. ENG. J. MED. 1212, 1213–14 (in Florida, North Carolina, Tennessee and Virginia, the uncompensated care burden is 50% to 90% higher at nonprofit hospitals than at investor-owned hospitals).

39. These numbers are derived from data collected by the AHA, as reported in NORTH CAROLINA CENTER FOR PUBLIC POLICY RESEARCH, COMPARING PERFORMANCE OF FOR-PROFIT AND NOT-FOR-PROFIT HOSPITALS IN NORTH CAROLINA 48 (1989). The AHA declined to provide similar data for subsequent years.

40. *See* Simpson & Lee, *supra* note 22. This estimate is based upon annual data from 1986 and 1988. *See also, Hospital Charity Care and Tax Exempt Status: Restoring the Commitment and Fairness, Hearings Before the Select Committee on Aging* 60 (1990) (estimating foregone revenues at $8 billion).

41. This assumption is a fair approximation for income and property taxes combined because even though nonprofits may have proportionately less income than for-profits, nonprofits tend to have higher valued property than for-profits. *See* Henry B. Hansmann, *The Effect of Tax Exemption and Other Factors on the Market Share of Nonprofit Versus For-Profit Firms*, 40 NAT'L TAX J. 71, 80 (1987).

42. INSTITUTE OF MEDICINE, *supra* note 38, at 114. Even this unfavorable comparison fails to account for property taxes paid by the proprietary hospitals, which would substantially increase the nonprofit deficit.

43. Pace Management Services, 1986 Financia/Charity/"Social Overhead" Performance of Wasatch Front [Utah] Hospitals 3 (1989) (unpublished study performed by private consulting firm).

44. NORTH CAROLINA CENTER FOR PUBLIC POLICY RESEARCH, *supra* note 39, at 168–91. In contrast, the United States General Accounting Office compared uncompensated care by nonprofit hospitals in five states (California, Florida, Iowa, Michigan and New York) with their estimated income tax liability had they not been exempt, and by this measure found that only 15% of the hospitals failed to render uncompensated care equal in value to the value of their exemption. GAO Report, *supra* note 24, at 143. This comparison, however, failed to account for the value of the property tax exemption, the charitable deduction, or tax-exempt bond financing, and also failed to measure nonprofit uncompensated care against a base from representative for-profit institutions.

45. MODERN HEALTHCARE, Nov. 1, 1993, at 3; Jay Wolfson & Scott L. Hopes, *What Makes Tax-Exempt Hospitals Special*, 48 HEALTHCARE FIN. MNGT. 56 (1994) This study was funded by a large for-profit chain in Florida.

46. Medical Center Hosp. v. City of Burlington, 152 Vt. 611, 566 A.2d 1352 (1989).

47. The U.S. General Accounting Office found that "many [nonprofit] hospitals' admissions and transfer policies limit elective care for those unable to pay." GAO REPORT, *supra* note 24, at 147. Moreover, because hospitals generally accept only those patients admitted by members of the medical staff, they can avoid charity cases without establishing elaborate screens merely by relying on the selfinterest of their physicians, who are under no obligation to render their services for free. Therefore, the passivity engendered by the open door test allows hospitals to shirk their share of charity care unless they take affirmative steps to advertise their open door policy and to require physicians to accept a reasonable number of charity cases.

5

Community Benefit
and the Nonprofit Ethic

Overview

The possible bases for charitable tax exemption surveyed so far face a pair of correlative problems under our criteria for evaluation. Using charitable trust law as the basis for exemption decisions is patently over-inclusive by failing to test for whether such entities provide social services that are worthy of the exemption in the modern milieu. In contrast, the relief of government burden theory, which does contain such a test, is too demanding for many traditionally exempt nonprofits to meet; if actually enforced, this theory would radically alter the scope of the exemption, and so fails the historical consistency test. It also performs poorly under the proportionality criterion. Recognizing these twin difficulties, many nonprofit entities maintain that the proper test for the exemption should consider whether they benefit the community in a variety of ways less obvious or tangible than direct quid-pro-quo relief of specific government burdens with free services to the community. Nonprofits maintain they benefit the community even when they charge for services by providing services superior to that of investor-owned competitors, by responding to community needs better than for-profits, or by fostering desirable values in ways that proprietary firms and government do not.

Unlike the categorical theory drawn from trust law, the community benefit test does not automatically validate the exemption of any nonprofit activity. Instead, this theory seeks to identify particular nonprofit activities in which the community values the special quality or ethic that the nonprofit enterprise offers. Perhaps the most forceful statement of the community benefit theory, made in the context of religious institutions, is this by a 19th century Georgia court:

> [Nonprofit institutions promote values] such as benevolence, charity, generosity, love of our fellowmen, . . . and all those comely virtues and

amiable qualities which clothe life 'in decent drapery' and impart a charm to existence, . . . furnish a sure basis on which the fabric of civil society can rest, and without which it could not endure. Take from it these supports, and it would tumble into chaos and ruin. Anarchy would follow order and regularity, and liberty, freed from its restraining influence, would soon degenerate into the wildest license, which would convert the beautiful earth into a howling pandemonium, fit only for the habitation of savage beasts and more savage men.[1]

Of like mind, but of less apocalyptic manner is Chauncey Belknap's explanation that:

[T]he only principle that affords a complete justification covering the entire field of [charitable] exemptions . . . is that government relieves from the tax burden religious, educational, and charitable activities because it wishes to encourage them as representing the highest and noblest achievements of mankind[,] . . . activities which by common understanding are agreed to rate among the highest in the scale of social values.[2]

Professor Rob Atkinson provides another, more measured, but particularly clear description of this view:

Charities are said to provide what I will call "metabenefits," benefits that derive not from what product is produced or to whom it is distributed, but rather from how it is produced or distributed. Traditional theory has identified two ways charities provide such "metabenefits." In the first place, they are said to deliver goods and services more efficiently, more innovatively, or otherwise better than other suppliers. In the second place, their very existence is said to promote pluralism and diversity, which are taken to be inherently desirable . . . . This theory rests on the fairly explicit premise that not only particular goods and services, but also particular modes of supplying them, can be identified as especially good for the public under neutral principles administrable by a government agency, the Internal Revenue Service, subject to judicial review.[3]

And Bruce Hopkins, one of the foremost authorities on exempt organizations, has stated that exemptions are "a bulwark against overdomination by government and a hallmark of a free society; they help nourish the voluntary sector of this nation and preserve individual initiative, and reflect the pluralistic philosophy that has been the guiding spirit of democratic America."[4]

The theory of exemption based on the superiority of the nonprofit ethic comes closer to meeting the deservedness criterion than simply relying on charitable trust law precedents because it requires a positive demonstration of a community benefit that profit-making firms do not offer. The community benefit theory also avoids the difficulty that the relief of government burden theory faced under the proportionality criterion regarding over- and under-subsidization. Because the community benefit theory postulates that a benefit inheres in all of the organization's services, a subsidy matched to the size of the operation—as income tax and property tax exemptions generally are—is well calibrated to the extent of deservedness under this theory. The more property a nonprofit organization has and the more income it earns, the more superior services it can render to the community, even if it charges at or above its costs. For the same reason, this theory addresses the universality criterion by seeking to justify all types of exemption as well as the charitable deduction. It also has the potential to explain a number of the restrictions on charitable status such as the prohibition on lobbying and the restraint on unfair competition, because these restrictions are apparently designed to protect the public's interest. This theory also comports with the historical consistency criterion to the extent that it draws from the notion of public benefit that exists in charitable trust law.

Nevertheless, the community benefit theory has its own problems with the proportionality criterion, and it fails entirely to satisfy one dimension of deservedness. To demonstrate why this is so, we will again focus on hospitals as an in-depth case study of one hotly contested exemption battleground. Hospitals maintain that they provide many unique benefits besides free care: they support physician education and medical research; provide a full range of services regardless of each service's profitability; and support community health education and preventative services such as childbirth classes, meals for the elderly, and immunization clinics.[5] More amorphously, they claim to foster an ethos more conducive to proper medical practice than that prevailing in profit-oriented environments.[6] While the focus of our discussion below is hospitals, we note that similar arguments are made by many other charitable organizations—private nonprofit universities and primary schools, for example.[7]

Deficiencies in the Community Benefit Theory

Deservedness

To fully meet the deservedness criterion, the community benefit theory should show that the social benefits claimed by nonprofit firms are real and that they would be lost without the exemption. Without this "but for" connection (that is, the claimed benefits would not exist without tax exemption), the economic benefit of tax exemption is a waste or a windfall.

In short, to fully assess the viability of the community benefit theory, one needs to ask first why an exempt entity is preferred for any given service or product to a for-profit one, and second why the exemption is needed to secure this preference. These two inquiries mirror the "worth" and "need" components of the deservedness criterion discussed earlier. Failing either prong undermines deservedness because the failure would establish either that nonprofits do not necessarily provide superior social services, or that a tax subsidy is not necessary for them to continue providing such services.

The hospital industry is an ideal testing ground for this analysis. Scholars of the nonprofit enterprise have long been fascinated with the hospital industry because it provides an intriguing mix of all three sectors of the economy operating in tandem: proprietary, government, and nonprofit firms.[8] These scholars have developed several competing explanations for why nonprofit hospitals have historically outnumbered for-profits. Some explanations relate to a plausible community benefit, while others do not. The explanations that see no inherent benefit in the nonprofit form directly refute the worth component of the community benefit theory—under these accounts, for-profits would be just as good for the community. On the other hand, even those accounts that support the notion of social benefit inherent in the nonprofit form must still pass the "but for" (need) component of the deservedness criterion—that is, they must show that the social benefits would not exist if exemption were taken away.

Positive Theories of Nonprofit Dominance. Some theorists claim that the nonprofit form predominates in certain economic sectors such as education and medical care because it is preferred by consumers of these services for socially valued reasons. One such theory is drawn from Professor Hansmann's pioneering work in which he explains that patrons tend to favor the nonprofit organizational form when complex and difficult-to-evaluate services are involved. Patrons prefer nonprofits because they have less trust in firms whose profit incentive provides them a stronger bias to behave opportunistically. Hansmann maintains nonprofits enjoy greater public confidence because a "nondistribution constraint" attaches to nonprofit status, precluding anyone from having a private interest in the organization's economic performance and requiring the institution to retain any net income to further its public service mission.[9]

The strongest application of this "trust theory" for the existence of nonprofit enterprise is that it explains why donors choose to make contributions exclusively to nonprofits when they desire to support traditional charitable services such as disaster relief and care for the poor.

Hansmann characterizes donors as "purchasing" these relief services for others, and observes that, as a consequence of the third-party nature of this transaction, donors are not in a position to monitor whether and how effectively the desired aid is rendered. Red Cross, for instance, is in the business of "selling" disaster relief services to contributors for delivery to third-party beneficiaries. As the contributors generally have no way of determining the quality of Red Cross's relief services or whether such services actually are performed, the "consumer" (the contributor) cannot engage in comparative shopping. As a result, the consumer is better off obtaining such services from a nonprofit entity, since the prohibition by a nonprofit on the distribution of profits to private individuals (the prohibition against private inurement) gives the consumer some assurance that the money paid to the organization will actually be used for the service rather than diverted to owners.

This trust explanation also holds for two-party commercial transactions in which consumers purchase services for themselves that are difficult to evaluate because of the intangible nature of the services. Prominent examples include child care and education. As these services are typically purchased on behalf of someone else in the family, they too are not pure two-party transactions, which may partially explain the difficulty of monitoring these services.[10] However, other scholars, such as Professor Ira Ellman, are skeptical of the assertion that services such as education and child care are inherently more difficult to evaluate than are many other ordinary consumer purchases.[11] Casual observation and intuition reveal that parents may be much more aware of the relative quality among the choices they make for these purchases than for automobiles or food.

Regardless, Hansmann's trust theory for the existence of nonprofit enterprise has superficial appeal in the medical arena because health care is indeed a service that is difficult for consumers to evaluate. Health care is difficult to monitor because of its inherently complex and qualitatively subjective nature, and because an individual patient rarely has an opportunity to experience how an alternative provider would have treated the same ailment.[12] It is thus surprising that Hansmann finds his theory is a poor fit in the hospital industry. The reason the trust theory does not readily extend to hospitals, however, is that patients rarely undertake to evaluate hospital services independently. Instead, they rely heavily on the judgment of their physicians in selecting a hospital. Indeed, it is sometimes said that the true consumers of hospital services are doctors, not patients. Because patients tend to follow the advice of learned intermediaries, they generally are indifferent to whether their hospital is a nonprofit or for-profit entity;

accordingly, nonprofit status would not be necessary to correct the market deficiencies in hospital care purchases by individuals.

On the other hand, the trust explanation still may be viable if *doctors* also have socially valued reasons to prefer nonprofit hospitals—reasons equivalent to consumer trust. According to one body of scholarship, doctors, and by derivation, their patients, do have such reasons. Patients trust their doctors' choice of hospitals in part because doctors are perceived to be guided by a professional ethos binding them to ethical norms of fiduciary responsibility to their patients. Hence, doctors have good reason to promote practice environments that foster this professional ethos. Nonprofits are considered "superior from the point of view of professional ideology and practice" because "[m]any features that are generally considered to be specific characteristics of the professions—altruism, autonomy, an emphasis on quality of service, and a certain anti-market and anti-bureaucratic ethos—have also been singled out, quite independently, as the *raisons d'etre* of nonprofit institutions."[13] Nonprofit hospitals stress these values because they tend to attract the managers whose values correspond with those of the founder.[14] For these reasons, "the nonprofit nature of a service organization tends to reinforce the fiduciary component in the relationship with clients, thus increasing professional authority and autonomy." This point is frequently made with negative emphasis by stressing the tendency of for-profits to debase professionalism:

> [P]rofit-making organizations do not possess the appropriate characteristics required for the social control function in the health care system. This is so mainly because the decision-making mechanism in profit-making organizations is inherently at cross purposes with the unique characteristics of the health care segment of society--namely, the unusual and personal nature of the physician-patient relationship and the centrality of health and disease to individuals and to society. Nonprofit organizations, on the other hand, do seem to possess—at least potentially—the social control mechanism required to protect individual patients and society.[15]

Although this explanation supports the notion that there is an inherent social benefit in the nonprofit form, it fails to satisfy the need ("but for") component of the deservedness criterion. The reason for this failure is that *why nonprofits exist* is a fundamentally different question than *whether they should be exempt*. As Burton Weisbrod has observed, "Public policy can be devised simply to permit nonprofit organizations to exist; to permit nonprofits to compete with for-profit firms; to provide for public subsidies for nonprofits; or to provide for specific forms of subsidies."[16] Many writings on the tax exemption reason in terms that assume the question is whether nonprofits should exist at all, as if the issue were whether they should be banned rather than subsidized.[17] This framing of the issue obscures careful focus on the more important issue from an exemption standpoint: whether nonprofit firms require the economic benefits of tax exemption to provide their socially superior services.

Looking that question squarely in the eye, the deservedness criterion is not fully met even granting the superiority of nonprofit hospitals because there is no reason to assume that nonprofits would not continue to predominate absent exemption. No one is suggesting that the nonprofit form of enterprise be outlawed; doctors or patients or others may have solid grounds to believe that the nonprofit form is a better vehicle for delivery of health care services, so be it. This does not necessarily mean, however, that government should subsidize those preferences.

Another example, this time from the education sector, may help drive home the point. Harvard University is a tax-exempt educational institution. Harvard would no doubt argue that it produces a variety of community benefits and offers a "special ethic" in education. But if consumers (students, parents or perhaps some combination of the two) truly prefer the special ethic in education provided by Harvard, wouldn't they continue to do so even if Harvard were not tax-exempt? Would Harvard really go out of business if tax exemption were repealed? True, absent exemption a Harvard education might cost more than it does now, thus restricting access by students who could not afford to go there. If this is a legitimate government concern, however, it can be addressed more directly and far more efficiently simply by providing needy students with direct financial aid. Under the current system, the economic benefits of exemption might not go toward reduced tuition, but rather to higher salaries for professors or administrators.[18]

The *Minneapolis Star* once asked facetiously: "Is just being a 'nice guy' enough to get you on the property-tax free list?"[19] The favorable view of nonprofit dominance would seem to so hold because it reasons that, wherever nonprofits prevail, this is because of the socially valued preference of consumers: doctors and patients in medicine, students and their parents in education, opera lovers for the Metropolitan Opera. But if there is no obstacle to effectuating these preferences, then there is no reason to subsidize them. Professor Jensen made this point over 60 years ago:

> [T]he service deserving [a tax subsidy] must be incapable of being fostered adequately on a commercial, quid pro quo basis . . . . Transportation is a necessary public service, but it is not, ordinarily, necessary to subsidize it.

The state has no interest in extending it beyond the point where the beneficiaries will pay for it.[20]

It is suprising that this point is not better recognized. Elsewhere, government is not in the habit of devoting large amounts of scarce public resources as gratuitous rewards for good deeds. The communities in which we live think it is socially desirable for us to mow our lawns, but no one thinks to reward us for this community benefit, nor do we think to ask for any such reward. No more should the government forego billions of dollars in revenue from nonprofit organizations for the simple reason that society values their services.

Negative Theories of Nonprofit Dominance. The preceding argument assumes as correct the assertion that nonprofits deliver services in some uniquely better way than government or for-profits. We would be remiss if we failed to observe that this assumption has not gone unchallenged, particularly in the arena of health care. Even defenders of the exemption concede that "self-satisfaction and self-righteousness . . . is perhaps an occupational hazard" among nonprofit hospital administrators, who tend to "have an almost reflexive belief in the inherent superiority of voluntary health care."[21]

This line of argument attacks the exemption squarely on the subcriterion of worth—that is, whether the assertion is in fact true that nonprofits offer a superior service to for-profit or governmental alternatives. It is this *comparative* dimension that nonprofit proponents often glance over in describing the inherent social benefits of their services. If those services are not uniquely provided by the nonprofit sector, then nonprofit provision does not deserve a public subsidy; even granting the social worth of those services in isolation.

Turning again to the hospital industry, extensive empirical studies exist comparing the performance of nonprofit and for-profit counterparts. By and large, this literature demonstrates that the two sectors are remarkably similar in their performance characteristics. The overriding consensus of these studies is that "available evidence on differences between for-profit and not-for-profit health care organizations is not sufficient to justify a recommendation that investor ownership of health care organizations be either opposed or supported by public policy."[22] For the most significant measures of hospital performance—quality and cost—there is little or no difference between the two sectors.[23]

Likewise, for the more amorphous grouping of services referred to as community services—health screening, community education, immunizations, temporary housing, transportation, and the like—nonprofit and for-profit hospitals perform approximately the same, primarily because these serve a valuable marketing function.[24] Hospital behavior is remarkably uniform because the two sectors share identical sources of financing: private and public health insurance.[25] The operational incentives created by these sources of revenue tend to swamp whatever contrasting incentives exist by virtue of organizational form, a likely result in any industry.[26]

The empirical evidence, therefore, fails to support the argument that exempt hospitals produce tangible community benefits in excess of their for-profit rivals. Nevertheless, supporters of exempt hospitals note that the exempt nonprofit form dominates hospital organization, and therefore conclude that there is a superior ethic of care in the nonprofit form that results in a social preference for these institutions over for-profit competititors. Our examination of the literature, however, reveals considerable debate over whether the dominance by nonprofit hospitals in fact reflects a valued social preference or instead serves the private interests of the industry.

We begin by observing that nothing is so special or different about health care as to preclude profit motivation altogether. Other essential goods and services in society—such as food, shelter, and transportation—are dominated by the for-profit sector.[27] Moreover, within medicine, "most physicians, dentists, optometrists, and pharmacists work for proprietary firms, many nursing homes are for-profit, [and] drug and medical devices are manufactured by such firms."[28] It is only within the hospital industry that the nonprofit form dominates, and this domination may be explained in two ways that have nothing to do with a superior ethic inherent in the nonprofit form.

First, some theorists blame the tax exemption itself for allowing nonprofits to maintain a higher market share.[29] Skeptics also point to the many other forms of governmental favoritism for nonprofit hospitals that permeate the regulatory and reimbursement environment. Nonprofits have received favorable treatment under labor laws, certificate of need rules, licensing statutes, the Hill-Burton Act (which subsidizes hospital construction), tort law, and by Blue Cross.[30] In short, these theorists find that market dominance results from the tax and other financial benefits conferred on nonprofit institutions, not from any inherent superiority. As a result, these critics characterize the exemption for hospitals as an anachronism that remains "in large part as a consequence of institutional inertia,"[31] or even as a mindless subsidy that perpetrates a fraud on the public.[32]

A second possible explanation for nonprofit dominance that is equally unflattering maintains that nonprofit hospitals proliferate because doctors prefer nonprofits for reasons of economic self-interest inconsistent with socially optimal patient care. The two principal theories that rely on physician self-interest are the "physician control theory" and the "managerial prestige theory." These differ in that the first posits physicians' financial interest as the primary determinant of hospital organization and operation, whereas the second views physician interest as derivative of nonprofit managers' utility function.[33]

The physician control theory holds that physicians prefer nonprofits because this institutional form tends to increase physicians' control over the medical staffing and financial affairs of hospitals by virtue of the absence of any shareholders with overriding or competing authority.[34] The "managerial prestige" theory of nonprofit preference posits that physicians enjoy derivative benefits from the way in which nonprofit managers naturally tend to behave. Nonprofit hospitals are thought to spend more than for-profits on physician and patient amenities because their professional prestige is determined not by profits but by institutional size and reputation.[35] In economic jargon, it is said that nonprofit institutions are "volume maximizers" or "output maximizers," rather than profit maximizers.[36] The same notion is captured in the colloquialism that accuses hospital managers of suffering from an "edifice complex."

Many of the arguments applied to the dominance of nonprofit hospitals can be transferred to other sectors of exempt charitable organizations. For example, it is not self-evident that nonprofit educational institutions are inherently superior to for-profit ones. For-profit institutions exist and even dominate certain parts of the educational sector, such as vocational training.[37] Some communities even have begun experimenting with hiring for-profit companies to run local primary schools.[38] Many of the same questions could be raised about the performing arts and about scientific research organizations, for example. As with hospitals, it could be that nonprofit organizations exist or dominate in these mixed-sector industries not because of any inherent superiority in the nonprofit form, but because that form maximizes the economic returns for the organizers. We illustrate this point at the end of Chapter 3 with the largely hypothetical example of exempt physician groups. A real example are the exempt nonprofit entities that provide skills seminars such as continuing legal education for lawyers. Even in the most sacrosanct of exempt arenas, religion, we hear numerous stories of unscrupulous individuals who form bogus churches solely for the economic benefits that flow from tax exemption and deductibility of charitable contributions.[39]

We do not necessarily maintain that these negative theories of nonprofit dominance are more convincing than the positive theories outlined earlier. Instead, we mean only to demonstrate that assertions by nonprofit proponents that the nonprofit form is inherently superior cannot be taken on faith alone.The problem is that nonprofit form often has a halo effect on public policy discussions that precludes any critical analysis of the motivations behind the form. Other commentators have referred to the community benefit standard as an "existential"[40] one that relies on concepts with "vague, emotive meanings" to express "rhetoric of intention . . . rather than any exact program or method."[41] In words that we do not endorse yet cannot refrain from quoting, the "ideals of private charity and voluntarism . . . act as the opiate of the American public, deluding a basically decent people into believing that . . . deeply troubling social problems requiring whole dollars for their solution can . . . be adequately addressed with just two bits' worth of trickle-down generosity."[42] Dissolving the halo that surrounds nonprofit status allows us to see more accurately whether in fact superior community benefits exist in a particular nonprofit sector. A close examination of the hospital sector reveals a hotly contested dispute that is not easily resolved either by empirical evidence or by abstract theory. The essential aspects of this dispute, moreover, apply to other charitable organizations. Even if the dispute is resolved in favor of nonprofits, this still does not satisfy the deservedness criterion unless there is some explanation of why the exemption is necessary in order to achieve this nonprofit preference.

The Commerciality Test and the Mission Test. Faced with the deservedness problems encountered by the community benefit test, both the IRS and the hospital industry have attempted to refine limiting principles. The IRS has attempted to segregate exempt activities from those conducted by for-profit firms by applying a "commerciality" test that seeks to determine in which sectors nonprofit organizations make unique contributions. In some fields such as education and health care, the Service has refused to extend the exemption to organizations that would otherwise qualify under the reasoning that the benefits they provide to the community are no different than those provided by commercial competitors.

The area in which the IRS has been most active in invoking this commerciality test is to deny exemption to educational organizations that it believes operate largely like for-profit publishing houses.[43] In *Scripture*

Press Foundation v. United States,[44] for example, the Court of Claims held that an organization that published teaching materials for Bible classes operated primarily for profit and only secondarily as an educational (and religious) institution. Accordingly, it was not exempt, having violated the primary purpose test.[45] Likewise, an organization that published two periodicals containing economic forecasts and securities analysis was held not exempt since its activities in essence amounted to investment advice to subscribers for a fee.[46] The IRS uses the commerciality doctrine in other areas, however: for example, the agency invoked the commerciality doctrine to deny exemption to a nonprofit pharmacy and to outpatient services and sales by otherwise exempt hospitals that were available from for-profit providers in the same geographic area.[47] States have also used this test: for example, to exclude residential homes for the aged from exemption.[48]

The commerciality test represents a valiant attempt by the Service to assess directly whether nonprofits deserve the exemption under a community benefit theory, since it seeks to compare their services and operation with for-profit competitors. The problem is that amorphous nature of community benefit and the case-by-case analysis employed by the courts and the IRS produce inexplicable variations in result.Thus activities that appear indistinguishable from one another are treated differently largely due to the gut reaction of the reviewing court concerning the motives of the founders of the organization. For example, in *Presbyterian & Reformed Publishing Co. v. Commissioner*,[49] the Third Circuit held exempt a religious publisher remarkably similar to that of *Scripture Press* noted above. The court stated in its opinion that "success in terms of audience reached and influence exerted, in and of itself, should not jeopardize the tax-exempt status" of the organization, and that large accumulations of cash should not be viewed suspiciously if reinvested in exempt activities.[50]

The Service has been equally inconsistent in its approach in other areas. For instance, nonprofit hospitals operate in just as commercial a manner as do nonprofit pharmacies and book publishers, yet the doctrine is not applied to them. Another example of inconsistency lies in the fact that a number of activities conducted by educational institutions, such as university bookstores or restaurants clearly compete with stand-alone businesses. If the focus of the commerciality doctrine is that goods and services provided by for-profit businesses are not appropriate subjects for tax-exemption, then any activity in an area populated by for-profit enterprise ought to lose exemption. This, however, clearly is not the existing law.

Another attempt to give the community benefit test some teeth is the approach being proposed in the hospital sector that looks to the manner in which the entity defines and carries out its "mission." The essential concept is that, if a hospital declares that its aim is to serve the community's benefit, and if it takes concrete steps to achieve that end, then the mere process and structure of a community oriented organization should suffice, regardless of the actual outcomes. This approach was conceived by David Seay at the United Hospital Fund,[51] and it has found its way into New York state legislation and into President Clinton's proposed health care reform plan. Under the Clinton version, a hospital qualifies as charitable if, at least once a year, "with the participation of community representatives [it] (1) assesses the health care needs of its community, and (2) develops a plan to meet those needs."[52] The problem is that this test simply does not differentiate in any meaningful way between the conduct of an exempt and a for-profit entity. For-profit entities must assess their markets and make changes in their products and services to satisfy consumer demand as a matter of daily market survival; if one wants a lesson concerning what happens to a for-profit entity that fails in this regard, take a look at the recent history of IBM.[53] Accordingly, courts, commentators, legislators and the IRS have all failed to generate a principled and predictable approach to policing the community benefit standard.

Proportionality

The community benefit theory faces a final set of problems under the proportionality criterion. Since proportionality seeks to test whether the size of the public subsidy is roughly commensurate with the size of the community benefit, it requires an articulation of community benefit that is measurable in at least some rough quantitative fashion. However, there is no methodologically sound way to measure the soft values that inhere in the claim of a superior nonprofit service ethic. "[H]istory has shown that these words [community, voluntary and charity] have long had vague, emotive meanings. They have expressed a rhetoric of intention . . . rather than any exact program or method."[54]

Without such specification, it is impossible to verify whether society is receiving its money's worth from the exemption. In Professor Bittker's words, "Lacking a method for measuring these appealing but elusive virtues, one must perforce rely on intuition in comparing the achievements of private charities with those of government [and profit-making enterprises], when they are performing similar functions."[55]

Not every decision of government need be made by calculator, particularly social policy decisions made by Congress, but a standard that relies entirely on intuition is inappropriate in an administrative arena that requires courts and agencies to apply a legislative mandate in a multitude of real world settings.[56] The degree of legislative abdication inherent in the community benefit standard is particularly troubling considering that it leaves to tax collectors—rather than departments of government legitimately concerned with substantive public policy—the task of determining what constitutes socially worthy activity across the broad range of nonprofit enterprise.[57] This arrangement has a high potential for producing capricious results, leading to the accusation that the IRS has decided "to abandon completely any attempt to administer the exemption and [has decided to] treat cases on an ad hoc, nonanalytical basis . . . using definitional strategies based on subjective, unarticulated factors rather than on objective, verifiable criteria."[58] The Supreme Court has warned that such a role is particularly troubling with respect to exemption for religious organizations because "inquiry into the particular contributions of each religious group 'would introduce an element of governmental evaluation and standards as to the worth of particular social welfare programs, thus producing a kind of continuing day-to-day relationship which the [first amendment] policy of [religious] neutrality seeks to minimize.'"[59]

A final reason the community benefit theory of the charitable exemption abdicates governmental responsibility is that the theory leaves decisions concerning priorities for spending the subsidy to the private entities that receive it. Thus, assuming that taxing authorities are capable of judging which industries are better structured on a nonprofit basis, once this determination is made, any further decisions about how the subsidy is spent are left to the firm's managers, constrained only by the requirements of maintaining nonprofit status. Thus, hospital managers can choose to use the subsidy to support facility refurbishment rather than meet the more pressing need of treating greater numbers of uninsured patients, or university presidents can choose to direct the benefits of exemption into higher faculty salaries rather than expanded student programs. This unfettered discretion given managers of tax-exempt institutions means that we can have no assurance that the level of support provided by an exemption even roughly matches the level of deservedness.

The community benefit theory constitutes the nonprofit sector's most sophisticated attempt to justify the present scope of the exemption. This theory makes its case on the inherently unquantifiable values that nonprofit enterprise serves. There is considerable merit to the view that nonprofit organizations offer advantages over both proprietary markets and the government; otherwise we would not have such a large nonprofit sector. On the other hand, the size of the nonprofit sector may largely result from the exemption itself. The existence of both possibilities demands some demonstration that society needs the exemption to effectuate its preference for the higher values and greater diversity that nonprofits offer. This demonstration is entirely absent. Obstacles to the optimal provision of some nonprofit goods and services may exist, but the theory does not attempt to identify them. Consequently, the community benefit theory fails to establish a coherent basis for the exemption, not only because of the difficulties it encounters in documenting the amorphous nature of the claimed benefits, but also because the theory is insensitive to whether a public subsidy is necessary to produce those benefits.

Notes

1. Trustees of the First Methodist Episcopal Church v. City of Atlanta, 76 Ga. 181, 192–93 (1886).

2. Chauncey Belknap, *The Federal Income Tax Exemption of Charitable Organizations: Its History and Underlying Policy*, in RESEARCH PAPERS SPONSORED BY THE COMMISSION ON PRIVATE PHILANTHROPY AND PUBLIC NEEDS 2025, 2033–35 (U.S. Dept. of the Treasury ed., 1977) (hereafter FILER COMMISSION PAPERS). This theory also has the imprimatur of the Supreme Court. *See* Walz v. Tax Comm'r, 397 U.S. 664, 672–73 (1970) ("[C]ertain entities that exist in a harmonious relationship to the community at large, and that foster its 'moral or mental improvement,' should not be inhibited in their activities by property taxation . . . . The State has an affirmative policy that considers these groups as beneficial and stabilizing influences in community life . . . .").

3. Rob Atkinson, *Altruism in Nonprofit Organizations*, 31 B.C.L. REV. 501, 605–06 n.266 (1990).

4. BRUCE R. HOPKINS, THE LAW OF TAX-EXEMPT ORGANIZATIONS 62 (6th ed. 1992).

5. J. David Seay & Bruce Vladeck, *Mission Matters*, in IN SICKNESS AND IN HEALTH: THE MISSION OF VOLUNTARY HEALTH CARE INSTITUTIONS 1, 6–7 (1988) (hereafter IN SICKNESS AND IN HEALTH); AMERICAN HOSPITAL ASSOCIATION, COMMUNITY BENEFIT AND TAX-EXEMPT STATUS: A SELF-ASSESSMENT GUIDE FOR HOSPITALS 36–38 (1988).

6. Stanley Jones & Charles Du Val, *What Distinguishes the Voluntary Hospital in an Increasingly Commercial Health Care Environment?*, in IN SICKNESS AND IN HEALTH, *supra* note 5, at 230 ("[T]he voluntary hospital embodies a set of values in health care that helps quicken the conscience of the community concerning the

sick and poor and inspires a vision of what medicine and health care can accomplish for mankind, beyond what the marketplace demands . . . ."); David Wikler, *The Virtuous Hospital: Do Nonprofit Institutions Have a Distinctive Moral Mission?*, *in* IN SICKNESS AND IN HEALTH, *supra* note 5 at 142 ("Nonprofit hospitals are often regarded as better for society than for-profit hospitals precisely because they aspire to, and often do, achieve virtue.").

7. John D. Colombo, *Why is Harvard Tax Exempt? (And Other Mysteries of Tax Exemption for Private Educational Institutions)*, 35 ARIZ. L. REV. 841, 865 (1993).

8. Over the past fifty years, the relative mix of these three sectors has remained remarkably stable, as follows (in number of beds): public (governmental) hospitals—20% to 25%; voluntary hospitals—around 70%; proprietary hospitals—from 5% to 10%. J. ROGERS HOLLINGSWORTH & ELLEN J. HOLLINGSWORTH, CONTROVERSY ABOUT AMERICAN HOSPITALS: FUNDING, OWNERSHIP AND PERFORMANCE 20–21 (1987).

9. Henry B. Hansmann, *The Role of Nonprofit Enterprise*, 89 YALE L.J. 835 (1980). For a more detailed examination of Hansmann's theories, see Chapter 6.

10. Michael Krashinsky, *Transaction Costs and a Theory of Nonprofit Organization*, *in* THE ECONOMICS OF NONPROFIT INSTITUTIONS 114, 117 (Susan Rose-Ackerman ed., 1986).

11. Ira M. Ellman, *Another Theory of Nonprofit Corporations*, 80 MICH. L. REV. 999, 1033 (1982) ("In fact, one's general impression is that, whether or not they are right, parents tend to think that they know whether their child's school or day care facility is doing a good job.")

12. *See* Kenneth Arrow, *Uncertainty and the Welfare Economics of Medical Care*, 53 AM. ECON. REV. 941 (1963).

13. Giandomenico Majone, *Professionalism and Nonprofit Organizations*, 8 J. HEALTH POL., POL'Y & LAW 639, 640 (1984).

14. *See* DENNIS R. YOUNG, IF NOT FOR PROFIT, FOR WHAT? (1983) (developing this sorting theory in some detail).

15. Merwyn Greenlick, *Profit and Nonprofit Organizations in Health Care: A Sociological Perspective*, *in* IN SICKNESS AND IN HEALTH, *supra* note 5, at 155, 175.

16. BURTON A. WEISBROD, THE NONPROFIT ECONOMY 88 (1988).

17. *E.g.*, Elizabeth Miller Guggenheimer, *Making the Case for Voluntary Health Care Institutions: Policy Theories and Legal Approaches*, *in* IN SICKNESS AND IN HEALTH, *supra* note 5, at 35, 36–41 (1988) (defending the exemption merely by observing why nonprofit hospitals should exist); Michael Horwitz, *Corporate Reorganizations: The Last Gasp or Last Clear Chance for the Tax-Exempt Nonprofit Hospital*, 13 AM. J. L. & MED. 527, 558–59 (arguing for "retention of the nonprofit concept").

18. In fact, evidence exists that this is precisely what happens, at least at major research universities. *See* GILBERT M. GAUL AND NEILL A. BOROWSKI, FREE RIDE: THE TAX-EXEMPT ECONOMY 67-73 (1993).

19. ALFRED BALK, THE FREE LIST 81 (1970); *see also* Steven Stone, *Federal Tax Support of Charities and Other Exempt Organizations: The Need for a National Policy,* 20 U. So. Cal. L. Center Tax Inst. 27, 45 (1968).

20. JENS JENSEN, PROPERTY TAXATION IN THE UNITED STATES 148 (1931).

21. Seay & Vladeck, *supra* note 5, at 4–5.

22. William Yoder, *Economic Theories of For-Profit and Not-for-Profit Organizations,* in INSTITUTE OF MEDICINE, FOR PROFIT ENTERPRISE IN HEALTH CARE 191 (Burton Gray ed., 1986).

23. HOLLINGSWORTH & HOLLINGSWORTH, *supra* note 8, at 111–14; Yoder, *supra* note 22, at 76–77; Mark Schlesinger et al., *Nonprofit and For-Profit Medical Care: Shifting Roles and Implications for Health Policy,* 12 J. HEALTH POL., POL'Y & L. 427, 437 (1987); Frank Sloan, *Property Rights in the Hospital Industry, in* HEALTH CARE IN AMERICA 103, 130 (1988); Daniel Ermann & Jonathon Gabel, *Multihospital Systems: Issues and Empirical Findings,* HEALTH AFF., Spr. 1984, at 50.

24. The U.S. General Accounting Office found that a majority of both types of hospitals offered a wide range of community services, but that nonprofits are modestly more likely to do so than for-profits. U.S. GENERAL ACCOUNTING OFFICE, NONPROFIT HOSPITALS AND THE NEED FOR BETTER STANDARDS FOR TAX EXEMPTION, REP. NO. 90-84, at 4 (May 30, 1990). However, nonprofit hospitals "were equally likely to charge a fee for community services [and] more likely to cover the costs of providing the services." *Id.*

25. *See generally* HOLLINGSWORTH & HOLLINGSWORTH, *supra* note 8 at 65–66.

26. Sloan, *supra* note 23, at 138–39.

27. PAUL J. FELDSTEIN, HEALTH CARE ECONOMICS 218 (2d ed. 1993); Hansmann, *supra* note 9, at 880–81.

28. Sloan, *supra* note 23, at 109.

29. *See generally* Robert C. Clark, *Does the Nonprofit Form Fit the Hospital Industry,* 93 HARV. L. REV. 1417, 1474; Henry B. Hansmann, *The Effect of Tax Exemption and Other Factors on the Market Share of Nonprofit Versus For-Profit Firms,* 40 NAT'L TAX J. 71, 76–77.

30.Robert Bays, *Why Most Private Hospitals are Nonprofit,* 2 J. POL'Y ANALYSIS & MGMT. 366, 367 (1983); Charles Foster, *Hospitals and the Choice of Organizational Form,* 3 FIN. ACCOUNTABILITY & MGMT. 343, 353–54 (1987); Thomas Marmor et al., *Nonprofit Organizations and Health Care, in* THE NONPROFIT SECTOR, A RESEARCH HANDBOOK 221, 224–27 (Walter W. Powell ed., 1987); Bruce Steinwald & Duncan Neuhauser, *The Role of the Proprietary Hospital,* 35 L. & CONTEMP. PROBS. 817, 835 n.27 (1970); Note, *The Quality of Mercy: "Charitable Torts" and Their Continuing Immunity,* 100 HARV. L. REV. 1382 (1987) (documenting the modified survival of charitable tort immunity for nonprofit hospitals).

31. Henry B.Hansmann, *The Evolving Law of Nonprofit Organizations: Do Current Trends Make Good Policy?,* 39 CASE W. RES. L. REV. 807, 814 (1989).

32. The two most vocal critics are Clark, *supra* note 29, at 1447; and Regina Herzlinger & William Krasker, *Who Profits from Nonprofits?*, 65 HARV. BUS. REV. 93, 104 (1987).

33. *See generally* FELDSTEIN, *supra* note 27, at 212–23.

34. Mark Pauly & Michael Redisch, *The Not-for-Profit Hospital as a Physicians' Cooperative*, 63 AM. ECON. REV. 87 (1973); *see also* James Blumstein & Frank Sloan, *Antitrust and Hospital Peer Review*, L. & CONTEMP. PROBS., Spr. 1988, at 7, 19–20; Bays, *supra* note 30, at 377; Clark, *supra* note 29, at 1436–37, 1441–47.

35. Marvin Lee, *A Conspicuous Production Theory of Hospital Behavior*, 28 S. ECON. J. 48, 49 (1971).

36. Joseph Newhouse, *Toward a Theory of Nonprofit Institutions: An Economic Model of a Hospital*, 60 AM. ECON. REV. 64, 64–65 (1970).

37. Colombo, *supra* note 7, at 863.

38. *E.g.*, William Whittle, *Massachusetts' Charter Awards Includ 3 Schools to be run For Profit*, WALL ST. J., March 18, 1994, at B3 (Boston City Schools).

39. Take, for example, the following case from California in the late 1980s:

> They say they are practicing the world's oldest religion. But police say their enterprise resembles the world's oldest profession. Such is the debate surrounding Will and Mary Ellen Tracy, a Canyon County couple who have hit the national talk-show circuit to promote the unorthodox theology of the Church of the Most High Goddess, a "sex church" the Tracys operate in West Los Angeles . . . . Mary Ellen Tracy says she and other women act as priestesses who absolve the sins of male followers through sexual religious rites that predate Christianity. So far, she says, she has brought more than 2,000 male converts into the church. "Anything God wants from me, I will give him," says Tracy, 46. "If he wants me to be monogamous, I'll be monagamous. If he says go have sex with 20,000 men, I'll do it."
>
> Last week, Los Angeles Police Department vice officers arrested the Tracys—Mary Ellen on suspicion of prostitution and Will on suspicion of pimping—citing the couple's request for donations to the church . . . . Will Tracy, 51, acknowledged the church followers must contribute money or services to participate in the rituals that involve sexual intercourse. But he said the contributions are religious sacrifices.

Steve Padilla, *Is Church Old Time Religion or Prostitution?*, L. A. TIMES, April 16, 1989, at 6, col. 1 (Metro section). The two ultimately were convicted. L.A. TIMES, Sept. 9, 1989, at 10, col. 4 (Metro section).

40. Robert L. Bromberg, *The Charitable Hospital*, 20 CATH. L. REV. 237, 248–51 (1970).

41. ROBERT STEVENS, IN SICKNESS AND IN WEALTH: AMERICAN HOSPITALS IN THE TWENTIETH CENTURY 354 (1989).

42. Uwe Reinhardt, *Charity at a Price*, N.Y. TIMES BOOK REV., Aug. 20, 1989, at 14.

43. *See* Rev. Rul. 67-4, 1967-1 C.B. 121 (publishing must be done in a manner "distinguishable from ordinary commercial publishing practices"). *See generally,* Daniel Shaviro, *From Big Mama Rag to National Geographic: The Controversy Regarding Exemptions for Educational Publications,* 41 TAX L. REV. 693 , 722–28 (1986); BORIS I. BITTKER & LAWRENCE LOKKEN, FEDERAL TAXATION OF INCOME, ESTATES AND GIFTS ¶103.2 at 103-5 to 103-8 (2d ed. 1992); HOPKINS, *supra* note 4, at 188–93.

44. 285 F.2d 800 (Ct. Cl. 1961), *cert. den.* 368 U.S. 985 (1962).

45. Similarly, in The Incorporated Trustees of the Gospel Worker Society v. United States, 501 F. Supp. 374 (D.D.C. 1981), *aff'd,* 672 F.2d 894 (D.C. Cir. 1981), *cert. denied,* 456 U.S. 944 (1982), the district court found that an exempt religious and educational organization engaged in dissemination of religious literature had evolved into the equivalent of a commercial press, generating an earned surplus of $5.3 million by 1978. *See also,* Fides Publishers Ass'n v. U.S., 263 F. Supp. 924, 935 (N.D. Ind. 1967) (publication and sale of religious literature at a profit cannot be exempt because "every publishing house would be entitled to an exemption on the ground that it furthers the education of the public.").

46. American Institute for Economic Research v. U.S., 302 F.2d 934 (Ct. Cl. 1962), *cert. denied,* 372 U.S. 976 (1963). Similarly, "investment clubs" formed to exchange investment information among members in order to promote their investment acumen are also not exempt even though they meet the broad definition of educational purposes. Rev. Rul. 76-366, 1976-2 C.B. 144.

47. Federation Pharmacy Servs. v. Comm'r., 625 F.2d 804 (8th Cir. 1980); Carle Found. v. United States, 611 F.2d 1192 (7th Cir. 1979), cert. denied, 449 U.S. 824; Rev. Rul. 85-110, 1985-2 C.B. 166, 168. But see Hi-Plains Hosp. v. United States, 670 F.2d 528 (5th cir. 1982) (pharmacy sales income exempt when sales help recruit physicians to rural hospital).

48. *E.g.,* Presbyterian Residence Center Corporation v. Wagner, 66 A.D. 2d 972, 974; 397 N.Y.S. 478, 486 (N.Y. App. 1977) (denying exemption for apartment complex for the elderly, finding complex was "indistinguishable from a commercial apartment complex having appurtenant recreational facilities").

49. 743 F.2d 148 (3d Cir. 1984).

50. *Id.* at 157–58.

51. *See* J. David Seay & Robert M. Sigmund, *Community Benefit Standards for Hospitals: Perceptions and Performance,* FRONTIERS HEALTH SERVICES MANAGE-MENT 30, Spring 1989; J. David Seay, *Tax Exemption for Hospitals: Towards an Understanding of Community Benefit,* 2 HEALTH MATRIX 35 (1992).

52. H.R. 3600, 103d Cong., 1st Sess. § 7601(a) (1993).

53. *See generally,* John Burgess, *IBM Reports a Record $5 Billion Loss,* WASH. POST, Final Edition, Jan. 20, 1993, at A1 (IBM decline attributable to "its failure to keep up with one of the world's fastest-changing industries."); Mark Clayton, *As IBM Faltered, the Slide Shows Grew Slicker,* CHRISTIAN SCIENCE MONITOR, Mar. 30, 1993, at 9 (attributing IBM woes to the fact that in the 1980's it simply ignored fundamental changes in its market).

54. STEVENS, *supra* note 41, at 354. J. David Seay, on the other hand, claims that the community benefit standard need not be inherently vague, and has proposed specific process-based criteria for exemption of hospitals. Seay & Sigmund, *supra* note 51, at 30; Seay, *supra* note 51 at 45–48. According to Seay, the key elements of this standard are that hospitals have processes to identify community needs and develop programs to meet those needs. But as we have observed in the text, this process-based standard does not attempt to quantify the community need or assess whether nonprofits outperform for-profits in this regard. One can argue, in fact, that for-profit institutions are likely to be *more* responsive to community needs, since for-profits are rely on customer patronage for financial success, and customer patronage requires selling a product the customer wants.

55. Boris I. Bittker & George K. Rahdert, *The Exemption of Nonprofit Organizations from Federal Income Taxation*, 85 YALE L.J. 299, 332–33 (1976).

56. See generally Donald A. Dripps, *Delegation and Due Process*, 1988 DUKE L.J. 657; Richard J. Pierce, Jr., *The Role of Constitutional and Political Theory in Administrative Law*, 64 TEX. L. REV. 469 (1985); David Schoenbrod, *The Delegation Doctrine: Could the Court Give It Substance?*, 83 MICH. L. REV. 1223 (1985); Symposium, *The Uneasy Constitutional Status of the Administrative Agencies: Part I, Delegation of Powers to Administrative Agencies*, 36 AM. U.L. REV. 295 (1987).

57. John P. Persons et al., *Criteria for Exemption Under Section 501(c)(3)*, in FILER COMMISSION PAPERS, *supra* note 2, at 1909, 1942 (IRS is forced to become the "arbiter of the public good"); Alvin C.Warren et al., *Property Tax Exemptions for Charitable, Educational, Religious and Governmental Institutions in Connecticut*, 4 Conn. L. Rev. 181, 302, 309 (1970) (describing as "legislative abdication" the decision to leave these important social policy decisions to the lowest level of the administrative echelon). *See* Daniel M. Fox & Daniel C. Schaffer, *Tax Policy as Social Policy: Cafeteria Plans*, 1978–1985, 12 J. HEALTH POL., POL'Y & LAW 609, 633, 653 (1987) (exploring this phenomenon in the context of tax deductions for health insurance).

We do not mean to imply that direct grants are inherently superior to tax incentives in all circumstances. To paraphrase an example used by Professor Zelinsky, it may well be that a tax credit to farmers for planting soybeans is preferable policy to a direct farm subsidy program or to a government-run farm. But this assumes that the tax subsidy at least has an identifiable purpose; as the above discussion illustrates, this simply is not true of the current state of tax exemption, in which Congress has created a subsidy mechanism but left to others the task of defining who are the objects of subsidy.

58. *See* Tommy F. Thompson, *The Unadministrability of the Federal Charitable Tax Exemption: Causes, Effects and Remedies*, 5, VA. TAX REV. 1, 56 (1985).

59. Texas Monthly, Inc. v. Bullock, 489 U.S. 1, 22 n.2 (1989).

6

Academic Theories

In addition to the conventional theories of the exemption critiqued in the earlier chapters, a growing body of academic scholarship has constructed novel explanations for charitable status. We already have examined one of those academic theories in depth: Boris Bittker and George Rahdert's theory discussed in Chapter 2 that exemption is the natural result of an inability to fit exempt organizations within the traditional income tax structure. In this chapter, we focus on two theories which, unlike Bittker and Rahdert's, adopt the mainstream view that exemption constitutes an implicit government subsidy to the exempt organization. These two theorists then develop unique explanations for why this subsidy should exist and which entites are deserving.

Henry Hansmann's Capital Subsidy Theory

In the early 1980's Professor Henry Hansmann wrote two articles examining the nature of nonprofit enterprise and the rationale for exemption.[1] As noted in Chapter 4, Hansmann began with the observation that nonprofit firms tend to dominate those markets characterized by "contract failure"—that is, where the private market fails to function properly. Contract failure occurs when the consumer of a product or service has difficulty either in comparing the quality of performance offered by competing providers before making a purchase, or else in determining after a purchase is made whether the service or good was actually delivered as promised.

Hansmann's classic examples are CARE and the Red Cross. In each of these cases, the "customers" are donors who "purchase" relief for third parties. The donor/purchasers, however, have no way to evaluate whether the promised relief services are actually delivered, because the persons actually consuming the relief services are not the purchasers themselves, but third parties often located in remote areas of the world. According to Hansmann, purchasers in these circumstances are more likely to trust a nonprofit firm for these services, because one of the basic elements of nonprofit status under state corporate or trust law is a prohibition on the entity distributing proceeds to its managers or founders—what Hansmann refers to as the "nondistribution constraint." One should note that the nondistribution constraint is imposed by laws governing the operation of nonprofit entities, *not by tax exemption laws*, although tax law refers to this same general concept in its prohibition against private inurement.[2] Because of this constraint, donor/purchasers have greater assurance that the money they pay to nonprofit firms actually will be used to produce the desired services, even though independent verification is difficult or impossible.

Hansmann's second major area of contract failure involves "complex personal services" such as education (or as discussed in Chapter 5, perhaps health care) where comparisons of quality between providers is difficult. Here, the problem is not the separation between purchaser and consumer, because the purchaser and consumer may be the same; rather, the market problem is that the goods or services purchased are so complex or difficult to value that the average consumer has difficulty evaluating competing providers. Accordingly, consumers in this position prefer nonprofit providers, because once again the nondistribution constraint gives the consumer some assurance that the purchase price is being devoted primarily to rendering the services requested.

While the contract failure hypothesis is an elegant explanation of why nonprofits exist, as we have previously noted, this issue is not the same as whether such entities should be subsidized through the tax system. Under Hansmann's theory, nonprofit firms dominate markets characterized by contract failure because they are preferred by purchasers of their services. As we observed in Chapter 5 with respect to nonprofit hospitals, if Hansmann's theory is correct, then presumably this preference would exist without the aid of tax exemption. "Nonprofit" and "tax-exempt" are not necessarily co-extensive; we can have one without the other. If a person prefers the Red Cross for disaster relief because of the nondistribution constraint imposed by state law, nothing in the decision to either tax or exempt Red Cross interferes with or fosters the donor's ability to exercise that preference. Hence, no necessary or sufficient connection exists between Hansmann's explanation for the existence of nonprofit firms and the government's grant of tax exemption.

Hansmann recognizes this latter point in the second of his two articles, where he develops his explanation for the connection between exemption and contract failure. The essence of this theory is that tax exemption is necessary for nonprofits to overcome the financial burdens imposed on them by the publicly valued nondistribution constraint. Hansmann notes that because of the nondistribution constraint, nonprofit firms are incapable of accessing the public capital markets (e.g., the stock markets). Since a nonprofit firm cannot distribute profits to shareholders, owning stock in a nonprofit firm would be distinctly unappealing. Instead, nonprofit firms are limited to debt, donations and retained earnings as capital sources. The exemption, therefore, is needed to overcome this comparative disadvantage in the capital markets.

The income tax exemption serves as a capital formation subsidy by permitting nonprofit firms to retain earnings as a capital source free of taxation. In theory, the value of this subsidy is equal to the marginal tax rate on income (currently 35%—if one ignores bumps in the rate schedule—for corporations at the federal level),[3] plus the marginal state tax rate on income (adjusted for the fact that state taxes are a deductible item for federal tax purposes, thus lowering the effective state tax rate), plus the state tax rate on taxable property adjusted in the same manner. Hansmann explained that in ideal market conditions, the income tax exemption provides the greatest subsidy in times of increasing demand for a nonprofit's services, because increasing demand will result in greater revenue, which in turn results in a larger dollar amount of taxes forgiven by exemption. Conversely, as demand falls off, so will revenues, and the subsidy effect of exemption decreases. These subsidy modulations also tend to follow the level of proportionate need for subsidy over time since periods of increased demand usually entail relative capital shortages. Therefore, Hansmann's capital subsidy theory elegantly addresses one part of the proportionality criterion, at least for income tax exemption.

Hansmann's theory, however, has severe shortcomings in other respects, as Hansmann recognizes. Under the need component of the deservedness criterion, the theory offers no test for determining which nonprofits suffer from a comparative capital disadvantage. This depends on how capital-intensive the particular service is, and the degree to which nonprofits must compete with for-profits. It also depends on how sensitive this product or service sector is to investor capital, as opposed to other available sources such as debt or retained earnings. The upshot is that many traditionally-exempt entities appear not to need the subsidy at all. Nonprofit hospitals, for instance, have ample sources of capital due to generous insurance systems.[4] Other nonprofits such as churches struggle for capital, but rely very little on retained earnings—the source of the income tax exemption subsidy. Instead, they rely on donations, and their primary source of subsidy comes from the distinct (but related) deduction under Code Section 170.

Thus in order for the capital subsidy theory to explain the exemption, some mechanism would be necessary to identify those entities actually suffering from capital formation problems that could be remedied through increased retained earnings. Hansmann offers no such mechanism.

Hansmann's theory appears stronger under the worth component of the deservedness criterion because he crisply explains the socially valued reasons for preferring the nonprofit status in terms of the nondistribution constraint, which also creates the capital shortage. Nevertheless, although this contract failure explanation for preferring nonprofits is certainly true in many instances, it is not universally or unquestionably the case. For example, Hansmann claims that the nonprofit form is preferred in the educational market to overcome two forms of contract failure: the market separation problem that results from parents purchasing education for third-party consumers (their children) and the evaluation problem that results from education as a complex personal service, where quality comparison is difficult. Market separation, however, clearly is not a major problem at the college/university level, where substanital numbers of students pay for their own education through loans, grants and work. Moreover, while quality comparisons between educational institutions may be more difficult than choosing a Ford over a Chevy, students and parents certainly do it, assisted by any number of private rankings, guidebooks and the like.[5] Professor Ellman has observed that even at the primary and secondary education levels, parents likely engage in far more quality evaluation than Hansmann appears to credit.[6] Likewise, as we observed in Chapter 4, both the market separation and monitoring problems may be overstated in the hospital sector. Hansman's theory provides us the analytical tools to debate these issues, but nothing in the theory itself answers who is a deserving charity, except to relegate us to an intensely empirical inquiry. The theory therefore does not easily lend itself to practical administration in a manner that will honor the worth criterion as applied.

Hansmann's theory is also flawed under the proportionality criterion. Although the subsidy modulates to fluctuations according to the level of capital need within one organization over time, it is not sensitive to differences in capital need among different deserving nonprofits. This defect exists because the theory uses income as a proxy for capital need. However, one organization with heavy capital needs may have little income (and hence a small subsidy), while another with only slight needs may have a large income. Therefore, as Hansmann concedes, the exemption operates as an "extremely crude mechanism" for conferring the subsidy.[7] A much more direct and efficient method for subsidizing capital formation exists through direct construction grants or tax-exempt bond financing, both of which are widely used in the hospital and education sectors.[8] Hansmann's theory does not explain why the income tax exemption should be used in preference, or even as a supplement, to these other methods that respond much more precisely to variations in the need for capital.

Finally, Hansmann's theory does not satisfy the universality and historical consistency criteria from the standpoint of explaining all dimensions of the exemption in terms of our intuitions about what charities are. While Hansmann argues that his theory could be applied to the state property tax exemption,[9] in fact it is a very poor fit. Like the relief of poverty theory, the capital subsidy theory has a perverse, upsidedown effect as applied to the property tax since that exemption provides the greatest subsidy to those entities that already have the largest capital base. As for its intuitive sense, the capital subsidy theory does a poor job of describing "charities." Hansmann offers no evidence that Congress, courts or taxing officials have ever considered the exemption as a subsidy for capital formation. While the classic charities are excellent examples of activities suffering contract failure and in need of a capital subsidy, it does not comport with common understanding to elevate these incidental characteristics into the *definition* of all charities.

In sum, Hansmann's capital subsidy theory fails to some degree on all four scores. It fails to track when an exemption is deserved because it offers no meaningful, administrable test for which nonprofits overcome market failure and when capital formation problems exist with respect to specific activities, it offers no explanation for why capital formation problems would not better be addressed by direct government subsidies for capital formation (as currently exist) and it fails to provide an adequate explanation for state property tax exemption or an intuitive concept of what is "charitable."

Rob Atkinson's Altruism Theory

Extending the Yale Law School dominance of academic theories of the income tax exemption, in a 1990 article Professor Rob Atkinson, a Yale graduate and former student of Professor Hansmann, defended exemption as a proper government encouragement of altruism in our society.[10] Criticizing Hansmann's theory as too narrow and economically driven, Atkinson theorized that all nonprofit organizations other than "mutual commercial nonprofits" (entities in which the founders directly benefit from the firm's production, such as parent-controlled day care) are valued for the very reason of their nonprofit status. This value adheres to the multiple ways in which nonprofits can be said to be altruistic institutions. Donative entities provide the clearest case by engaging in worthy causes supported largely by donations. Even in the case of commercial nonprofits, however, Atkinson finds that the initial decision by the founder to adopt the nonprofit form and thereby forego the distribution of future profits constitutes an altruistic subsidization of consumption by the institution's customers. In effect, the altruism is inherent in the founder's decision to plow all earnings back into the enterprise, thereby improving the quality or lowering the costs of the goods or services sold.

According to Atkinson, altruism is something that is (or should be) highly valued by our society, in either its pure or in this implicit, "plow-back" form. The tax exemption exists, then, as a means to support this socially valued altruism in all of its forms, and regardless of the underlying activity. "Under this theory, there would be no inquiry into the merits of such [consumption], no search for public benefits flowing from it. The metabenefit of altruistic production would suffice."[11]

Atkinson's theory has the great benefit of certainty and administrability, items lacking in any of the theories of exemption advanced so far. In essence, Atkinson would grant exemption to any nonprofit entity other than a "mutual commercial nonprofit," which would be exempt from income tax in any event under a tax-base rationale that it earns no income. In so doing, however, Atkinson would expand the scope of exemption beyond any current boundary. We think, therefore, that it is incumbent upon Atkinson to justify this expansion by rigorously defending his theory under the deservedness criterion, and this is where we encounter two crucial flaws in his approach.

In order to meet the deservedness criterion, Atkinson must show first that altruism is valued by society and second that a tax subsidy is necessary to effectuate this public policy. Atkinson declines on both counts. As to the first, he concedes that "[i]t would be logical for me here to prove that altruism [in the special sense of foregoing the distribution of profits] really is a good thing and thus worthy of tax favors," but he states that the task "is too ambitious" because it entails ascertaining "what is ultimately good." He therefore leaves the matter to one of "faith, of freely chosen values and visions."[12] To assume without argument or explanation that society places great value on nonprofit enterprise per se, simply because no profit is distributed, is to adopt a question-begging posture that argues in favor of expanding the exemption based on a bare description of the present state of the nonprofit sector.

Certainly, this leap of faith might be in order for the pure altruism inherent in classic donative institutions, but it is not so easily accepted for the special form of altruism contained in the plow-back argument. It is difficult to accept on face value the assertion that nearly all nonprofit organizations exhibit altruism by virtue of the founder's decision to forego profits when there are a variety of reasons why organizers might choose the nonprofit form for purely self-serving motives. In the hospital industry, for example, many commentators conclude that the nonprofit form predominates because doctors prefer it, not because of altruistic motivation but because they earn more and face less oversight.[13] The nonprofit form might be chosen in labor intensive service businesses that can pay out virtually all the net revenues as salaries to employees, simply because the resulting exemption would provide more such revenues—in essence a distribution of profit, though one not prohibited by nonprofit corporate or tax law as long as the salary is reasonable.[14] Under Atkinson's theory, this possibility would label as "altruistic" the purely strategic adoption of the nonprofit form and then justify the very exemption that motivates this strategy by bare reference to this label.

We do not mean by this cynical account necessarily to discredit Atkinson's "metabenefit" version of altruism. Rather, we use it only to show that he fails to make a convincing case for *all* nonprofits in the mere abstract assertion that such altruism is possibile for some. Whether or not such altruism in fact motivates most or all nonprofit founders is of course an intensely empirical inquiry. A related problem is that Atkinson assumes that a one-time decision to forego profits justifies exemption essentially forever. This would require us to grant exemption in perpetuity with no right to reconsider whether the initial decision is still relevant in terms of future values. Racially segregated parks and swimming pools were once legitimate targets of philanthropy;[15] Atkinson would agree that societal mores have changed to the point that we would no longer consider a government subsidy for such activities, but he is unable to integrate this side constraint as part of his basic exemption theory.[16]

We need not resolve these empirical and social policy complexities here because the second prong of deservedness is so clearly lacking under Atkinson's theory in any event. Even granting the worth of metabenefit altruism, this still fails to offer an explanation for why it is necessary to subsidize altruism via a tax exemption. No one is suggesting that we somehow outlaw altruism in society; people are free to pursue their altruistic motivations without government intervention or help.

This point is precisely the same point as that made at length in Chapter 5 with respect to the community benefit theory of exemption, only here Professor Atkinson maintains that the implicit altruism which exists in virtually all nonprofits is what constitutes the community benefit. In order for this assertion of community preference to justify the exemption, Atkinson must explain why tax exemption is necessary to achieve this preference. This requires showing some barrier to forming or operating a nonprofit entity which the tax exemption would help overcome. Atkinson does not do so, but one obvious possibility is the founder's loss of profits that results from devoting future income streams back to the enterprise. This loss of earnings does not constitute a strong case for the exemption, however, because the exemption rewards the institution, not the founder. Where the exemption itself motivates the founder to adopt the nonprofit form, it is likely there were no significant profits at stake to begin with, and so this argument for needing the exemption is self-defeating.

The Public Trust Variant

Another possible justification for exempting all nonprofits exists in yet another variation on the community benefit theme. We refer to this as the "public trust" variant. One might overcome the central flaw in Atkinson's position by arguing that nonprofits are deterred or hindered by virtue of state law provisions that impose more stringent organizational and operational constraints on nonprofit than for-profit enterprises. These laws are designed in part to ensure attention to community rather than private interests.[17] For example, managers of nonprofit corporations have a fiduciary responsibility to the public to exercise care in managing the corporation's assets, a public trust duty enforceable by state attorneys general. The exemption might be viewed as an exchange for the imposition of these greater public responsibilities.[18]

This "public trust" theory, however, does not solve Atkinson's deservedness problem. Although the law remains somewhat unsettled, nonprofit organizations simply are not under any unique corporate duties. Nonprofits generally owe no greater fiduciary responsibility to the public than for-profits owe to their shareholders.[19] A number of older cases, drawing by analogy from the law of charitable trusts, have applied heightened "trust-like" duties to nonprofit corporations classified as charitable.[20] This distinction between trusts and corporations exists primarily to give the founder of a charity a choice between two organizational forms, one that is more flexible but less protective than the other. Nevertheless, "the modern trend is to apply corporate rather than trust principles in determining the liability of the directors of charitable corporations, because their functions are virtually indistinguishable from those of their 'pure' corporate counterparts."[21] The leading decision, for instance, judged a nonprofit hospital's managers by the same rules concerning mismanagement and delegation of duties that govern all corporations.

Even where this decision is not followed, the additional restrictions placed on "noncharitable" nonprofits do not accrue to the net benefit of society. Instead, the restrictions exist primarily to compensate for the fact that nonprofit managers are not subject to shareholder oversight and therefore they may present a greater risk of misbehavior than managers of investor-owned companies.[22] A prime example of such a compensatory rule is the authority of state attorneys general to challenge nonprofits for breach of their duties. A second example is a prophylactic rule against self-dealing transactions by nonprofit directors.[23] These rules exist, not because nonprofits have any greater public duties as a class, but because the absence of owners means there is not one available to challenge mismanagement or to consent to self-dealing.

Implicit in much of the argument that underlies the public trust variant is that nonprofits somehow better represent the entire community's interests precisely because they do not have to answer to private shareholders. This assumption peculiarly posits that the interests of shareholders and customers of proprietary establishments differ from the public interest at large. Granting this assumption, nonprofits nevertheless are under the same distorting influences. Those nonprofits that primarily sell products and services must also satisfy the demands of their customers. Moreover, nonprofits must respond to the demands of the investment community because commercial nonprofits still must rely on borrowed capital to substitute for lack of equity or donated capital. The similarity in the sources of operating and capital funds helps to explain the essentially indistinguishable behavior of the two sectors where they coexist in the same industry.[24] Ultimately, therefore, there simply is no good explanation for why society should subsidize nonprofits merely because of the nonprofit form.

Exempting all nonprofits also fails the historical consistency and universality criteria. It is not historically correct because it contradicts the established understanding that "charitable" encompasses a smaller set of activities than do all nonprofits; otherwise the very complex structure of § 501 that differentiates among the various categories of charitable and noncharitable tax exemption would be largely redundant. As for universality, it is not met because Atkinson fails to explain the significant limitations on tax exemption, such as the public policy doctrine or the unrelated business income tax, except as side constraints to exempt status. His argument that nonprofits deserve exemption if they put their profits to good use, for example, would apply to profits so devoted regardless of the source of those profits and would render unnecessary the imposition of the UBIT, returning the law to its pre-1950 stage where exemption was determined by a "destination-of-income" test.[25]

We do not wish to overemphasize our disagreements with Professors Hansmann and Atkinson. Ultimately, the donative theory of exemption that we develop in the remainder of this book shares much in common with both of their theories, since they each advocate subsidizing activities motivated by altruism. But a careful development of why this is appropriate is needed in order to develop the administrable standards for exemption qualification that Hansmann's and Atkinson's theories lack.

Recapitulation

We will recapitulate the many strands of argument in the first part of this book by referring to our four criteria for evaluating theories of the charitable tax exemption. The most important criterion is deservedness, which has two distinct components: whether the theory identifies activities that are both worthy of and in need of a social subsidy. The chief example of a conventional theory that fails the worth component of deservedness is the theory that uses charitable trust law to define the scope of the tax exemption. This body of law, which has evolved since before the enactment of the 1601 Statute of Charitable Uses, contains essentially no subject matter limits to its coverage. It indiscriminately enforces trusts that pursue any *public* purpose that a founder might choose, a conception that is "broad enough to include whatever will promote, in a legitimate way, the comfort, happiness, and improvement of an indefinite number of persons."[26] Beyond this basic requirement of publicness, the only limits charitable trust law sets are organizational and operational constraints on the manner in which the activity is conducted, constraints such as nonprofit status and a prohibition of operating the entity for the benefit of those who control it. It is manifestly absurd to confer billions of dollars of public subsidy on activities for no other reason than that, if they were organized as trusts, the law would not refuse to enforce the trust terms.

Other theories more discriminating in their determination of worth are nevertheless flawed under the deservedness criterion because they do not explain why valued activities *need* support to exist at a socially optimal level. A prime example is the community benefit theory, which seeks to ascertain which activities are more desirably offered on a nonprofit than a for-profit basis. This theory is flawed because, even assuming society has a preference for nonprofit enterprise (either generally or in particular industries), the community benefit theory fails to explain why a subsidy is needed to effectuate this preference. For instance, even if we accept the (unproven) argument that nonprofit hospitals are superior to for-profits, doctors and patients are free to patronize nonprofits to the full extent they desire. Therefore, there is no basis for providing a social subsidy to assist in realizing this choice. The exemption is either a waste or a windfall.

After determining what activities deserve a social subsidy, the next difficulty in understanding the charitable exemption is to formulate a theory that reasonably tailors the level of subsidy to the level of deservedness so as not to grossly over- or undersubsidize the activity. The primary hurdle this proportionality inquiry presents is why should deserving activities be subsidized through the tax system rather than by a more targeted form of direct subsidy that would almost surely be more accurate? A leading example of a theory that fails this proportionality criterion is one that limits the exemption to organizations that provide some measure of free services to the poor. Under this theory of the exemption, a tax subsidy produces an upside down effect as between qualifying entities that provide a small percentage of free services and those that provide a large percentage: those charities that provide the least free services will have the most exempt property and income, all else being equal. Therefore, the charity care theory perversely aids those activities the most that least deserve support, among the entities that qualify. Other theories of the exemption distribute support randomly or unpredictably with respect to their definition of deservedness.

Existing theories of the exemption also perform poorly under the universality and historical consistency criteria. For instance, Professors Bittker and Hansmann have proposed competing theories that would explain the federal income tax exemption but that have no relationship to the state property tax exemption. Moreover, their theories fail to explain major restrictions on the exemption and give no coherent meaning to the term "charitable" that accords with established history and common sense understandings. Even the government burden theory as applied to the relief of poverty suffers from historical inaccuracy since the exemption has always extended to a far broader range of activities.

This analysis might be attacked by observing that our criteria for evaluation are too demanding. No social program could live up to the exacting scrutiny we have just given the charitable exemption. This may be true, but our objective is not to impose an unrealistic degree of theoretical rigor. Instead, it is to highlight by contrast the remarkable ability that the donative theory developed in the following chapters has to satisfy this array of analytical screens. If a theory can be constructed that avoids most of the foregoing objections, then it must be given strong credence, if not on absolute terms, then at least compared with the alternatives.

Notes

1. Henry B. Hansmann, *The Role of Nonprofit Enterprise*, 89 YALE L.J. 835 (1980) (hereafter *Nonprofit Enterprise*); Henry B. Hansmann, *The Rationale for Exempting Nonprofit Organizations from Federal Income Taxation*, 91 YALE L.J. 54 (1981) (hereafter *Exempting Nonprofits*).

2. *E.g.*, I.R.C. § 501(c)(3) (permitting exemption for an entity only if "no part" of its revenues "inures to the benefit of any private shareholder or individual . . . .").

3. I.R.C. § 11.

4. *See generally,* DONALD COHODES & BRIAN KINKEAD, HOSPITAL CAPITAL FORMATION IN THE 1980S (1984). This situation may change, though, as a result of sweeping limitations in public and private health insurance. *See* J. ROGERS HOLLINGSWORTH & ELLEN J. HOLLINGSWORTH, CONTROVERSY ABOUT AMERICAN HOSPITALS: FUNDING, OWNERSHIP AND PERFORMANCE 40–42 (1987). On the other hand, continuing a capital subsidy would defeat the purpose of these reimbursement reforms, namely to eliminate excess duplication and force hospitals to operate more efficiently.

5. *E.g.*, BARRON'S EDUCATIONAL SERIES, INC., BARRON'S PROFILES OF AMERICAN COLLEGES (19th ed., 1992); JAMES CASS & MAX BIRNBAUM, COMPARATIVE GUIDE TO AMERICAN COLLEGES (15th ed., 1991); COLLEGE BOARD, THE COLLEGE HANDBOOK 1993 (1992); PETERSON'S GUIDE TO FOUR-YEAR COLLEGES 1993 (Susan W. Dilts ed., 1991); EDWARD B. FISKE, THE FISKE GUIDE TO COLLEGES 1993 (1992); MACMILLAN PUBLISHING CO., THE COLLEGE BLUEBOOK (23d ed., 1991); CHARLES T. STRAUGHN II & BARBARASUE LOVEJOY STRAUGHN, LOVEJOY'S COLLEGE GUIDE (21st ed., 1992).

6. *See* Ira M. Ellman, *Another Theory of Nonprofit Corporations*, 80 MICH. L. REV. 999, 1033 (1982) ("In fact, one's general impression is that, whether or not they are right, parents tend to think that they know whether their child's school or day care facility is doing a good job.").

7. Hansmann, *Exempting Nonprofits, supra* note 1, at 92.

8. According to the 1994 U.S. Budget, the lost revenue from exempting interest on bonds issued by private nonprofit hospitals and educational organizations was $2 *billion.* BUDGET OF THE UNITED STATES GOVERNMENT, ANALYTICAL PERSPECTIVES, Fiscal Year 1995, at 66. In addition, the federal government and states provide direct capital assistance to educational institutions in the form of grants for building facilities for handicapped students, free textbooks and instructional materials and transportation services (such as buses) that otherwise would require substantial capital investment. DANIEL J. SULLIVAN, PUBLIC AID TO NONPUBLIC SCHOOLS 92–95 (1974). *See generally,* NATIONAL CENTER FOR EDUCATION

STATISTICS, FEDERAL SUPPORT FOR EDUCATION FISCAL YEARS 1980–1992 (1993) (detailing direct federal expenditures on education).

9. Hansmann, *Exempting Nonprofits, supra* note 1, at 93.

10. Rob Atkinson, *Altruism in Nonprofit Organizations*, 31 B.C.L. REV. 501 (1990).

11. *Id.* at 619.

12. *Id.* at 628–30. He continues: "I must admit my suspicion that the question of inherent goodness may not be subject to proof, in the case of either altruism or other proposed desiderata." *Id.* In a later article on morality and ethics, Atkinson further explains his position that these matters are simply incapable of objective proof and thus must rest with shared personal commitment. Rob Atkinson, *Beyond the New Role Morality for Lawyers*, 52 MD. L. REV. 853, 872–889.

13. *See* Mark A. Hall & John D. Colombo, *The Charitable Status of Nonprofit Hospitals: Toward a Donative Theory of Tax Exemption*, 66 WASH. L. REV. 307, 367–74 (1990) and sources cited therein.

14. Mark A. Hall & John D. Colombo, *The Donative Theory of the Charitable Tax Exemption*, 52 OHIO ST. L.J. 1379, 1419–20 (1991). To be fair, Professor Atkinson does recognize that certain nonprofits may exhibit a material quid pro quo for their managers, and would deny exemption in these cases. Atkinson, *supra* note 13, at 544–45, n.125, 553–54 (doctor controlled hospitals). He does not, however, provide any operational criteria to distinguish such organizations, although he does believe that such criteria could be developed (donations, perhaps?). *Id.* at 554.

15. The famous case of Senator Augustus O. Bacon of Georgia is one example. Upon his death, Senator Bacon left a large tract of land to the city of Macon, Georgia, for use as a segregated park. When African-Americans sought admission to the park in 1963, litigation ensued which ultimately ended in the United States Supreme Court ordering desegregation of the park. Evans v. Newton, 382 U.S. 296 (1966). In its discussion concerning whether the administration of the park constituted "state action" subject to the Fourteenth Amendment, the Court noted that the park enjoyed tax-exempt status. *Id.* at 301.

16. *See* Atkinson, *supra* note 10, at 636-37 (possible room for public policy doctrine in the altruism theory as an "extraneous" constraint).

17. Elizabeth Miller Guggenheimer, *Making the Case for Voluntary Health Care Institutions: Policy, Theories and Legal Approaches, in* IN SICKNESS AND IN HEALTH: THE MISSION OF VOLUNTARY HEALTH CARE INSTITUTIONS 35, 48–49 (1988) (hereafter IN SICKNES AND IN HEALTH); J David Seay & Bruce Vladeck, *Mission Matters, in* IN SICKNESS AND IN HEALTH, *supra*, at 15–17.

18. Ellman, *supra* note 6, at 1006 n.22 (collecting cases); *see* American Hosp. Ass'n v. Hansbarger, 600 F. Supp. 465, 473 (N.D.W.V. 1984), *aff'd*, 783 F.2d 1184 (4th Cir.), *cert. denied*, 479 U.S. 820 (1986) (tax exemption compensates for the burden that nonprofits have of maintaining community representation on their governing board).

19. Ellman, *supra* note 6, at 1006 n.25; Henry B. Hansmann, *Reforming Nonprofit Corporation Law*, 129 U. PA. L. REV. 497, 567 (1981).

20. Ellman, *supra* note 6, at 1006 n.22.

21. Stern v. Lucy Webb Hayes Nat'l Training School for Deaconesses & Missionaries, 381 F.Supp. 1003, 1013 (D.C.D.C. 1974).

22. *See* CLARK C. HAVIGHURST, HEALTH CARE LAW AND POLICY 209 (1988); Kenneth Karst, *The Efficiency of the Charitable Dollar: An Unfulfilled State Responsibility*, 73 HARV. L. REV. 433, 436 (1960) (charities lack any "interested... individual to call the charitable fiduciary to account").

23. *See* Ellman, *supra* note 6, at 1007–08.

24. *See* HOLLINGSWORTH & HOLLINGSWORTH, *supra* note 4, at 66–67 (1987); Cyril Chang & Howard Tuckman, *The Profits of Not-for-Profit Hospitals*, 13 J. HEALTH POL., POL'Y & L. 547, 549–50 (1988).

25. *Cf.* Trinidad v. Sagrada Orden de Predicadores, 263 U.S. 578 (1924).

26. Harrington v. Pier, 105 Wis. 485, 520, 82 N.W. 345.

PART TWO

The Donative Theory

7

Theoretical Foundations of the Donative Theory

In the first half of this book, we provide an exhaustive (and exhausting) survey of the many flaws in the numerous conventional and academic theories for exempting charitable institutions from taxes. Our analysis produces a frustrating stalemate. Defining charitable in the popular sense of poverty relief is countered by examples of symphonies and prep schools; broadening the exemption to cover the relief of any government burden overlooks the separation of church and state; and the search for a concrete sense of community benefit fails to keep the exemption within administrable bounds. In frustration, most conventional thinkers have resorted to a superstitious faith in the mystical guidance of the 1601 Statute of Charitable Uses, while academicians have proposed theories that ignore our basic intuitions about what constitutes a charity.

In the remainder of this book, we propose a new "donative theory" of exemption that would limit exempt status to those entities that receive a substantial level of donative support from the public. Actually, this theory is not new; the role of donations in nonprofit enterprise has been noted in the previous literature and several major antecedent works have laid the framework for a theory of exemption based upon donative activity.[1] Nevertheless, no one has yet fully articulated as we do why tax exemption should be limited to those "charities" that attract substantial donations, and no one has yet explained as we do why this theory satisfactorily ties together a convincing understanding of why nonprofit organizations exist, why they should be exempt from tax, and the origins of the legal concept of charity.

This part of the book proceeds by first describing in this chapter the two foundations for the donative theory: (1) economic theory for which market failures produce voluntary donations and why significant free riding behavior attaches to donative support; and (2) political theory about why governments fail to adequately fund objects of charity. This "twin-failure" argument provides the paradigm case for a shadow subsidy administered through the tax system. In subsequent chapters, we then explore the extent to which this explanation for a donative subsidy loses its force when applied to cases of less than pure public goods status and to adulterated motives for giving. We conclude that the donative theory has the power to apply generally to all instances of true giving, but that it does not apply to the mere retention of earnings by a nonprofit entity. We also demonstrate that an exemption for donative organizations employs concept of charity that best meets the four criteria developed above—deservedness, proportionality, universality, and historical consistency. In particular, the donative theory is consistent with charitable trust law, from which tax exemption jurisprudence draws its concept of charity, and it explains the major limitations on charitable status. Finally, our examination of moral theory reveals that the foundation of the donative theory is not exclusively economic; it is strongly buttressed by the leading theories of distributive justice and by the pluralistic values that characterize the third sector.

Economic Theory: The Paradigm Case

A stimulating body of economic and political theory has emerged over the past decade attempting to explain why the United States has such a large "third sector" as an alternative to proprietary firms and the government. These scholars have identified three major categories of nonprofit institutions, which are characterized by their sources of income: donative nonprofits, such as the Salvation Army, rely on contributions; commercial nonprofits, such as National Geographic, generate most of their receipts from sales; and mutual benefit organizations, such as a country club, derive revenue from dues-paying members. Our focus in this chapter, obviously, is donative nonprofits. For this subset, scholars have developed a combined theory of market and government failure to explain their existence. Donations arise where the two principal sectors of society fail adequately to supply desired goods and services, for reasons that lie at the intersection of classic microeconomic and political theory. A closer examination of this "twin failure" explanation for why donative nonprofits exist reveals that they present the strongest normative case for deserving a tax exemption subsidy.

Market Theory

Economists theorize that donative organizations exist to facilitate the production of certain "public goods" (which can be either products or services).[2] Pure public goods in the economic sense are those characterized by two conditions: (1) *durability*—the cost of supplying everyone is no more than the cost of supplying a single person because the good does not wear out as others use it; and (2) *indivisibility*—the nature of the good is such that, once it is produced for one consumer, it is impossible to exclude its use by any other consumer. Classic examples of nearly pure public goods include air pollution control and border defense. The cost to clean the air in a particular geographic region is the same whether one person or one million live there; once clean, moreover, everyone enjoys the benefit.

Because of these characteristics, the private market will not supply public goods either at all[3] or at an optimal level[4] because no one has an incentive to pay for them. If one supposes that someone else will pay for the public good, then one can "free ride" on that other person's payment. If I know that Sarah next door will pay to support the PBS program I watch, there is no need for me to pay, as well, because once PBS sends out it signal, I can watch "for free." Moreover, even if no one else will pay, there is still no incentive to purchase the goods, because the purchaser knows there is no way to exclude others from enjoying the purchase —that is, there is no way to prohibit *others* from free-riding. Even if Sarah won't pay to support PBS, neither, logically, should I, because if I do, Sarah can watch on my nickel. "Regardless of how the individual estimates the behavior of others, he must always rationally choose the free-rider alterative."[5]

The same thought is also captured in terms of extreme "positive externalities": individual purchases will always fail to produce public goods at the optimal level since one who chooses to pay for such a good will realize only an infinitesimal fraction of the benefits that the good offers to society at large.[6] As a consequence of these severe free-riding incentives and positive externalities, classic economic theory postulates that the government is in the best position to provide public goods (either directly, or by subsidizing private production) since government can coerce "purchase" by everyone via the power of taxation.

Political Theory

If government is able to correct the free-rider defect through its power to tax, why then should donors ever need to contribute to the private production of public goods? The answer lies in the vagaries of majoritarian voting logic, which result in the government systematically undersupplying certain public goods. Economist Burton Weisbrod first had this insight.[7] Drawing on previous observations about government-provided goods and voting patterns, he demonstrated that certain blocs of voters will predictably lack the voting strength to force the government to meet their public goods needs. This is true because governmental decisions in a democracy are roughly shaped by the desires of the majority of the electorate.[8] The government will therefore supply any given public good at a level approximating that desired by the median voter.

As illustrated in Figure 7.1 for a hypothetical public good, if the government were to move much beyond the median demand to a level of production Q_b, then the number of voters who prefer a lower level of the public good would vote down the increase (V_{nb} versus V_{pb}). Conversely, high demanders prevent the government from lowering the provision of public goods to, say, Q_a (V_{pa} versus V_{na}). As a result, the voting equilibrium settles near the middle of the range of voter tastes (Q_m).

This system of majoritarian politics works reasonably well provided the desire for a public good is fairly homogeneous. In that case, the level of median demand is close to the level of demand at either extreme.[9] This logic does not hold, though, for public goods for which there are heterogeneous, widely divergent tastes. In such situations, voting logic predicts an undersupplied minority of high demanders, indicated by the shaded area of Figure 7.1. This supramedian group has no ready alternative other than to make voluntary contributions to a private organization to provide additional production. Put more concretely, there may exist in society a group that has a high demand for opera. The median voter, however, does not value opera nearly as much as this high-demand group. Ergo, the majority of the electorate will not vote for government-supplied opera at a level sufficient to satisfy the high-demand group. Thus in order to satisfy its demand, this group contributes to the Metropolitan Opera Society. One can contrast this situation to, say, public highways, in which demand is relatively homogeneous (nearly everyone has a car and wants good roads); in this case, there is no great difference between the median voter's demand and extreme demand, and the result will be that the government will supply roads at a level great enough to satisfy the "nearly everyone" who has a car. For this reason, no "public highway society" exists, because no additional private road production is necessary to meet extreme demand otherwise unmet by government provision.

These observations about when donative behavior occurs are not dependent on the exact reason for government failure. The above description hypothesizes a situation in which a high-demanding group asks government for more production and is turned down by an indifferent majority. But government failure may also occur because dissatisfied voters may simply decide as a matter of transaction costs that it is easier to

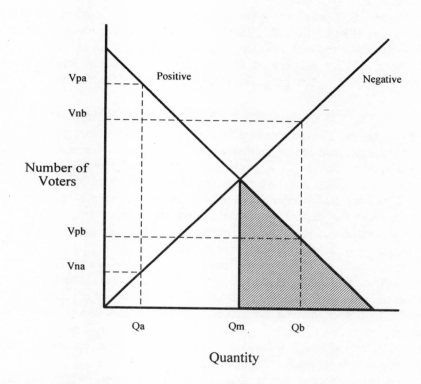

FIGURE 7.1 Quantity of a public good supplied by government as a function of positive and negative voter demand.

encourage contributions than to solicit the government, or voters may conclude that production through government coercion diminishes the value of production that obtains from the mere existence of voluntarism. In developing the latter point, theoretical economists have demonstrated that direct government provision of public goods may actually decrease overall societal welfare by depriving donors of the opportunity to give themselves, which they value to the extent that giving is motivated by act utility.[10]

Confirmation of the relationship between government failure and donative behavior comes from observing whether rapid drops in donative activity follow sharp increases in government spending. Several economists have posited that government spending has a "crowding out" effect on donations, such that as government spending increases, the need for charities to solicit donations, and the willingness of donors to give, diminishes.[11] Although some studies have found less crowding out effect than theorists had predicted,[12] they do confirm that government spending is inversely correlated with the level of donative support. For instance, giving to social welfare services dropped rather precipitously following the government's New Deal programs that grew out of the Depression.[13]

The Charitable Exemption and Deduction as Shadow Subsidies

Government failure combined with private market failure provides the most rigorous case for explaining why donative nonprofits exist and what function they serve. This explanation does not, however, make the normative case that donative nonprofits should be subsidized through the taxing system. In fact, the above explanation might support a conclusion that because the majority of the electorate has refused to provide direct government production of a given public good, that same majority will also refuse to provide indirect government production through a tax subsidy. Thus we need to answer two questions at this juncture. First, if the intersection of private market failure and government failure produces donative behavior to increase production, then why is any government help needed to further increase production beyond that supplied by donations? Second, even if such help is needed, why would the majority, whom we have just hypothesized refused to provide the good at optimum levels, approve an indirect subsidy?

The first question has a relatively simple answer. Where donative behavior exists, we can be relatively sure that donations alone will not provide the desired good in great enough quantity to satisfy all demand. The reason for this relates back to the free-rider hypothesis: if a good is a public good, and therefore has the twin characteristics of durability and indivisibility, the rational economic behavior of any individual is not to pay for the good but rather "free ride" on someone else's payment. Thus economic theory would predict that not everyone that wants the particular good will pay for it through donations, resulting in chronic undersupply.

Of course, taken to its extreme, classic economic theory would predict that no donative behavior would occur at all because of the free-rider incentive. As a practical matter, we know that this prediction is wrong: a considerable number of people are willing to pick up litter or staff fire protection services, for example. As Gerald Marwell has commented, "[a]ny look at the real world demonstrates that the problem of collective action is frequently 'solved,' at least to the extent of permitting some collective goods, if not an optimal amount, to be provided . . . . In fact, voluntary collective action seems endemic."[14] Thus, donors contribute to education, which entails the public good of raising society's level of knowledge and bolstering the economy with skilled workers. Another classic object of philanthropy—disaster relief and aid to the poor—provides the public good of assuaging society's collective concern over the plight of the nation's or world's destitute.[15]

This arm-chair empiricism has been verified by more carefully controlled and rigorously designed social experiments, which demonstrate that free riding behavior is severely dampened by a set of motives loosely described as altruism—a willingness to take a collective view of social benefit and set aside narrow, individual self-interest.[16] For example, in one study the researchers gave groups of nine volunteers five dollars apiece and told them that if at least five members gave up their stakes, each of the nine would receive a ten-dollar bonus. The income maximizing strategy for each individual under these rules is to keep the money, hoping others will contribute, whereas the group strategy is to somehow designate five donors. Under varying conditions (group discussion, no discussion) the rate of contributing ranged from 47% to 84%, with the resulting voluntary provision of the "public good" (i.e., qualifying for the group bonus) ranging from 60% to 100%.[17] In a similar study, the researchers varied the constituencies of a dozen groups according to academic majors. Each of the groups showed some, but only a moderate, level of free riding behavior, except for the study group consisting of graduate students in economics, who free rode almost entirely.[18]

There are various accounts of what motive overcomes free-riding. In the language of sociology, the motive derives from a group dynamic or inbred sociality.[19] Psychologists tend to speak more in terms of a person's sense of elemental fairness, perhaps a product of the Superego.[20] Economists postulate that some individuals' utility functions are dependent on the utilities of others.[21] And biologists theorize about an evolutionary basis for altruism, which enhances the odds of species survival.[22] No matter what the hypothesis regarding donative behavior, however, each of the empirical studies confirms that free riding occurs to some degree, just as common observation finds that voluntarism falls short of ideal aspirations. Thus even though some mechanism works to overcome free-riding in its absolute form, that mechanism is not sufficient to overcome all free-riding, and some consumers will fail to pay their fair share for the good in question.

Where donative support for public goods exists, therefore, one can anticipate persistent undersupply of that good. This is illustrated in Figure

7.2, where Q_g represents the level of a hypothetical public good provided by the government, and Q_d the additional quantity produced through private donations. The shaded area represents a remaining level of unsatisfied demand. Therefore, some form of funding is needed that matches private donations with an additional subsidy to amplify the donations, in order to take up the slack left by the free-rider disincentive and move the level of production further toward Q_s.

This matching, or shadow subsidy, function is precisely the explanation that Weisbrod has offered for the charitable deduction.[23] A deduction from personal income taxes for donations to charities is, in economic analysis, a

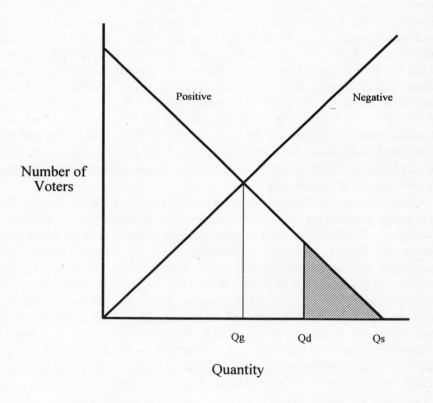

FIGURE 7.2 The effect of donations and a donative subsidy on the production of a public good.

system that provides a proportionate government subsidy for each dollar of private philanthropy. Thus, in a thirty percent tax bracket, a taxpayer who donates $100 is in effect contributing only $70, because absent the donation the taxpayer would have paid $30 in tax on those earnings. By forgiving part of the tax bill, the government is in effect providing the taxpayer with a rebate in lieu of writing a check directly to the charity. This government assistance is funded by increasing the tax burden on the public, including those members of the public who take a free-ride by choosing not to donate. "Tax subsidies therefore represent, in effect, contributions from low demanders to stimulate the high demanders to contribute."[24]

Weisbrod's insights about the deduction can be extended to the exemption from income and property taxes. The exemption is also capable of providing a form of shadow subsidy if it is administered with this donative theory in mind. Exempting donative nonprofits from income and property taxation helps to remedy the systematic underprovision of public goods by allowing the donation to be more productive than it would be if it, or its earnings, were taxed.

This "twin failure" theory neatly satisfies both the worth and the need components of our deservedness criterion when the tax subsidy is applied to donative nonprofits. The existence of a significant level of giving signals a collective benefit that is not being supplied at a sufficient level—in short, a worthy object of subsidy. However, the free riding incentive tells us that these donations systematically fall short of supplying the objects of philanthropy at an optimally desired level—in short, that an additional subsidy is necessary. A tax exemption for donative institutions helps to take up this donative slack by using the tax system as a form of shadow subsidy, that is, by amplifying the effect of private donations. This is an explanation that meshes perfectly with the rationale for the charitable deduction. The deduction encourages individuals to give more, and the exemption helps the institution to make the gift go further.

The second question posited above, why the majority of the electorate would go along with such a subsidy, can also be explained easily through economic analysis. The answer here is that although a majority of voters may resist paying the full cost of government directly providing certain goods and services, a majority may be willing for government to "contribute" to such production because, while they do not value the particular good or service enough to pay for all of it, they recognize that they would receive some marginal benefit from increased production and hence would be willing to pay for a portion of that increased production, especially if such agreement would permit a partial cross-subsidy of their own special interest.[25] Because exemption is "worth" only the tax rate on taxable income or property, it is only a fraction of the cost of direct government provision of the desired goods and services; accordingly, consumers who do not value a particular good or service enough to pay for its full cost but attach some marginal value to increased production should be willing to use exemption to accomplish this purpose. Moreover, even those consumers who attach no value to increased production of a particular good in isolation might go along with a partial subsidy of that production as a political cost of receiving their cross-subsidy.

Viewed in this light, exemption is a sort of "I'll scratch your back if you'll scratch mine" social compact among high-demanding groups with widely divergent preferences. Opera lovers are not willing to pay the full cost of the government studying ruffled grouse and vice-versa; but many ruffled-grouse lovers wouldn't mind paying a little for more opera, and many opera lovers wouldn't mind paying a little for a bit of ruffled grouse study, especially if the bargain results in each group getting some help for its own preferred interest. Because everyone who has a particular interest subject to government failure benefits from exemption, and because virtually all segments of society either have such an interest or directly benefit from such an interest,[26] from the standpoint of social policy exemption becomes a method for government to assist *all* of society in providing goods and services that the private market cannot provide (since by definition we are dealing with a private market failure situation), and which the government cannot fully provide directly because of structural deficiencies in the democratic system.[27]

Imperfections in the Paradigm:
Generalizing the Public Goods Basis for Donations

So far, we have demonstrated the theoretical basis for using exemption as a shadow subsidy for public goods. This paradigm case, however, does not cover many (if any) real-world situations. The classic objects of philanthropy are not pure public goods. Although education entails the public good of bolstering the economy with skilled workers and religion promotes moral values, both entail significant private goods: schools educate the children of donors, and religion provides salvation (or at least spiritual guidance) to the faithful. In the more economic terminology introduced at the outset, neither is completely durable: at some point, the church hall and the classroom fills and another must be built. Nor are they indivisible: admission could be charged (as it partially is by colleges). Even welfare relief, whose public good aspect is more pure (helping the poor assuages a societal conscience, a psychic benefit available to all), partakes only partially of public good characterization. At least an incidental motivating factor for donations to the poor is the localized distress that one person has in seeing another in a destitute condition. Relief of the *donor's* specific distress is not a benefit shared by the public at large. "When Thomas Hobbes was asked why he contributed to a beggar, and was this not due to Christ's commandment, he responded that he did so 'with the sole intent of relieving his own misery at the sight of the beggar.'"[28] If the donative theory is to stand a legitimate explanation of the exemption, therefore, it must comport with these real-world cases.

In fact, these imperfections do not present problems for the donative theory. What these cases illustrate is that donative activity occurs with respect to impure as well as pure public goods. "Strictly speaking, no good or service fits the extreme or polar definition in any genuinely descriptive sense. In real-world fiscal systems, those goods and services that are financed publicly always exhibit less than such pure publicness."[29] Indeed, if this were not so, the strong free-rider hypothesis would be correct and we would see no donative support whatsoever. Thus, these impurities in the public good characteristic of the objects of philanthropy may be necessary in order for there to be any philanthropy. This does not alter the economic conclusion that philanthropy signals an undersupplied good of some sort, and that because of the free rider incentive, philanthropy alone will be insufficient to produce the good at an optimal level.

In fact, this basic conclusion is true even for situations that cannot be characterized as involving public goods at all without straining the meaning of this term. The essential connection between donative activity and public goods is some form of combined private market and government failure. Public goods dramatize a particular form of market failure—they present a polar case of free riding associated with positive externalities—but the same rationale exists in any case where market imperfections result in free riding activity.[30] Indeed, stated even more broadly, donations are a generic tool for overcoming any number of market defects regardless of their free riding characterization. Consequently, the essential fact in the donative theory is the existence of donations per se and not any a priori assessment of the nature of the market defect that produces the donation. Where there is significant donative behavior, there is necessarily a market defect that gives rise to the donation. The free-riding associated with *giving*, not with the particular market defect that *produces* the giving, is the essential component of the rationale for subsidizing donative institutions.

Transaction cost analysis helps explain that the classic incidents of pure public good status (indivisibility and durability) are not the sole economic determinants of donative activity.[31] Many services that are said to be public goods do not actually face an absolute indivisibility problem. Instead, it is merely difficult or uneconomical to assess each consumer's benefit and, therefore, charge him or her appropriately. For instance, when the government builds a road, it sometimes erects a toll booth that charges the particular drivers who use the road, suggesting that a private good is involved. It is not impossible to do this for every road, but in most circumstances this form of revenue collection is less efficient than simply taxing all residents. Thus, some goods become "public" at one price (or level of production) but not at another. Similarly, while it is technically feasible for churches and synagogues to charge admission (and some in fact do so),[32] such crass commercialism could be viewed as destroying the spiritual values enhanced by individual contribution. This loss of spiritual value is a transaction cost of treating religious services as a private good. Likewise, although government provision is often the first and more efficient alternative to the market failure associated with public goods, in some cases voluntary provision through donations may be preferred because coerced provision through taxation entails the transaction cost of destroying the enjoyment that comes from a sense of good citizenship. In the words of Dean Calabresi (also of Yale Law School), "There is a whole category of goods or characteristics whose production cannot be bought or coerced and yet whose presence in the society gives individuals pleasure. These goods are often attitudes like trust, love and altruism whose value depends on their being freely given and which are therefore destroyed if they are bought or coerced."[33]

Professor Hansmann provides another example where the language of public goods does not illuminate the reasons for giving, yet a donative subsidy is deserving nevertheless. He observes that the public goods explanation does not easily fit philanthropic support of the performing arts because the primary benefit accrues to individuals in the audience rather than the community at large.[34] Nevertheless, significant philanthropy occurs.[35] Hansmann theorizes that the nonprofit performing arts rely on contributions to supplement ticket sales as a means of voluntary price discrimination by those who value the performance more than the average ticket holder. The performing arts find it difficult to justify charging widely different amounts for their tickets (perhaps the public outcry would be a transaction cost of doing so). Instead, via targeted fund raising, they extract higher payments from patrons who place the highest value on the arts.

Arts organizations prefer this financing mechanism, despite the burden of soliciting contributions, because it helps to overcome a form of market failure that inheres in the fact that the *marginal* costs of admitting additional members into the audience (or of staging more performances of the work once it is rehearsed) is far below the *average* cost per ticket holder of producing the show.[36] Assuming the ticket price is set so the marginal cost of enlarging the audience equals the marginal benefit to additional attendees, as competitive markets tend to do, then total revenues from ticket sales would be too low in many instances for the performance to be produced. The same point is more commonly illustrated by observing that, if an airline were to set a uniform price at the marginal—rather than the average—cost of boarding an additional passenger, it could never afford to take off the ground since marginal costs only compensate for an extra meal, a tiny increment of fuel, etc., not the already sunk costs of buying a plane, hiring a pilot, etc. The performing arts use donations as a mechanism to achieve the same result airlines achieve through discriminatory pricing schemes that tend to charge more to business travelers who place a higher value on flying than do recreational tourists who can fly for less by reserving much further in advance. This revenue scheme offers some advantage wherever there is a marked differential between average and marginal costs.[37] Indeed, one way of describing public goods is those which have extreme economies of scale. This is precisely the "durability" component of the classic definition. Such a system of voluntary price discrimination, however, allows some patrons to take a free ride on the generosity of others. Therefore, a donative subsidy is needed to assist the scheme in reaching its optimal funding level.

The preceding analysis, by harkening to the form of market failure typified by natural monopolies, suggests a further application of the generalized economic basis for donations. Natural monopolies exist in those goods and services where competition is destructive because it tends to drive prices below a level that will sustain even a single producer. The paradigm natural monopoly is a product with large economies of scale, that is, one with large sunk costs of initial capital investment but low costs of additional production, in other words, one where the average costs far exceed the marginal costs. The result of the rapidly increasing returns from ever-expanding production is that a single firm can meet increased market demand more cheaply than can several competing producers. Competition thus becomes self-destructive: it leads either to an inefficient solution, or, in more extreme cases, to a cyclical pattern that polarizes between monopoly pricing and rampant market entry. Such a paradigm is found in the classic public utilities (electric, gas, water and local telephone services), for which it is uneconomical to have several service lines running down each street. The traditional remedy is government intervention and protection, but Hansmann's analysis of giving to the performing arts illustrates that an alternative to government intervention is voluntary support of prices above those which market forces generate. The performing arts also illustrate that the incidents of extreme natural monopoly conditions—as with the characteristics of pure public goods—are not necessary for significant philanthropy to exist. Hospitals are another such enterprise,[38] and historically received substantial donative support until the government displaced most of this financing.

A final example of the ability to generalize the public goods explanation for subsidizing the objects of donations comes from charitable contributions to public television and radio. Professor Mark Gergen maintains that such contributions do not deserve personal income tax deduction because broadcasting is not an indivisible service (pay-per-view technology now exists, but was not available when radio and television began).[39] This misconceives the basis for a tax subsidy as depending too strictly on the purity of public goods characteristics. Despite the technical ability to charge for public broadcast services, the fact remains that, for whatever reason, those who devised the public broadcast system found it preferable to rely on donations rather than subscriber fees.[40] As a consequence, we can anticipate that some free-riding will occur, and we know the service will be systematically underfunded relative to the benefits donors and nondonors would be willing to pay for if the service were sold.

To further illustrate, one could just as well argue that it is more logical for churches and synagogues to organize like social clubs and charge admission to those who attend services since the primary motive for filling the collection plate is the self-interested desire to have a place to congregate each week. Nevertheless, whether for ideological or practical reasons, churches and synagogues choose to rely primarily on voluntary contributions, which signals that some degree of free-riding is present. Gergen argues that religions have a weak case for the charitable deduction because they "probably do not suffer greatly from free-riding, or at least do not suffer as much from freeriding as do most other charities."[41] But this would only be a basis for providing less of a subsidy, or increasing the level of support required to justify a subsidy, not for denying the exemption altogether.

The critical observation is that, because giving in any form is voluntary, potential donors can enjoy the organization's benefits for free. Otherwise, if the organization refused service to noncontributors, payments would not be donations at all; they would be purchases. The organization's decision to rely on gifts rather than sales is bound to create a free-rider opportunity on which at least some significant number of people who benefit from the organization's services will capitalize. As a consequence, all donative organizations will be underfunded to some degree.

The above discussion sets the theoretical foundation for the donative theory. We observe that donations constitute a signal by the donors that some good or service is undersupplied by both the private market and direct government funding. Moreover, because of the free-rider incentive, donations alone will never provide the level of production actually required to meet demand. Thus, donative entities need additional financial support, and this support is provided by the indirect subsidy of tax exemption (as well as through the charitable deduction). In the next chapter, we examine more closely our assertion that donations perform the signalling function we ascribe to them.

Notes

1. Professor Hansmann's acknowledgement that the exemption is justified for donative nonprofits comes closest to our donative theory of exemption. Henry B. Hansmann, *The Role of Nonprofit Enterprise*, 89 YALE L.J. 835, 887–889 (1980). Hansmann's discussion, however, fails to capture important aspects of the justification for subsidizing donative nonprofits through the tax system rather than through direct government grants, fails to tie the donative exemption to the law of charitable trusts, and fails to demonstrate the ability of the donative theory to integrate all major components of the taxation of charitable organizations. Economist Burton Weisbrod, whose work also strongly influenced our development of this theory, more thoroughly establishes the theoretical groundwork for subsidizing donations, but he does so in the limited context of the charitable *deduction*. BURTON A. WEISBROD, THE NONPROFIT ECONOMY (1988). He does not extend his explanation to the exemption, and does not incorporate the common law concept of charity. Another major work upon which the donative theory relies, but which also falls short of recognizing the full dimensions of the theory, is JAMES DOUGLAS, WHY CHARITY? THE CASE FOR A THIRD SECTOR (1983). Finally, Professor Rob Atkinson's work also stresses the role of altruism, although he does not undertake the rigorous economic analysis we do nor develop a normative argument to explain why the exemption should attach to altruistic activities. Rob Atkinson, *Altruism in Nonprofit Organizations*, 31 B.C.L. REV. 501 (1990).

2. Leading discussions of this public goods theory of the existence of nonprofit enterprise include DOUGLAS, *supra* note 1, at 129–30 (1983); WEISBROD, *supra* note 1, at 59–60 (hereafter NONPROFIT ECONOMY); BURTON A. WEISBROD, THE VOLUNTARY NONPROFIT SECTOR 51–76 (1977) (hereafter VOLUNTARY SECTOR); Mark Gergen, *The Case for a Charitable Contributions Deduction*, 74 VA. L. REV. 1393, 1397–98 (1988); Hansmann, supra note 1, at 848; and Edward Krashinsky, *Transaction Costs and a Theory of Nonprofit Organization*, *in* THE ECONOMICS OF NONPROFIT INSTITUTIONS: STUDIES IN STRUCTURE AND POLICY 119–21 (Susan Rose-Ackerman ed., 1986).

3. The classic statements of this theory are MANCUR OLSON, THE LOGIC OF COLLECTIVE ACTION (1968) and John Hardin, *The Tragedy of the Commons*, 162 SCIENCE 1243 (1968).

4. Gerald Marwell & Jeffrey Ames, *Experiments on the Provision of Public Goods*, 84 AM. J. SOC. 1335, 1337–38 (1979).

5. JAMES BUCHANAN, THE DEMAND AND SUPPLY OF PUBLIC GOODS 88–89 (1968).

6. *See* JOHN RAWLS, A THEORY OF JUSTICE 268 (1971).

7. *See generally* WEISBROD, VOLUNTARY SECTOR, *supra* note 2, at 53–61; Burton A. Weisbrod, *Toward a Theory of the Voluntary Non-Profit Sector*, *in* ALTRUISM, MORALITY, AND ECONOMIC THEORY 171 (Edmund S. Phelps ed., 1975).

8. *See* JAMES BUCHANAN & GORDON TULLOCK, THE CALCULUS OF CONSENT 136 (1962).

9. The positive-voter line would be more vertical; the negative line would be lower and more horizontal.

10. James Andreoni, *Impure Altruism and Donations to Public Goods: A Theory of Warm-Glow Giving*, 100 ECON. J. 464, 470 (1990); Dwight Lee & Richard McKenzie, *Second Thoughts on the Public-Good Justification for Government Poverty Programs*, 19 J. LEGAL STUD. 189, 198.

11. *See, e.g.*, Burton Abrams & Mark D. Schmitz, *The Crowding-Out Effect of Governmental Transfers on Private, Charitable Contributions*, *in* THE ECONOMICS OF NONPROFIT INSTITUTIONS 303 (Susan Rose-Ackerman ed., 1986).

12. *See* James Andreoni, *Giving and Impure Altruism: Applications to Charity and Ricardian Equivalence*, 97 J. POL. ECON. 1447 (1989).

13. Russel D. Roberts, *A Positive Model of Private Charity and Public Transfers*, 92 J. POL. ECON. 136, 141 (1984).

14. Gerald Marwell, *Altruism and the Problem of Collective Action*, *in* COOPERATION AND HELPING BEHAVIOR 207, 224 (Valerian Derlega & Janusz Grzelak eds., 1982).

15. *See* Peter L. Swords, CHARITABLE REAL PROPERTY TAX EXEMPTION IN NEW YORK STATE 217–21 (1981) (discussing public goods nature of poverty relief, education, and cultural activities); Roberts, *supra* note 13, at 139 (characterizing redistribution to the poor as a "public good" for which the "private solution is inefficient"). *See generally*, DOUGLAS, *supra* note 1, at 57–58 (observing that the Statute of Charitable Uses contains several obvious instances of public goods).

16. Most of these studies are reviewed and critiqued in Oliver Kim & Mark Walker, *The Free Rider Problem: Experimental Evidence*, 43 PUBLIC CHOICE 3 (1984); R. Mark Isaac et al., *Divergent Evidence on Free Riding: An Experimental Examination of Possible Explanations*, 43 PUBLIC CHOICE 113 (1984).

17. Linda Caporael et al., *Selfishness Examined: Cooperation in the Absence of Egoistic Incentives*, 12 BEHAV. & BRAIN SCI. 683 (1989).

18. Gerald Marwell & Jeffrey Ames, *Economists Free Ride, Does Anyone Else?*, 15 J. PUB. ECO. 295 (1981).

19. *See* Corporael et al., supra note 17, at 695–96; *see generally*, DEVELOPMENT AND MAINTENANCE OF PROSOCIAL BEHAVIOR (Ervin Staub et al. eds., 1984) (collection of essays by sociologists).

20. *See* Harold Margolis, SELFISHNESS, ALTRUISM, AND RATIONALITY 54–55 (1982).

21. Armen Alchian & William Allen, *The Pure Economics of Giving*, in THE ECONOMICS OF CHARITY 5 (Inst. Econ. Affairs 1973) ("the postulates of economic theory do not say that man is concerned only about himself. He can be concerned about other people's situations also."); *see generally* Robert Sugden, *Reciprocity: The Supply of Public Goods Through Voluntary Contributions*, 94 ECON. J. 772 (1984); Robert Sugden, *On the Economics of Philanthropy*, 92 ECON. J. 341 (1982).

22. *See* RICHARD DAWKINS, THE SELFISH GENE (2d ed. 1989); SCOTT A. BOORMAN & PAUL LEVITT, THE GENETICS OF ALTRUISM (1980); ERVIN STAUB, I POSITIVE SOCIAL BEHAVIOR AND MORALITY 26–34 (1974); EDWARD WILSON, SOCIOBIOLOGY: THE NEW SYNTHESIS (1975); Edward Wilson, *Genetic Basis of Behavior—Especially Altruism*, 31 AM. PSYCHOLOGIST 370 (1976).

23. WEISBROD, NONPROFIT ECONOMY, *supra* note 1, at 29–30.

24. WEISBROD, NONPROFIT ECONOMY, *supra* note 1, at 30.

25. WEISBROD, VOLUNTARY SECTOR, *supra* note 2, at 66. Think of a typical demand curve, in which demand increases as price decreases. If we replace "price" with "tax cost," then demand will increase as the tax cost decreases. Thus as one moves from government providing the full cost of additional production to a cost of, say, $.30 on the dollar, demand will increase.

26. As we note above, donations signal that a group has unmet demands for an entity's goods or services, and the vast majority of United States residents donate to some exempt organization. A 1989 Gallup poll on contributions and volunteering, for example, found that 75.1% of all households surveyed contributed to some exempt organization. VIRGINIA A. HODGKINSON & MURRAY S. WEITZMAN, GIVING AND VOLUNTEERING IN THE UNITED STATES 25, Table 1.1 (1990). As might be expected, contribution activity varied significantly by income level with households reporting income of under $10,000 per year having the lowest percentage of contributions (49%). *Id.* at 55, Table 2.1. Even at the relatively modest income level of $10-20,000, however, 65.1% of surveyed households made donations. Thus even the relatively poor have special demands for goods and services signified by their donative activity. Moreover, a number of donative institutions directly aid the poor (the United Way, the Salvation Army, etc.); thus although lower income households

donate at a lower rate, they tend to be the beneficiaries of donations.

27. *See* WEISBROD, NONPROFIT ECONOMY, *supra* note 1, at 25–26; WEISBROD, VOLUNTARY SECTOR, *supra* note 2, at 51. In theory, it might be possible to provide a direct subsidy to various organizations equal in amount to the indirect subsidy provided by exemption. Such a system would require that government in effect measure each person's elasticity of demand for a particular good or service, assess taxes based upon that demand and then apportion tax dollars based upon that assessment. As a practical matter, of course, such a system would be impossible to administer. In absence of making people pay individually for, say, the right to breath clean air, there is no way to measure an individual's marginal valuation of particular public or quasi-public goods. Moreover, the free-riding problem inherent in these goods would lead people to lie about their preferences, even if they knew them. *See id.* at 53–54.

28. AMITAI ETZIONI, THE MORAL DIMENSION: TOWARD A NEW ECONOMICS 51 (1988). *See also* Alasdai MacIntyre, *Egoism and Altruism, in* I THE ENCYCLOPEDIA OF PHILOSOPHY 462, 463 (Paul Edwards ed., 1967). Gergen incorrectly reasons that aid to the poor is an impure public good because the primary benefit is to the individual who receives the aid rather than to society. Gergen, *supra* note 2, at 1398. This is incorrect because the individuals who receive the aid do not purchase this good; therefore, the benefit to them is also an externality. It is simply more concentrated in them than in society at large. A good loses its public characteristic only to the extent that the consumer is willing (and able) to pay for it. Only then are the benefits internalized to the purchaser.

29. BUCHANAN, *supra* note 5, at 49. *See also* Gergen, *supra* note 2, at 1398.

30. One should note, though, that some forms of market failure do not produce donations, perhaps because they are self-correcting within the market, perhaps because they are corrected by government intervention, or perhaps because the contributing public views them as insignificant or less significant than other defects that do receive donations. The point, again, is that the focus ultimately is on the existence of the donation, not on theorized cases for some form of subsidy.

31. *See* Krashinsky, *supra* note 2, at 114 (advocating this analytical framework as providing a superior terminology for understanding nonprofits); DOUGLAS, *supra* note 1, at 37–38 (observing that "market failure," "public goods," "externalities," and "transaction costs" are flexible terms that provide alternative forms for expressing a range of similar ideas; "unlike the dichotomous pair of 'public' versus 'private' goods, [the other terms] emphasize the graduated nature of the choice between supply through a commercial market, through voluntary action or through coercive government action").

32. Many Jewish synagogues raise from twenty percent to all of their income through annual dues charged on a per family basis for membership in the local synagogue. For seats on High Holy Days there is often a separate charge that varies with the number and location of seats. Typical seat fees in 1982 ranged from $200 to $2000. Synagogues also often charge special fees to participate in Passover services and meals. Pew rental is another form of sales, one that has a mainstream

Christian history in the United States. The payment of Mass stipends, fees fixed by the Catholic Church for Masses said in the name of or on behalf of the payor, also involves sale of services. Note, *Religious Nonprofits and the Commercial Manner Test*, 99 YALE L. J. 1631, 1641–42 (1990).

33. Guido Calabresi, *Comment [on Arrow's "Gifts and Exchanges"]*, in ALTRUISM, MORALITY, AND ECONOMIC THEORY 58, 59 (Edmund S. Phelps ed., 1975).

34. Henry B. Hansmann, *Nonprofit Enterprise in the Performing Arts*, 12 BELL J. ECON. 341 (1981). Some arts organizations, such as symphony orchestras, are recognized as providing some public benefit by enhancing a community's overall attractiveness to residents and newcomers, but Hansmann argues correctly that, much like a professional sports team, this benefit is incidental to the individual audience benefit.

35. According to data from a sample of Form 990's analyzed by the Independent Sector, arts and cultural organizations received 35% of their total revenues from private donations in 1989, or about $7.5 billion. VIRGINIA A. HODGKINSON ET AL., A PORTRAIT OF THE INDEPENDENT SECTOR 33 (1993); VIRGINIA A. HODGKINSON ET AL., NONPROFIT ALMANAC 1992–1993 at 147, Table 4.2 (1992).

36. As long as there are seats in the hall, the marginal cost of adding an audience member is close to zero (simply the administrative costs related to the ticket).

37. *See* ESTELLE JAMES & SUSAN ROSE-ACKERMAN, THE NONPROFIT ENTERPRISE IN MARKET ECONOMICS 28 (1986).

38. PAUL FELDSTEIN, HEALTH CARE ECONOMICS 212 (2d ed. 1982) (discussing natural monopoly characteristics of rural hospitals, but observing that in urban areas, there are only "slight economies of scale"); WEISBROD, VOLUNTARY SECTOR, *supra* note 2, at 93–98 (describing hospital services that represent "investment indivisibilities," i.e., "facilities [that] come in sufficiently large and costly units that marginal cost pricing would likely mean unprofitable operations").

39. Gergen, *supra* note 2, at 1443–44.

40. This behavior might be explained by the price discrimination rationale that Hansmann develops for the performing arts or by the natural monopoly explanation developed in the text above, because the marginal costs of serving additional viewers is essentially zero. Also, the commercialization of these channels might be viewed as a transaction cost that would detract from the public spiritedness associated with PBS (although, here, the authors agree wholeheartedly with Gergen that the obnoxiousness of most PBS-affiliate fund raising campaigns imposes a far greater cost).

41. Gergen, *supra* note 2, at 1438.

8

What Counts as a Donation

In the previous chapter, we examined the broad theoretical foundations of the donative theory, positing that donations to an entity signal an unmet need for that entity's product, and at the same time signal that such needs will not be met by direct government intervention. In this chapter, we develop further our contention that donations in whatever form (provided they truly are donations) in fact perform this twin signalling function.

Critical to the donative theory are the following assertions, which we so far have left primarily to intuition: (1) all donations signal socially desirable services; and (2) significant free-riding behavior attaches to giving in all of its manifestations. Neither assertion is necessarily true. People may give for reasons other than pure altruism. If the reasons are sufficiently personal, then the benefit may not be shared by others' in society at a level to justify a social subsidy, and if the motives for giving are primarily selfish, there may be no significant free-riding. Even where there is a true social benefit, whatever motive overcomes the free-rider disincentive to give could in theory be capable of correcting altogether the market defect that produces the need to give.

We are (presently) incapable of resolving these quandaries at a level of theory, which seems to leave to messy empiricism the task of establishing a rigorous basis for deciding which objects of philanthropy to subsidize. Fortunately, significant work by sociologists and psychologists that more closely examines the actual motives for giving greatly eases this task by pointing a way towards clearly and predictably drawing the proper bounds of the donative theory.[1] Our review of this literature reveals that, in most instances, selfish and adulterated motives for giving do not undermine the basis for the donative theory, with the exception of donations that are not true gifts but instead constitute implicit purchases.

Mixed Motives for Giving

The Cynical View of Altruism

Those who speak of altruism usually intend some moral assessment about the quality of motivation that prompts a gift, suggesting that it is made without reference to self interest. However, economic theorists have observed that, morals aside, giving is never truly altruistic because for giving to occur there must be some positive or negative incentive that operates selectively on the donor to induce the gift. As Ervin Staub explains, "An actor may behave prosocially to gain material rewards for his act, . . . to gain social approval and praise (or avoid social disapproval and even ostracism), . . . [to] feel good (gain self-reward) because he acted according to his values and principles (thus he maintains a positive self-concept), or when he expects empathic reinforcement (a reduction of the distress he felt as a result of vicariously experiencing another person's distress or an increase in his own positive feeling by vicariously experiencing the positive feelings of another that would result from his prosocial act)."[2]

While it is undoubtedly true that some form of self interest broadly defined always motivates giving, this tells us little of analytical importance. Obviously, *something* always motivates us to act. In Rapoport's words, "The proponents of [egoism] are always ready to . . . extend . . . the concept of 'selfishness' to include any demonstrable source of motivation not previously subsumed under the concept. It seems advisable, therefore, to concede the [egoistic] dogma once and for all, thus rendering the hypothesis unfalsifiable and, therefore, sterile. Then one can go about the business of examining the rich variety of sources of human motivation governing choices where the outcomes of those choices result in the distribution of costs and benefits to self and others."[3]

This criticism accepted, nevertheless, the economist's challenge to the altruist is still troubling for it says that the mere presence of a gift does not reveal what motivates the giver. Rejecting the strong egoistic premise that all gifts are selfish does nothing to validate that all gifts are socially valued, nor does it demonstrate which ones are which, or to what degree. As one court summarized:

> Community good will, the desire to avoid community bad will, public pressures of other kinds, tax avoidance, prestige, conscience-salving, a vindictive desire to prevent relatives from inheriting family

wealth—these are only some of the motives which may lie close to the heart, or so-called heart, of one who gives to a charity.[4]

This cynical view of altruism creates two difficulties for the donative theory in meeting the deservedness criterion. First, if the incentive to donate does not arise from the public benefit that the supported activity conveys, but rather is in the nature of a "side payment" to the donor such as naming a building,[5] the ability of donations to signal socially worthy objects potentially is impaired. We would have a hard case to make for a social subsidy if the cynical view of philanthropy were true that donations result more from the self-interest of donors who desire to participate in a private benefit than from the public benefit their gift provides to others.[6] Second, if the incentive to donate is strong enough, it may override the free-rider problem, and donations themselves might be enough to fund the good or service at the socially optimal level. In this latter case, exemption would be unnecessary as a "shadow subsidy" to provide optimal production. Stated more succinctly, the challenge is to determine whether certain payments are spurious donations, more in the nature of purchases than gifts. If so, our rationale for subsidy disintegrates because our theory holds that no subsidy is appropriate where private markets are functioning. If the donative theory can be shown to survive even the most skeptical views of altruism, however, then we have great assurance that all objects of donations deserve some additional social subsidy. In the following sections, we will examine successively four categories of private benefit that potentially motivate donors:

1. Direct, tangible benefits the donor receives from the supported services. For instance, Professor Gergen argues that viewers' gifts to public television are more in the nature of personal consumption than disinterested altruism. Likewise, one might speculate that the primary motive for giving to religion is for the donor to provide himself a spiritual clubhouse, or, as Aldous Huxley is reputed to have said, "Charity is a peculiar species of fire insurance."[7]
2. Psychic benefits the donor receives merely from the act of giving itself, without regard to whether the gift does anyone any material good. Thus, one might repeatedly donate to famine relief in Somalia despite news accounts of rampant corruption in the manner in which this relief is distributed, because one feels good about even a futile attempt to do something about this human travesty, almost as a form of sacrificial offering accompanying a prayer.

3. Purely selfish benefits the donor receives indirectly by giving. Thus, it is sometimes alleged that the primary motive for giving to education is the reputational benefit from naming a building or the selfish interest of enhancing the value of one's own degree, rather than the donor's disinterested recognition of the value of education to society. Corporate giving is the best example of entirely self-interested motivation since it would be an abuse of the fiduciary obligation to shareholders for management to donate for any reason other than enhancing the corporate image.[8]

4. Benefits in the nature of an exchange, where the motive for the gift is a material quid pro quo return to the donor. A nice example occurs in a Supreme Court case that considered whether fees paid to the Church of Scientology for spiritual "auditing" and training sessions were deductible charitable contributions.[9]

Donors Who Benefit Directly: Altruism versus Egoism

One cynical version of philanthropy argues that self-interested gifts to activities the donor engages in do not deserve a subsidy because the donor partakes in the benefit he supports. Examples include gifts to the symphony by ticket-holders and religious contributions from the congregation. At the extreme, some theorists maintain that all giving is, by nature, egoistic because it necessarily satisfies at least a desire to give. In Mark Kelman's words, "charitable donors are the same as everyone else in an individualistic society: they use their money for their own relative benefit. Even the most sincere altruist buys the scarce resource of looking altruistic."[10] Even under less tautological definitions of altruism, some researchers contend that most giving is prompted by the egoistic desire to benefit oneself, as by avoiding guilt or sadness, not by the simple desire to benefit another as an end in itself.[11] This view is said to have originated in 1651 from a discussion by Thomas Hobbes in *Leviathan*. There are two versions of this egoistic position: that no one is ever motivated by a concern for another as an end in itself, and that this motive is sometimes present but is outweighed by concern for one's own welfare.[12]

The debate between altruism and egoism has occupied moral philosophers since the writings of Kant, so we hold no pretense of being able to resolve it here.[13] But resolving it is not necessary to the present inquiry because the judgment here is not a moral one; it is one of economics and social policy. The properly formulated question for present examination is, putting aside labels and moral judgments, are donations still capable of signalling an activity that deserves a social subsidy despite the potentially private consumption nature of a donation? It might be thought that this question could be answered empirically simply by observing whether everyone who consumes the good in fact contributes to it. But, for some goods, such as psychic gratification from the betterment of society, it is impossible to make this determination. And, even if it were, there is no mechanism for determining whether those who contribute do so to the full level of their benefit.

Professor Gergen's work provides an apt illustration of the confusion that unnecessarily confounds this inquiry. Gergen's distinction between altruism and egoism misconceives the issue by supposing that a tax subsidy is not deserved when giving is motivated by the donor's desire to benefit personally from the supported service rather than to benefit someone else. For instance, it is incorrect, or at least incomplete, to assert that those who contribute to public television do so because they enjoy watching it.[14] This is a nonsequitor. Except for those stricken by severe guilt, viewers who donate are perfectly able to enjoy the service without paying, or, as the case with the present authors, to give less than they would pay if forced to subscribe. Few people would believe that their individual gift makes a tangible difference in their actual enjoyment of the programming. "If Smith contributes $25 to public television, no sensible observer will suppose that he does so expecting this will lead to $25 worth of improvement in his private viewing of television, or indeed that his contribution will have any perceptible effect at all. Such behavior looks extremely puzzling in terms of a nontautological interpretation of self-interest."[15] Therefore, the desire to watch cannot, strictly speaking, be said to motivate the decision to give.

More likely, viewers of public television give because of a sense of moral obligation that makes the act of giving itself satisfying. That they obtain this satisfaction from giving to a service they use themselves does not deprive the gift of its ability to signal either worth or need. The fact that the donor has an interest in the service she supports verifies that the service has real benefit, and, if donations are widespread, the benefit is one shared by a significant portion of society at large.

Indeed, it can be argued from another perspective that egoism presents a *stronger* case for a donative subsidy than does altruism, considering that a donative subsidy requires a government as well as a market failure (as discussed in Chapter 7). The more localized benefit associated with egoistic giving is more likely to suffer from such government failure for the very reason that the benefit is less widely shared by voters at large. Hospitals, for example, nicely illustrate this relationship between insularity and giving. They received a much greater portion of their revenues from donations at an earlier time in the century when they primarily served closely knit ethnic and religious groups whose members desired to assure for themselves a place to receive care that accommodated their particular practices and beliefs. As community hospitals began to assume a more homogenous quality and private insurance became more widespread, the basis for hospital giving became more purely altruistic, but it also diminished greatly in response to the government's increased funding.[16]

Thus, a gift to cancer research motivated by the hope that the donor one day may benefit personally from a cancer cure cannot be discounted even if this motive is considered self-interested. The fact that the support occurs through a *donation* rather than a *purchase* means that a sacrifice was made.[17] Even under the cynical view of giving to schools and churches, the fact that enhancing the value of one's own educational degree is a benefit shared by many, as is the construction of a spiritual clubhouse, tells us that the donation identifies a service with a shared social benefit, however jaundiced or idealistic a spin we might place on the benefit. At the same time the donor enhances his own welfare, he enhances the welfare of others similarly situated. This satisfaction of the worth criterion will be predictably true of all donations, regardless of the particular motive.[18] The fact that the organization relies on donations rather than sales signals that the good by nature is one which benefits a number of people in a shared fashion. And the fact that the donor might have chosen to enjoy the same benefits by relying on the contributions of others tells us that contributions will be suppressed, at least somewhat, below the optimal level of desired shared benefits (with optimality defined as the hypothetical level the public would purchase or vote to support through taxes if market or government failure did not exist.)

Nevertheless, Gergen observes that, in certain circumstances, the private benefit may be large enough in comparison to the external benefit to the public that voluntary action would not result in undersupport.[19] For instance, we can expect no disinclination among adjacent property owners to call in a fire alarm because the benefit to the one who voluntarily calls greatly exceeds the minimal cost. But even if these extreme situations are classified as true donative acts (rather than quid pro quo exchanges), the very slight effort required means that they will receive very little value in the measurement of donative activity (in the example given, the value of the volunteer phone call would be 25 cents) and therefore will have an undiscernible effect on the availability of a subsidy.

The degree of self-abnegation in a gift is relevant, if at all, only to the *amount* of subsidy that is deserved. A gift to an activity from which the donor derives no tangible benefits might be thought to suffer relatively more from the free-rider inclination not to give. But it is doubtful whether it is worth the effort to fine-tune the system of donative support to the extent that Gergen attempts. Absent the ability to read minds, it is impossible to know with any precision the level of self interest and free-riding in personal motivations for giving. Consider, for instance, untangling the motives that Marwell articulates for one act of giving: "You might buy a family television set not only because you enjoy it, or because you enjoy seeing your spouse enjoy it, but because your spouse enjoys your own enjoyment, and you enjoy the pleasure he or she receives in that indirect fashion. In other words, rewards tend to reverberate through an interdependent, altruistic system . . . ."[20] The donative theory can survive these psychological complexities just as we saw in Chapter 7 that it accommodates the imperfections in the public goods rationale for giving.

This view has significant support in the decisions that wrestle with whether particular payments qualify for the charitable deduction from personal income tax. As explained by the Supreme Court, the IRS "has customarily examined the *external* features of the transaction in question. This practice has the advantage of obviating the need for the IRS to conduct imprecise inquiries into the motivations of individual taxpayers. The lower courts have generally embraced this structural analysis."[21] In the words of a lower court, "Were the deductibility of a contribution . . . to depend on 'detached and disinterested generosity,' [language from the famous *Commissioner v. Duberstein* decision[22]] an important area of tax law would become a mare's nest of uncertainty woven of judicial value judgments irrelevant to eleemosynary reality.").[23]

The point of this analysis, simply put, is that the donor's subjective motivation, standing alone, does not disqualify the gift since all gifts partake of some form of self-interest. Otherwise, the gift would not have been made.[24] The quality of the motivation that the egoism/altruism distinction attempts to capture is a moral assessment, not an instrumental one that determines whether the donation signals a worthy and needy activity; therefore, this assessment is not relevant to the justification for a tax subsidy.

Still, the cynic maintains that some motivations are so crassly self-satisfying or so unrelated to the worth of the recipient as to deprive the gift of any ability to signal a deserving activity. These further attacks on the donative theory can be countered more effectively, however, by abandoning egoism/altruism and turning to a more useful distinction some theorists draw between the "act utility" and the "result utility" of voluntary activity.

Giving for Giving's Sake: Act versus Result Utility

A number of theorists have postulated another polarized categorization of the motivation for giving, one that operates on a somewhat different spectrum.[25] A gift satisfies a donor's "act utility function" if the donor desires to participate personally in addressing a social need. Such donors give perhaps because they derive a sense of righteousness,[26] perhaps because their names are attached to the projects supported, perhaps to avoid social ostracism,[27] or perhaps to advance their careers. By contrast, charity satisfies a potential donor's "result utility function" if he desires only the social good that the charity produces. At the extreme, act utility stresses means—the donor is satisfied by participation and without regard to whether participation produces a beneficial end—whereas result utility stresses ends: satisfaction occurs by bettering some social condition and regardless of the individual's actual participation in bringing about this result. The act utility of a particular gift is individualized to the donor, whereas the result utility is shared broadly by other like-minded concerned citizens.

To illustrate, poverty relief organizations such as CARE often solicit support by creating the sense of "adopting" a particular child, along with a picture and personal information, so that the donor feels more involved than if aggregate statistics of third-world aid were reported. This tactic has been carried over to other arenas, such as the Adopt-a-Whale program by the International Wildlife coalition and the short-lived Adopt-a-Cow program to help farmers afflicted by drought.[28] The proliferation of these programs attests to the significance of the act/result distinction.

The act/result distinction is similar to egoism/altruism but is more revealing for our purposes because it directs our focus away from a primarily moral assessment of donative motive. Egoism seems to align with act utility and altruism with result utility, but this is not necessarily the case. One could view as selfish an individual's purely abstract interest in the betterment of society because such a person has no interest in doing anything personally to help, or one could view as noble a person's desire to contribute to a charitable cause despite its certain failure. These ethical characterizations, however, are irrelevant to our purpose, which is to examine the psychological and social dimensions of what prompts a person to donate and what public policy significance to attach to this behavior.

If *pure* act utility characterized a significant number of donations, the donative theory of the exemption would be seriously weakened.[29] If one gives to Somalia famine relief solely because the act of giving is gratifying and wholly without regard to whether the food ever reaches the starving population, then the donation meets neither the worth nor the need components of deservedness. The existence of such a gift does not serve as a reliable indicator of public need; it is more in the nature of a sacrificial offering. Like a prayer, the only benefit it definitely provides is the donor's private psychic gratification. No free-riding attaches to such pure act-utility donations. The donor reaps all of the benefits of giving but does so only if he gives. Because the full benefit of this gratification is internalized to the donor, he can be expected to contribute up to the desired level, and because the benefit obtains only if the donor participates personally, an indirect tax subsidy to the recipient would not enhance this private benefit.

It is only in this hypothesized world of extreme act utility, however, that the donative exemption would be a complete waste. It seems quite likely that virtually all gifts are motivated by a mix of act and result utilities.[30] Unless there were some form of act utility, the donor would have no reason to make the personal sacrifice of a gift. Moreover, unless the object of the donation were at least somewhat successful in achieving its desired ends, the donor would not likely derive any pleasure from personal participation, or at least would not continue to support the particular object in the future. In short, one can suppose that, all else being equal, those charities that do the most good will also produce the strongest act utility.

One telling method for determining the relative mix of act and result utility is the extent to which an increase in government expenditures on a public good "crowd out" private donations. If government spending crowds out at a 1:1 ratio, it is likely then that donors are concerned only with the result, and not their personal participation. However, if increased government expenditures fail to displace *any* private giving, pure act utility is suggested. Empirical findings suggest that the crowding-out effect is somewhere between these two extremes, confirming our hypothesis that act and result utilities are mixed to some degree in virtually all instances of giving.[31]

This mixture of personal satisfaction in helping, with an eye to the results that obtain, is precisely the condition that characterizes the paradigm case for the economic theory of the donative subsidy. Act utility can be thought of as the private good aspect of giving that motivates individual donors to reveal the existence of some unmet public need, whereas result utility can be thought of as the public good aspect of giving that maintains a free-rider disinclination to meet the need at an optimal level.[32] Without the personal gratification that comes from helping to address world hunger, there might not be any donations to signal the public's concern, but if there were no generalized gratification that society at large receives in the abstract knowledge that fewer people are starving, there would be no need to subsidize donations that do occur.

Still, it is a matter of psychological empiricism whether act utility fails to match result utility, that is, whether one's pleasure in participating is less than the actual social value in avoiding starvation (value as measured by hypothesized market or political spending decisions). In the cases examined earlier of support for public television and religion, the donor received directly the societal benefit supported. Because the donor's portion of the benefit in those cases is a small fraction of the whole, there is a predictable basis for concluding that the private benefit will induce a suboptimal level of support. Here, however, the private benefit is of a secondary nature: it is the donor's *gratification* in doing something to make *others* better off that induces a gift.[33] But the exemption does not subsidize this private gratification (nor, in rigorous theory, does it subsidize the welfare of the primary recipients); rather, the exemption addresses *society's shared concern* over the welfare of the primary recipients. Therefore, it is technically not on point to argue that the donor's empathetic experience of the recipient's suffering is likely to be less than the actuality of that suffering. The case for a donative subsidy turns on showing that donors contribute less than they and others empathize.

The Market in Altruism

The difficulty is that there is no necessary relationship between the donative proxy and the unexpressed desire. Conceivably, the level of gratification that donors receive from gifts to pediatric oncology wards could (1) fall short of, (2) equal, or (3) exceed the reality of how much society as a whole actually benefits from saving children from cancer. As Thomas Ireland explains, "This dichotomy leads to the paradox that individuals might voluntarily contribute for the provision of a public good in excess of the amount of the public good which would be justified by [result utility] efficiency conditions."[34] This is possible despite the free-riding that attends public goods because, if donors are motivated by non-public-goods considerations, the private benefit they derive merely from the act of giving conceivably is sufficient to *exceed* the desire by those who enjoy, but do not pay for, the social benefits.[35]

This is a troubling observation because it means that, although mixed act/result donations signal worthy causes, they do not necessarily signal needy causes: the level of donations may already be sufficient to meet the hypothesized societal optimum. Nevertheless, we believe there is a mechanism that tends to not only weed out excessive donations but also to depress most donations below socially optimal levels. We call this mechanism a market in altruism.

The market in altruism works as follows. Those donors who desire to make some personal contribution to the betterment of society will have many choices from which to satisfy this desire. They will naturally tend to choose the outlet that provides the most satisfaction. We can generally assume that, for most donors, this will be the worthy object they perceive as needing the most support. However, as gifts combined with subsidies begin to approach the socially desired level of production for the particular object of charity (as measured through the perceptions of those inclined to give), gifts to that object will begin to taper off and shift to other objects. In stable social settings, these countervailing forces may settle at an equilibrium, but as social conditions change, this market in altruism redirects philanthropy and the accompanying tax subsidy to new objects.

Placing altruism in a market context raises the troubling possibility that some giving is uninformed, over-reactive, or otherwise might come from donors who are oblivious to social worth or need, but these facts are no more troubling than similar defects in the private or political markets. Moreover, the donative theory can screen out minor aberrational patterns by requiring an entity to show a *substantial* level of donative support before qualifying for the charitable exemption.

Promotional Gifts: Self-regarding versus Other-regarding Motives

The prior section demonstrates that dividing the universe of donative motives between act and result utilities further reinforces the conclusion that motive does not matter. However, we still have not addressed the most troubling case: where the motive to donate is entirely selfish. To clarify, we introduce a third distinction in donative motives: self-regarding versus other-regarding motives.[36] Both egoism and altruism, and both act utility and result utility, can be reconciled with the assumption that the motive to give springs from some regard for the welfare of another being, which regard forms the basis for the gift's signalling function. Some giving, however, can be shown to be *entirely* selfish in the sense that the donor's gratification is wholly driven by his own personal material or psychological wellbeing. This might be termed either a strong version of egoism or an extreme form of act utility.[37] To illustrate, a donor may give large sums to education solely as an act of crass self-promotion to obtain the community recognition that comes from naming a building or a professorship, caring nothing about the quality of education or even the values of gift-giving.

Even this case, we believe, does not rob gifts of their ability to signal worth for the simple reason that the social approval desired by the donor would not be forthcoming unless the object of the publicized gift were considered worthy by a broad segment of the public. Thus, even the most self-interested donation qualifies under our deservedness criterion if the private reputational benefit enjoyed by the donor serves as a proxy for social worth, in the same way that act utility serves as a proxy for result utility. By way of analogy, it makes no difference if the present authors are motivated to write this book solely by the professional prestige that attaches to its publication by this esteemed press, rather than by any consideration of the good our ideas might do for society or for the body of academic knowledge. If the prestige associated with this press depends on the worth of its books, our (hypothesized?) selfish motives reflect this worth by inducing us to improve the quality of our work in order that it might be accepted by this press.

The epitome of purely self-interested giving is corporate philanthropy, which occurs primarily (if not solely) as a marketing strategy to enhance the corporation's image in the community.[38] "Few corporations engage in philanthropy because others need money, as though a corporation were a well-heeled uncle who should spread his good fortune around the family. For the most part, corporations give because it serves their own interests—or appears to."[39] To verify this, one study "found that the percentage of a utility's gross income contributed to nonprofit organizations is strongly correlated with the company's advertising and customer service expenditures, . . . [indicating] that charity is, in part, an extension of advertising and customer relations . . . . Industries with high levels of contact with the public, such as insurance, retail, and lodging, maintain significantly larger advertising and contributions programs than do mining, construction, primary metals, and other industries whose contact with the public is far more limited."[40] Indeed, any other motive would be a breach of the corporate managers' fiduciary duty to use corporate funds to benefit shareholders' economic interests. This public relations strategy, however, is successful only to the extent that the objects supported by corporate philanthropy are perceived by the public as being worthwhile.

Still, a reputation-driven donor does not signal an object in *need* of a social subsidy if the rewards from public reputation happen to be strong enough to induce the optimal amount of giving. Theory cannot guarantee that slippage always exists; if it does not, there is, in effect, no free-riding since the private rewards from giving (reputation enhancement) are enough to overcome fully the market defect that gave rise to the donation. Nevertheless, there is strong reason to suppose that purely selfish giving signals an object that needs subsidy. Again, this likely assurance is found in the concept of a market in altruism. One who gives for crass self promotion will choose the object of giving that produces the most bang for the buck, all other factors being equal. This choice will likely be the worthy object among the donor's range of choices that is perceived by the target population as being the most in need of support. It can be expected that, as the perceived need is more closely met, the reputational value of giving will gradually fall off, shifting reputational value and attendant donors' dollars to other, more recognized causes. This rough market in altruism creates some confidence (but not a guarantee) that the money of even the most selfish donors is not wasted on unneedy objects.

Only in rare instances will the motivation for giving be wholly divorced from an assessment of the object's worth. One example is a gift prompted entirely by the nuisance value of avoiding harassing solicitation, with no thought to the cause being served. Consider, for instance, the harried traveler accosted in an airport by religious fanatics. The traveler might give some small change rather than pausing to consider how to extract himself politely. Although such a gift arguably supports a public benefit, this benefit plays absolutely no role—either direct or indirect—in motivating the gift (other than perhaps to raise the intensity of harassment). Therefore, the gift serves no worth-signalling function. The donor might be entirely ambivalent, or even hostile, to the cause.[41]

Undoubtedly, a nuisance element plays some role in many instances of giving. But unless an organization relies entirely on pure nuisance gifts, this simply becomes a partial impurity in the process. This might affect the *level* of tax support we should provide donative institutions, but it does not eliminate the case for exemption altogether. Even then, it is questionable whether it is worth the administrative costs of detecting this minor noise factor in the philanthropic sector.

This analysis demonstrates that, even in the extreme case of a pure act utility donor motivated entirely by selfish considerations of personal reputation, the object of the donation probably deserves subsidy. This being true for the weakest imaginable case for social subsidy, we can be confident that donations generally deserve subsidy without engaging in close empirical examination of the precise motives behind individual acts or categories of philanthropy.

Spurious Gifts

Donors Who Receive a Quid Pro Quo: Gifts versus Purchases

Are there any situations, then, in which apparent donations fail to satisfy the requirements for subsidy? There are, but they may be considered cases of spurious donations in which it is proper to say that no gift exists at all; rather something is purchased from the recipient. The test for such pseudo gifts is whether the gift is prompted by a quid pro quo, not merely an incentive.[42] By quid pro quo, we mean an exchange between the giver and the recipient, where the value of the return consideration is independent of the gift itself. Thus, what distinguishes a social club from a church is not a theoretical analysis of the presence of a public good, altruistic motive, or private benefit, but the simple fact that the club chooses to charge membership fees, excluding those who do not pay, whereas the church chooses to rely on donations, making its services and facilities available even to those who do not contribute.

The quid pro quo test is familiar to courts that have wrestled with gift characterization problems for purposes of the charitable deduction.[43] A developer who dedicates park land to the city in order to obtain zoning concessions makes no donation,[44] nor do parents who contribute to the costs of their children's private school education.[45] However, the purchase of a ticket to the policeman's ball does constitute a gift to the extent that the ticket price exceeds its market value.[46]

In a leading case, the Supreme Court held that payments for spiritual "auditing" sessions conducted by the Church of Scientology do not constitute gifts because the services are not rendered unless the payments are made. "As the Tax Court found, these payments were part of a quintessential quid pro quo exchange: in return for their money, petitioners received an identifiable benefit, namely, auditing and training sessions in each branch church. . . . Each of these practices reveals the inherently reciprocal nature of the exchange."[47] We would hold the same for churches and synagogues that charge for pews, membership or special services.[48] Naturally, this presents issues of line-drawing when the requirement of payment is not overt, yet strong pressure is exerted to make the payment. Administering these lines is nothing new to tax authorities and courts, however, even if they do sometimes reach inconsistent or controversial results.[49]

The participation enjoyment derived by an act utility donor might be characterized as a form of quid pro quo: the donor purchases psychic gratification in exchange for the gift. But this is a benefit integral to the act of giving. By analogy to the doctrine of consideration, it is not given in return *by the recipient* and so cannot be characterized as having been bargained for.[50] A closer case is presented by one who receives a naming opportunity for an educational building in exchange for a large gift—a return benefit which, if it were bargained for, would likely be viewed as legal consideration.[51] However, because the reputational value associated with the naming opportunity flows from the very act of making the gift and serves as a proxy for the social worth of the recipient, the value is not independent of the gift itself. Consequently, we classify it as a true donation. With these prototypes in mind, the quid pro quo test should serve as a reliable guide for differentiating true purchases from the self-interest that might be said to attend any donation.

Retained Earnings as Donations

The preceding discussion addresses objections that the donative theory is too generous to charities by covering too many objects of philanthropy. In reality, few such critics are likely to surface since our theory will be seen as a significant retraction of the existing scope of the charitable exemption. Nevertheless, answering these objections is essential to establishing the donative theory on a firm analytical foundation. Of more immediate significance, however, are objections that the donative theory does not go far enough. Principally, it is possible to argue, following the comprehensive discussion of altruism recently published by Professor Atkinson,[52] that our application of the donative theory incorrectly excludes from its coverage some organizations that deserve subsidy even under its own terms. We maintain that the only nonprofits that qualify for an exemption are those that receive a significant portion of their revenues from donations. Atkinson, however, argues that virtually *all* nonprofit organizations[53] should be exempt as charities because implicit in their formation is an act of altruism that deserves a social subsidy: in choosing the nonprofit over the proprietary institutional form, the organizers are agreeing in advance to devote the entirety of their potential stream of earnings to the enterprise that the institution is established to further. "Thus, the founders' initial contribution of their potential earnings has an on-going aspect; the organization embodies their altruism."[54] This donative act is implicit in the formation decision by virtue of the core defining characteristic of nonprofit corporations—that they are prohibited by law from distributing their earnings and so must retain them for use within the institution. Therefore,

even if the organization receives no donations whatsoever but derives all of
its income from sales in the commercial marketplace, Atkinson would still
classify it as a donative ("altruistic") institution.

Earlier, we critiqued Atkinson's theory on its own terms as an academic
version of the amorphous community benefit notion. Here, we examine
whether Atkinson's argument can be adapted to the donative theory to
produce the same results, albeit for somewhat different reasons. We
demonstrate that this expansive interpretation of altruism is flawed because,
based upon the principles we have just set forth, it adopts an incorrect view
of what constitutes a true donation.

If the mere existence of nonprofit enterprise is to constitute donative
activity, it is only by virtue of the initial organizational decision, not by
virtue of the annual retention of earnings.[55] An entity's yearly act of
retaining its earnings is in no sense a form of philanthropy for the very fact
that this retention is compelled by law. This lack of choice in the matter
means that a nonprofit organization's annual retention of earnings neither
serves as a disinterested assessment of its own social worth in that year nor
is it accompanied by a disincentive to "give"—the two qualities necessary
for donations to deserve tax-exempt support.

This point does not apply, however, to the initial organizational decision.
Nonprofit founders are free to choose whatever corporate form they wish,
and their election of the nondistribution constraint could be viewed as a
donation of their expected future stream of earnings. Nevertheless, at least
two reasons exist to reject the organizational decision as a form of donation.
First, a corporate organizer who foregoes a stream of potential profits gives
away something that she never had. This decision does not partake of the
same level of self-sacrifice as one who pays hard-earned cash out of pocket.
Second, for many nonprofit organizations, there are several reasons to
suppose that the organizational choice was strongly influenced by the
organizers' own financial interests.

Professor Hansmann offers one such reason. He explains that nonprofit
organizations exist in most of their manifestations[56] to overcome consumers' concerns about being unable to monitor the quality of services they
purchase from the organization. The constraint on distributing profits that
attaches to nonprofit firms helps accomplish this objective by removing
managers' ability to divert the firm's funds to their own pockets—the major
form of abuse.[57] The principal application of this trust theory is to donative
nonprofits since the "patrons" of these companies have the least ability to
monitor what happens to their payments. But Hansmann also applies the
theory to commercial nonprofits, arguing that consumers prefer to patronize

nonprofits for complex services whose quality is difficult to monitor.[58] Thus, some commercial entrepreneurs may choose the nonprofit form simply to attract more customers.

This possibility is nicely illustrated by the explanation in Chapter 3 of why nonprofit hospitals predominate over for-profits. Nonprofit enterprise is thought by many to proliferate in the hospital industry because doctors find it more attractive. There are varying accounts, different in their positive and negative emphases, on why doctors have this preference, but they all share in common the premise that hospital organizers choose the nonprofit form in order to attract the most doctors, which maximizes the flow of patients. Therefore, this organizational motive is fully justified on a quid pro quo basis and so signals no need for a subsidy. Since there is no systemic bar to organizers' self-interested choice of an organizational form that maximizes its receipts, a subsidy is superfluous. True enough, barriers to entry and expansion may exist in particular areas of nonprofit activity. For instance, Hansmann explains why some commercial nonprofits may suffer from a comparative disadvantage in accessing capital markets.[59] But these and other conceivable barriers do not apply to all nonprofits. Therefore, they do not provide a convincing reason to link tax exemption to nonprofit status generally.[60]

Another welfare-maximizing reason for organizers to choose the nonprofit form is simply to obtain the exemption itself. Witness the periodic news reports of "self-declared religious leaders whose faith emerges only at tax time."[61] For instance, 88 percent of the residents of Hardenburgh, New York once became ordained ministers of the "Universal Life Church" in order to turn their homes into temples and thereby claim a tax exemption.[62] The same abusive motivations can exist in legitimate business settings. If the combined financial benefits of the property, sales and income tax exemptions, together with reduced postal rates, access to tax-exempt bond financing, and other economic advantages that come with charitable status are greater than the enterprise's expected earnings, then the trade-off of profits for exemption is nothing more than a purchase of an exemption. In labor-intensive service businesses, for example, the business organizers often pay out most, if not all, of the potential profit in the form of salaries to employee/owners.[63] If the exemption helps avoid an entity-level tax,[64] more money is left to distribute as salary or to pay for workplace amenities. The consequence of applying the donative theory in this scenario would be an entirely self-justifying, viciously circular application of the exemption that would rob it of any test for deservedness: the exemption would go to whatever organization chooses the nonprofit form for purposes of obtaining the exemption—in other words, to whomever wanted it.

Nevertheless, one can attempt to rehabilitate the argument for exempting commercial nonprofits under the donative theory by observing that a valid social signalling function occurs in the decision of *customers* to patronize a nonprofit over a competing for-profit facility. Some people may choose to give their business to the nonprofit simply because they approve of the nonprofit's activities. For instance, in *United States v. American Bar Endowment*,[65] the Supreme Court considered whether American Bar Association members make deductible contributions when they purchase insurance policies sponsored by the ABA Foundation (its charitable research arm). The Court held no; the policies were competitively priced and therefore the members received a full, quid pro quo exchange. Nevertheless, one could argue that the members' decision to shop with the ABA operates as a quasi-donation because it signals their approval of ABA activities.

However, the problems under this variant argument for crediting retained earnings as donations are the same as under the main line. We have no easy way to determine whether customers make their shopping decisions based solely on self-interest (perhaps because of Hansmann's trust rationale for preferring commercial nonprofits) or from a sense of public spiritedness. Even if we assume some level of eleemosynary intent, we face the difficulty of measuring the significance of this intent. Actual donations, and even the main line of the retained-earnings argument, offer us some basis for hard quantification of the size of public support, but this variant argument leaves us to pure speculation. It is *not* correct, under this variant argument, to measure the value either of gross revenues or of the net income generated by sympathetic sales. Most of the gross price reflects the value of the goods sold. Even the profit portion of the sales should not count as donations since customers would have had to pay this portion in any event as a cost of for-profit capital. Therefore, the only portion of the sales price that could be credited as a true donation would be any "excess" profits, as measured by comparing the prices charged by for-profit competitors. If there is no such excess, then there is no basis for quantifying the level of public recognition.

Likewise, for nonprofit formation, we lack any objective method to test for the accuracy of assertions that the founders' motives were altruistic. The fact that significant numbers of commercial nonprofits do not deserve the exemption counsels that, if only for prophylactic reasons, the mere organizational decision should not be counted as a donation.[66]

An additional factor puts the case to rest. Even for worthy organizational motives, crediting the organizational decision as a once-and-for-all donation would have the result of *forever* exempting the organization's stream of income, no matter how it fits into the changing social milieu. This is proper only if we are convinced that the organizer's initial decision operates as a continuing signal of social need, but at some point down the road, this initial decision loses its social significance as it becomes more distant from the contemporaneous scene. For instance, racially segregated parks and swimming pools were once legitimate targets of philanthropy.[67] Crediting organizational decisions made generations ago undermines the deservedness criterion because these organizations in effect are removed from the marketplace in altruism, which serves as a barometer of present social needs and preferences. Therefore, the same policies against dead-hand rule that prohibit various restraints on alienation also counsel against forever exempting all nonprofits at the outset of their corporate lives.

Perhaps the one arena in which the retained earnings argument potentially merits acceptance is for commercial organizations that serve a redistributive function. A charity that uses a large portion of its retained earnings to support free services to the poor can safely be assumed to be pursuing a worthy purpose since helping the indigent is the quintessential charitable activity, one that has enjoyed categorical charitable status for over four centuries. This status is not likely to change soon. Therefore, it is safe to assume that a founder who chooses a nonprofit form in order to better serve the poor acts from public spiritedness and that her decision has continuing social validity into the future. Only by this convoluted route is the donative theory arguably capable of covering a nonprofit entity that serves the poor, yet receives no overt donative support.

Accepting this argument, however, creates several difficulties. First, one must be able to draw the boundaries of this special category of cases. Precisely who are the poor, and how much aid must go to them in order to qualify? These are the type of ad hoc, normative decisions that revenue agents make in the present, unhappy state of affairs which the donative theory seeks to avoid. Second, assuming a valid case of deservedness can be established, the resulting subsidy suffers under the proportionality criterion since, without the presence of donations to measure the extent of the entity's beneficence, there is no mechanism for adjusting the level of subsidy to the level of deservedness. Thus, a very large commercial nonprofit enterprise that happens to generate very little income might enjoy tremendous property tax relief simply by giving away all of its earnings to the poor. Finally, one must ask, if such an organization is really deserving, why is it not able to structure its operations in a manner that would qualify under the main line of the donative theory? The lack of donative support suggests that we may be too generous in assuming its worth or need. A more accurate way to subsidize such an entity's donative spirit would be to give it a deduction for donating its earnings to a recognized charity, something that the law already does. Therefore, there is no obvious need for expanding the charitable exemption to cover such cases, although a plausible case can be made.

Summary

The paradigm case for subsidizing the objects of donations is established by the role of altruism in rectifying the market failure that afflicts public goods. However, this paradigm covers few instances of actual giving. There are two imperfections: the objects of most gifts are not true public goods, and the motives for giving are not purely altruistic. The donative theory avoids these difficulties because of its power of generalizeability: it applies to virtually any act of giving, regardless of the object or the motive. The existence of a significant level of giving identifies a product or service the production of which is desired but not available through private markets. And, due to the free-rider disinclination to give, we know that donations systematically will fail to support the optimal level of production (as measured by production if there were no market or government failure).

The power of this theory is that we need not understand why orchestras solicit and baseball teams do not, why social clubs charge admission but churches do not, or what is altruism and what is egoism. Motive matters only for the limited purpose of separating donations from purchases, but this is best done by looking for objective manifestations of an exchange whose return value is unrelated to the mere making of the gift. Discussion in terms of egoism confuses the self-interest that is always present to some degree in every transaction with a quid pro quo that indicates an act of pure private consumption.

This distinction is most easily seen in the case of donors who receive tangible benefits from the services they support. Their direct participation in the benefits makes their gifts stronger, not weaker signals of social worth. Subtler forms of self-interest, such as the donor who receives only psychic benefits from giving, and crasser forms, such as the donor who cares only about the reputational value of giving, are more challenging, however, because the proxy relationship between the motive to give and social worth tends to weaken our confidence that donations necessarily reveal causes that are both socially valued and in need of additional support. Nevertheless, even these motivations can be rehabilitated by observing that a market in altruism operates to direct these gifts to roughly those objects that society perceives as more deserving. Like other markets, this one will not operate flawlessly, but it should operate predictably enough that we can avoid the need in most cases to engage in intensive empirical examination of the subjective reasons for giving. On the other hand, there are some limits to the donative concept. A quid pro quo exchange is not a donation, nor is merely an annual retention of earnings by a nonprofit entity.

Notes

1. In addition to the citations in the notes below, the following sources review various motivations for giving and other cooperative behavior, and they provide extensive citations to the theoretical and empirical literature: DANIEL BAR-TAL, PROSOCIAL BEHAVIOR 39–50 (1976); NANCY EISENBERG, ALTRUISTIC EMOTION, COGNITION & BEHAVIOR 30–56 (1986); VIRGINIA HODGKINSON, MOTIVATIONS FOR GIVING AND VOLUNTEERING (1990); J. PHILIPPE RUSHTON, ALTRUISM, SOCIALIZATION & SOCIETY 36–57 (1980); JAMES Q. WILSON, THE MORAL SENSE 29–39 (1993); LAUREN WISPE, ALTRUISM, SYMPATHY & HELPING 303 (1978); ROBERT WUTHNOW, ACTS OF COMPASSION (1992); William Amos, *Empirical Analysis of Motivations Underlying Individual Contributions to Charity*, 10 ATLANTIC ECON. J. 45 (1988); Mark Gergen, *The Case for a Charitable Contributions Deduction*, 74 VA. L. REV. 1393, 1430 (1988); Jerzy Karylowski, *Focus of Attention and Altruism: Endocentric and Exocentric Sources of Altruistic Behavior*, in DEVELOPMENT AND MAINTENANCE OF PROSOCIAL BEHAVIOR 382 (Ervin Staub et al. eds., 1984); Joel Newman, *A Proposal for Direct, Deductible Charitable Contributions*, 96 DICKINSON L. REV. 209 (1992); Janusz Reykowski, *Motivation of Prosocial Behavior*, in COOPERATION AND HELPING BEHAVIOR 355–56 (Valerian Derlega & Janusz Grzelak eds., 1982). An excellent discussion and extensive bibliography are contained in MORTON HUNT, THE COMPASSIONATE BEAST (1990).

2. ERVIN STAUB, POSITIVE SOCIAL BEHAVIOR AND MORALITY 139–140 (1974). *See also* David Johnson, *The Charity Market: Theory and Practice*, in INSTITUTE OF ECONOMIC AFFAIRS, THE ECONOMICS OF CHARITY 94 (1973); Douglas Kenrick, *Selflessness Examined: Is Avoiding Tar and Feathers Nonegoistic?*, 12 BEHAV. & BRAIN SCI. 711, 712 (1989); Pamela Oliver, *Rewards and Punishments as Selective Incentives for Collective Action: Theoretical Investigations*, 85 AM. J. SOC. 1356, 1357 (1980) (a thoughtful examination of the way in which such incentives operate).

3. Anatol Rapoport, *Egoistic Incentive: A Hypothesis or an Ideological Tenet?*, 12 BEHAV. & BRAIN SCI. 719 (1989). *Accord*, AMITAI ETZIONI, THE MORAL DIMENSION: TOWARD A NEW ECONOMICS 27–28 (1988); Jeffrey Harrison, *Egoism, Altruism, and Market Illusions: The Limits of Law and Economics*, 33 UCLA L. REV. 1309, 1311 (1986); Amartya Sen, *Rational Fools: A Critique of the Behavioral Foundations of Economic Theory*, 6 PHIL. & PUB. AFF. 317, 322–24

(1977).

4. Crosby Valve & Gage Co. v. Commissioner, 380 F.2d 146, 146–47 (1st Cir.), *cert. denied*, 389 U.S. 976 (1967).

5. We take this term from Gerald Marwell, *Altruism and the Problem of Collective Action, in* COOPERATION AND HELPING BEHAVIOR 207, 221 (Valerian Derlega & Janusz Grzelak eds., 1982).

6. *See* TERESA ODENDAHL, CHARITY BEGINS AT HOME: GENEROSITY AND SELF-INTEREST AMONG THE PHILANTHROPIC ELITE 25, 41 (1990); Donald Bauman et al., *Altruism as Hedonism: Helping and Self-Gratification as Equivalent Responses*, 40 J. PERSON. & SOC. PSYCH. 1039 (1981); Stephen Worchel, *The Darker Side of Giving, in* DEVELOPMENT AND MAINTENANCE OF PROSOCIAL BEHAVIOR, *supra* note 1, at 382.

7. *Cf.* Johnson, *supra* note 2, at 92–93.

8. This motive was suggested to us by a colleague, Ira Ellman. (We are not so cynical as to have thought of it ourselves.) *See also* Rob Atkinson, *Altruism in Nonprofit Organizations*, 31 B.C.L. REV. 501, 541–42 (1990) ("Some donors no doubt glory in having their names attached, literally or otherwise, to ivied walls; others certainly seek to bask in the reflected glory of their alma mater's faculty and future alumni.").

9. Hernandez v. Commissioner, 104 L.Ed.2d 766, 781 (1989).

10. Mark Kelman, *Personal Deductions Revisited*, 31 STAN. L. REV. 831, 880 (1979).

11. *See, e.g.*, Robert Cialdini et al., *Empathy-Based Helping: Is it Selflessly or Selfishly Motivated?*, 52 J. PERSONALITY & SOC. PSYCH. 749 (1987) (presenting experimental results that indicate "that it is the egoistic desire to relieve sadness, rather than the selfless desire to relieve the sufferer, that motivates helping").

12. *See generally* Ronald Milo, *Introduction, in* EGOISM AND ALTRUISM 3–11 (Ronald Milo ed., 1973); Alasdai MacIntyre, *Egoism and Altruism, in* I THE ENCYCLOPEDIA OF PHILOSOPHY 462–63 (Paul Edwards ed., 1967).

13. *See generally* the 30 pages of commentary following Linda Caporael et al., *Selfishness Examined: Cooperation in the Absence of Egoistic Incentives*, 12 BEHAV. & BRAIN SCI. 683 (1989).

14. Gergen, *supra* note 1, at 1443–44 (most giving to public television "is easily explained as the value donors place on the programming"). *See also* MICHAEL CHESTERMAN, CHARITIES, TRUSTS AND SOCIAL WELFARE 408 (1979) ("only genuinely altruistic, redistributive and socially useful projects [should be] labelled charitable"; arguing that elite private schools, museums and the performing arts do not deserve the exemption).

15. HOWARD MARGOLIS, SELFISHNESS, ALTRUISM, AND RATIONALITY 12 (1982).

16. *See* Mark A. Hall & John D. Colombo, *The Charitable Status of Nonprofit Hospitals: Toward a Donative Theory of Tax Exemption*, 66 WASH L. REV. 307, 400–03 (1990).

17. *See* Thomas Nagel, *Comment [on Arrow, "Gifts and Exchanges"]*, *in* ALTRUISM, MORALITY, AND ECONOMIC THEORY 59 (Edmund Phelps, ed. 1975). The moral objection that might be raised if the benefitted group is small and elite is considered below in Chapter 9.

18. However, if a donation is made in contemplation of death, there may be a case for scrutinizing the degree of self interest because there may be less self sacrifice in disposing of wealth that the donor can no longer use personally (other than to give it to her family). In fact, the primary object of the law of charitable trusts is to determine whether a trust benefits the public or instead whether a disqualifying private benefit is present. For instance, a trust to maintain the testator's grave (or that of his family) is invalid, whereas one to maintain an entire graveyard is enforceable. RESTATEMENT (SECOND) OF TRUSTS, § 367, comment a (1958). Similarly, a trust to benefit employees of the founder's company is noncharitable because, like a gift to his family, it primarily is intended to enhance the founder's legacy. CHESTERMAN, *supra* note 14, at 313. These fine distinctions are not necessary for inter vivos gifts, especially if giving to a particular object is widespread.

19. Gergen, *supra* note 1, at 1410–12.

20. Marwell, *supra* note 5, at 220. *See also* John G. Simon, *The Tax Treatment of Nonprofit Organizations: A Review of Federal and State Policies*, *in* THE NONPROFIT SECTOR: A RESEARCH HANDBOOK 67, 86 (Walter W. Powell ed., 1987) ("Ignoring motive may be a necessity for the tax system; the search for purity of charitable intention would be an unmanageable task, even ignoring the complications caused by psychoanalytic theory.").

21. Hernandez v. Commissioner, 104 L.Ed.2d 766, 781 (1989) (collecting citations).

22. 363 U.S. 278 (1960). Justice Brennan might be thought to express a contrary view in this famous opinion, which maintains that the gift characterization for purposes of what counts as income turns on an assessment of "affection, respect, admiration, charity or the like impulses," an assessment that must be left to the "mainsprings of human experience." This opinion makes clear, however, that objective factors are important in measuring intent. *Id.* at 287 ("There must be an objective inquiry as to whether what is called a gift amounts to it in reality"). *See generally* James W. Colliton, *The Meaning of "Contribution or Gift" for Charitable Contribution Deduction Purposes*, 41 OHIO ST. L.J. 973 (1980); Joseph Sliskovich, *Charitable Contributions or Gifts: A Contemporaneous Look Back to the Future*, 57 U. MO. K.C. L. REV. 437, 470–87 (1989).

23. Crosby Valve & Gage Co. v. Comm'r, 380 F.2d 146, 146–47 (1st Cir.), *cert. denied*, 389 U.S. 976 (1967).

24. STAUB, *supra* note 2, at 7 ("If behavior that demands various sacrifices is not reinforced in any way, it would extinguish over time . . . . When a person behaves prosocially out of altruistic intentions, purely to benefit another, he is still likely to have some anticipation of, and certainly the experience of, such reinforcement."); Charles Broad, *Egoism as a Theory of Human Motives*, *in* EGOISM AND ALTRUISM,

supra note 12, at 97–98 (all giving is ultimately self-regarding in some sense).

25. This distinction is recognized and developed in a number of sources using varying terminology. The source from which we borrow this particular terminology is Thomas Ireland, *The Calculus of Philanthropy, in* THE ECONOMICS OF CHARITY, *supra* note 2, at 70–71, who observes that act utility is sometimes called the "Kantian" motive. *Id.* at 67–68. The same distinction has been drawn in terms on "endocentric" versus "exocentric" motives for giving. Jerzy Karylowski, *Two Types of Altruistic Behavior: Doing Good to Feel Good or to Make the Other Feel Good, in* COOPERATION AND HELPING BEHAVIOR, *supra* note 1, at 397. Recent economic theory has focused on "pure" versus "impure" altruism. *E.g.,* James Andreoni, *Impure Altruism and Donations to Public Goods: A Theory of Warm-Glow Giving,* 100 ECON. J. 464 (1990); James Andreoni, *Giving with Impure Altruism: Applications to Charity and Ricardian Equivalence,* 97 J. POL. ECON. 1447 (1989). *See also* Kenneth Arrow, *Gifts and Exchanges, in* ALTRUISM, MORALITY, AND ECONOMIC THEORY, *supra* note 17 at 13, 17–18; Guido Calabresi, *Comment [on Arrow's "Gifts and Exchanges"], in id.* at 58–59; Howard Margolis, *supra* note 15, at 21. For particularly helpful illustrations that give flesh and bones to this distinction by showing how it classifies specific motivations taken from real-world hypotheticals, see Karylowski, *supra,* at 407; Jerzy Karylowski, *Focus of Attention and Altruism: Endocentric and Exocentric Sources of Altruistic Behavior, supra* note 1, at 141–43.

26. ESTELLE JAMES & SUSAN ROSE-ACKERMAN, THE NONPROFIT ENTERPRISE IN MARKET ECONOMICS 25–26 (1986) (describing the "buying-in" mentality that allows donors to feel good about the charity's activities and claim them partially as their own).

27. "An arts fund may reward contributors . . . by printing their names in a program. Workers ensure cooperation with a strike by threatening to ostracize or beat up strikebreakers." Oliver, *supra* note 2, at 1356.

28. Newman, *supra* note 1, at 225–26.

29. *See* Calabresi, *supra* note 26, at 59 (such giving entails no public good, free-rider problem); Dwight Lee & Richard McKenzie, *Second Thoughts on the Public-Good Justification for Government Poverty Programs,* 19 J. LEG. STUD. 189, 194 (1990) (same). The theory would not be destroyed unless *all* donations fell at this polar extreme.

30. Jerzy Karylowski, *Two Types of Altruistic Behavior: Doing Good to Feel Good or to Make the Other Feel Good, supra* note 25, at 397–98; Richard Steinberg, *Voluntary Donations and Public Expenditures in a Federalist System,* 77 AM. ECO. REV. 24 (1987).

31. Bruce Kingma, *An Accurate Measurement of the Crowd-Out Effect, Income Effect, and Price Effect for Charitable Contributions,* 97 J. POL. ECON. 1197 (1989).

32. *See* Ireland, *supra* note 25, at 70.

33. The demarcation between these two cases is not as sharp in reality as we have drawn it here for purposes of illustration. We have already observed that, because the direct, tangible benefit to a viewer who supports public television is

actually quite small, it is probably the psychic value of giving that serves as the prime motivation. Nevertheless, we use this as one analytical peg because of its contrast with instances of giving for which the motivation can *only* be psychic.

34. *See* Ireland, *supra* note 25, at 71.

35. *See* Lee & McKenzie, *supra* note 25, at 194.

36. This is suggested by the discussion in MacIntyre, *supra* note 12, at 463.

37. Ireland, *supra* note 25, at 74.

38. *See* Joseph Galaskiewicz, *Corporate Contributions to Charity: Nothing More than a Marketing Strategy?*, *in* PHILANTHROPIC GIVING: STUDIES IN VARIETIES AND GOALS 246 (Richard Magat ed., 1989).

39. Ronald Smith, *The Unsentimental Corporate Giver*, FORTUNE (Sept. 1981), at 121.

40. Amer Useem, *Corporate Philanthropy*, *in* THE NONPROFIT SECTOR: A RESEARCH HANDBOOK, *supra* note 20, at 340, 348 (containing extensive bibliography).

41. Another application of this principle is found in Ottawa Silica Co. v. U.S., 699 F.2d 1124 (Fed. Cir. 1983), which considered the deductibility of a property owner/developer's donation of land for a new high school. The court found no qualifying gift because the IRS determined that the primary motive was that construction of the school would necessitate building access roads adjacent to the owner's property, which would increase the value of his land. Because this benefit is unrelated to the value of the school, it does not serve as a valid proxy of the donation's worth.

42. Atkinson adopts this test in his extensive discussion of altruism: "What is distinct about my donors is not that they give without gain, but that any satisfaction they derive from giving is not in the form of a material quid pro quo for their donation." Atkinson, *supra* note 8, at 526.

43. The most oft-quoted test for what constitutes a "contribution" under § 170 of the Code is the "detached and disinterested generosity" language contained in the Supreme Court's opinion in Commissioner v. Duberstein, 363 U.S. 278, 285 (1960) (to be a gift, transaction must proceed from a "detached and disinterested generosity" on the part of the taxpayer), a case that dealt with when an economic receipt constitutes a gift excluded from income under § 102 of the Code, rather than what constitutes a "contribution" under § 170. *See* BORIS I. BITTKER & LAWRENCE LOKKEN, FEDERAL INCOME TAXATION OF INCOME, ESTATES AND GIFTS ¶ 35.1.3 at page 35-8 (1990); MICHAEL J. GRAETZ, FEDERAL INCOME TAXATION: PRINCIPLES AND POLICIES 482 (2d ed. 1989). Although this test implies an analysis of subjective intent, courts generally have looked to objective factors signifying motive when applying it to charitable contributions. *See* Dockery v. Comm'r, 37 T.C.M. 317, 321 (1978) (reviewing a number of alternative tests for charitable contributions, especially for contributions by business entities). *See generally* Colliton, *supra* note 22; Sliskovich, *supra* note 22.

44. Stubbs v. U.S., 428 F.2d 885 (9th Cir. 1970), *cert. denied*, 400 U.S. 1009 (1971); Sliskovich, *supra* note 22, at 460–70.

45. *See* Rev. Rul. 83-104, 1983-2 C.B. 46.

46. Rev. Rul. 67-246, 1967-2 C.B. 104 (bifurcating charity ball ticket price into sales and contribution elements).

47. Hernandez v. Commissioner, 104 L.Ed.2d 766, 781–82 (1989). For an example of truly sham religious donations, see Chapter 5, at note 39, regarding the "sex church" operated by a couple from Los Angeles.

48. The IRS does not necessarily agree, however. *See* Powell v. United States, 945 F.2d 374 (11th Cir. 1991) (describing IRS practice of allowing deductions for these types of contributions).

49. *See* Davis v. United States, 110 S.Ct. 2014 (1990) (disallowing deduction to Mormon Church for family's contribution of funds to support their son's missionary work); Powell v. United States, 945 F.2d 374 (11th Cir. 1991) (alleging wildly inconsistent practices by IRS in whether to disallow church contributions that carry a quid pro quo). Perhaps this clarification of the purpose of the deduction will help to clarify this confusion.

50. *See* E. ALLAN FARNSWORTH, CONTRACTS 41–49 (1982). For instance, surely one reason Texaco has sponsored the Metropolitan Opera broadcasts for over 50 years is the image-polishing publicity it receives. Nevertheless, case law establishes that such incidental benefits do not disqualify a payment from donation status. BITTKER & LOKKEN, *supra* note 43, at *id.* (collecting cases).

51. Allegheny College v. National Chautaugua County Bank, 246 N.Y 369, 159 N.E. 173 (1927).

52. Atkinson, *supra* note 8, at 542–57, 616–20.

53. The sole exception is for "mutual benefit organizations"—social clubs, mutual insurance companies, and the like—which are exempt anyway for other reasons contained in the non-charitable subsections of I.R.C. § 501. *E.g.*, I.R.C. § 501(c)(6) (business leagues), (c)(7) (clubs), and (c)(8) (fraternal organizations).

54. Atkinson, *supra* note 8, at 556. *See* Buton L.Weisbrod, *Private Goods, Collective Goods: The Role of the Nonprofit Sector, in* THE ECONOMICS OF NONPROPRIETARY ORGANIZATIONS 151 (Kennth Clarkson & Donald Martin eds., 1980). Atkinson offers as an example the Orton Ceramic Company, a trust founded by Mr. Orton at his death with instructions to continue his life's work researching and producing parts used in the ceramic firing process. One can speculate that Mr. Orton's desire to promote the craft of ceramics motivated him to make an enduring donation to this enterprise of all its future earnings. However, the argument for this entity's exempt status does not rest solely with the organizational decision to retain future earnings, for the formation of the trust itself entailed the making of an actual, substantial donation from Mr. Orton's estate. Ultimately, though, we would not find this company to be donative because, for reasons explained in the text and in Chapter 11, we would require greater evidence of deservedness than simply one gift from a single donor.

55. The analytical path we follow here is identical to that used by the Supreme Court in the analogous context of determining whether purchasers of insurance policies from the ABA could claim tax deductible contributions for allowing the

ABA to keep the dividends that the insurance policies earned. U.S. v. American Bar Foundation, 477 U.S. 105 (1986). The Court rejected the ABA's argument that the policyholders' decision to forego dividends reflected their desire to further the ABA's public service mission. The Court reasoned that no donations occurred from year-to-year because the policyholders were bound by contract to forego the dividends, and that no donation occurred at the time policyholders signed up because there was no evidence they were motivated by generosity as opposed to the inconvenience of bargaining more aggressively with the Foundation.

56. Hansmann recognizes that there are exceptions to this theory, primarily for "mutual benefit organizations" described in note 53, *supra*. Hansmann concludes that these organizations are peripheral to the nonprofit form because they more accurately represent a third and distinct form of organization—cooperative corporations. Henry B. Hansmann, *Reforming Nonprofit Corporation Law*, 129 U. PENN. L. REV. 497, 582–83 (1981). Ellman, however, sees mutual benefit organizations as central to the nonprofit form. Ira M. Ellman, *Another Theory of Nonprofit Corporations*, 80 MICH. L. REV. 999 (1982). This debate is not germane to our analysis since the exemption of mutual benefit nonprofits stands on separate footing from the subsidy theories that this article discusses.

57. Hansmann, *supra* note 56, at 506. For a further elaboration of Hansmann's trust rationale, see Chapter 5.

58. As we noted in Chapter 6, several scholars disagree with this assertion, noting that many complex services are not nonprofit and that those that are nonprofit are not uniquely difficult to evaluate. *See* JAMES DOUGLAS, WHY CHARITY: THE CASE FOR A THIRD SECTOR 23 (1983) ("Private medical practice, dentistry, the law, the learned professions generally, the supply of pharmaceutical drugs, electrical contracting, any number of building trade crafts, automobile and television repairs are all fields in which the for-profit form is dominant."); Ellman, *supra* note 56, at 1032–33 (parents routinely evaluate child care services); William Yoder, *Economic Theories of For-Profit and Not-for-Profit Organizations*, in INSTITUTE OF MEDICINE, FOR-PROFIT ENTERPRISE IN HEALTH CARE 20 (Bradford H. Gray ed., 1986) (noting that for-profits have large share of child care and nursing home markets and no share of legal services, personal computers, or used cars). For purposes of our argument, however, it is not necessary either that all complex services be nonprofit or that all commercial nonprofits entail complex services. Our argument stands as long as this explanation applies to some nonprofits.

59. Henry B. Hansmann, *The Rationale for Exempting Nonprofit Organizations from Corporate Income Tax*, 91 YALE L.J. 54, 84 (1981).

60. Atkinson responds to the financial motives to chose a nonprofit form by arguing they are irrelevant since, regardless of the founder's motive, the organizational decision is still altruistic since the institution's earnings will be used to subsidize the purchases by its customers. Atkinson, *supra* note 8, at 553. This explanation seriously misunderstands the significance of a donation to the eligibility for a tax subsidy. It is nice that retained earnings are so used, but, the question is why such an operation deserves a *further* subsidy from taxpayers.

61. Ira M. Ellman, *Driven from the Tribunal: Judicial Resolution of Internal Church Disputes*, 69 MICH. L. REV. 1378, 1442 (1981).

62. *Id.* at 1442 n.182.

63. Atkinsion, *supra* note 8, at 544–45.

64. Observe, though, that such enterprises can be organized in a manner that avoids an entity-level *income* tax even without charitable status. For instance, because the 1986 Tax Reform Act put corporate tax rates below personal rates and repealed the *General Utilities* doctrine that had permitted corporate owners to pay a single capital gains tax on corporate income upon sale or liquidation of the corporation, conventional tax advice for service businesses has been to organize as a partnership or Subchapter S corporation to avoid the double level of tax inherent in the regular corporate structure. *See* Louis S. Freeman, *Some Early Strategies for the Methodical Disincorporation of America After the Tax Reform Act of 1986*, 64 TAXES 962 (December 1986); Jeffrey M. Gonyo, *Tax Planning Opportunities Using S Corporations Under the Tax Reform Act of 1986*, 65 TAXES 552 (August 1987). These alternative structures, however, have their own limitations: partnerships require at least one person with unlimited liability, while Subchapter S limits the number and kind of investors. *See* I.R.C. § 1361; WILLIAM S. MCKEE, WILLIAM F. NELSON & ROBERT L. WHITMIRE, FEDERAL TAXATION OF PARTNERSHIPS AND PARTNERS ¶ 3.06 (2d ed. 1990). Moreover, neither avoids a property tax. Therefore, one can easily conceive of situations in which a regular corporation with a tax exemption remains the most attractive form.

65. 477 U.S. 105 (1986).

66. Throughout this section we refer strictly to the decision to organize, not to any actual donations of start-up capital that are made at the organizational stage. These latter out-of-pocket contributions do qualify as donations.

67. The famous case of Senator Augustus O. Bacon of Georgia is one example. Upon his death, Senator Bacon left a large tract of land to the city of Macon, Georgia, for use as a segregated park. When African-Americans sought admission to the park in 1963, litigation ensued which ultimately ended in the United States Supreme Court ordering desegregation of the park. Evans v. Newton, 382 U.S. 296 (1966). In its discussion concerning whether the administration of the park constituted "state action" subject to the Fourteenth Amendment, the Court noted that the park enjoyed tax-exempt status. *Id.* at 301.

9

Moral Theory

In the view of some, the style of reasoning we have employed so far is antithetical to its subject because altruism operates on a plane of human experience that is removed from baser considerations of economic efficiency and analytical logic. This section responds to this attitude by demonstrating that the charitable tax exemption also gathers strong support from moral theory, support that depends on the donative status of exempt organizations. This support is all the more impressive because it comes from each of the several opposing schools of thought that dominate present moral and political debate, as well as from more classic forms of liberalism.

To demonstrate this compatibility, we will respond to the two moral and political objections to the donative theory raised in Chapter 7. The first is the anti-majoritarian objection, which applies to any subsidy-based theory of the charitable exemption. This objection holds that it is unfair to raise taxes on the majority of the public to benefit a small minority, particularly where the majority of voters have implicitly rejected a direct subsidy. The second is the elitism objection, which is unique to the donative theory. It observes that allocating governmental support according to the degree of private donative support gives more weight to the needs and tastes of those with the greatest financial ability to give and therefore distributes the subsidy in an elitist and regressive fashion. Earlier, we responded to these objections using the economic and political bases employed to establish the donative theory. Here, we take up these objections under several branches of moral political theory. We will demonstrate that, under each of several, opposing theories of distributive justice, the anti-majoritarian objection to subsidy theories generally is best answered by the donative theory, and that the donative theory survives the more specific attack of the elitism objection.

In the 1970s and 1980s, two competing liberal theories of distributive justice—contractarian and libertarian—were crystallized in two modern masterpieces: John Rawls' *A Theory of Justice* (1971) and Robert Nozick's *Anarchy, State and Utopia* (1974).[1] Rawls draws from the "social compact" theories of Locke and Rousseau to posit that those principles of justice should control by which every rational, self-interested person would agree in advance to be bound, under certain idealized conditions that Rawls describes as the "original position."[2] For instance, Rawls argues that anyone in the original position, not knowing his actual status in society, would follow a "maximin" strategy and adopt a principle that requires society to distribute its resources to the advantage of the least well-off individuals.[3] In sharp disagreement, Nozick maintains that Rawls' original position is a loaded theoretical construct designed to produce a set of redistributive principles in conflict with the preeminent moral principle: that the state must "treat[] us as inviolate individuals, who may not be used in certain ways by others as means or tools or instruments or resources, [and must] treat[] us as persons having individual rights with the dignity this constitutes."[4] More recently, a body of thought known as communitarian theory has criticized the individualistic foundations of both of these branches of liberalism and their assumptions that it is even possible to derive meaningful principles of rights and distributive justice in such an abstract fashion. Communitarians instead argue that moral principles are contingent on particular historical and social settings and on particular groupings within those settings.[5] Remarkably, a charitable tax exemption derived from the donative theory fits comfortably within all three of these opposing theories of distributive justice, as well as with more classic liberal principles.

Rawls' Contractarian Theory of Justice

A Rawlsian analysis directly responds to both the anti-majoritarian and the elitism objections. The donative theory serves as a model for Rawlsian justice because the government failure component of the theory so nicely exemplifies the effect of imposing the "veil of ignorance"—the principal condition that characterizes the original position, from which the terms of the idealized social contract are generated. The core of Rawls' unique insight[6] is that principles of justice derived by hypothesized societal consensus must be blind to the contracting parties' knowledge of their particular circumstances in life, so that "no one is able to design principles to favor his particular condition." Among the essential features of this original position are that no one knows "his place in society, his class position or social status, nor does any one know his fortune in the distribution of natural assets and abilities, his intelligence, strength, and the like. I shall even assume that the parties do not know their conceptions of the good or their special psychological propensities."[7]

Applying this analytical framework to particular laws, Professor Deborah Merritt explains that we "should ask whether the challenged legislation could reasonably have been adopted by community members if no one in the community knew, at the time the law was adopted, whether they would be in the advantaged or disadvantaged class. If the law might have been adopted by voters operating behind this 'veil of ignorance,' then [it is just]."[8] As Merritt observes, "Rawls himself saw that the idea of the original position can be used to measure the fairness of specific laws."[9] Rawls describes a "four-stage sequence" by which the technique of the hypothesized consensus in an original position is applied, first to produce very general principles of justice (such as "each person is to have an equal right to the most extensive basic liberty compatible with a similar liberty for others"), second to construct a constitution and a basic political form, third to enact specific laws, and fourth to apply those laws in particular situations. Each step is to be governed by the dictates produced by the prior: the constitution must be consistent with general principles of justice, laws consistent with the constitution, and adjudication consistent with laws. Thus, Rawls does not advocate that we harken back to the rarified original position at each stage. Nevertheless, he retains elements of the original position at each stage, since at each the decision makers are still subject to a form of the veil of ignorance. The veil is nearly (but not absolutely) complete at the first stage, it is partially lifted in order to form the constitution, and lifted still further to enact legislation—all as needed to make the decision with the particularity required at each stage. But we are still to suppose that, in crafting just legislation, legislators (acting as model ethicists and not as political representatives) are not to consider the particulars about themselves or their constituents.[10]

In our context, the veil of ignorance provides a convincing answer to why low demanding majorities are required to pay higher taxes in order to support the public good desires of high demanding minorities. Under the veil of ignorance, we have no notion of whether, for a particular collective good, we will be in the majority of the electorate that subsidizes high demanders or whether we will be in the minority that is forced to rely on voluntary initiative. Therefore, from the position of the ideal legislator, we should be eager to endorse a use of the exemption that spreads over society generally a portion of the cost of providing a needed public service that the majoritarian political process is structurally incapable of subsidizing directly. We are protected if we should land in the disenfranchised group, but the burden is not oppressive if we do not. Thus, the charitable tax exemption might be thought of as a form of mutual social insurance that most people would agree to opt into.[11]

The donative theory is also consistent with Rawls' "difference principle," which in essence is a much stronger, but more controversial, application of the preceding analysis. In simplified form, Rawls reasons that one of the two primary principles of justice that derives directly from the idealized original position is that an unequal distribution of economic privileges is just only if it is reasonably calculated to enhance the position of those who are in the worst position.[12] Thus, Rawls assumes that everyone in the original position is an extreme risk avoider: each chooses governing principles according to the "maximin rule" which assumes that one's place in society is selected by his worst enemy.[13] A use of the exemption that protects political minorities satisfies this condition. However, Rawlsian support for the donative theory does not depend on his controversial difference principle or maximin strategy. A donative theory is derivable directly from the original position analysis without adopting the extreme assumptions of risk aversion that underlie these arguments.[14]

The donative theory is necessary for this Rawlsian justification of the charitable exemption to hold because, from the ideal original position, it is impossible to compile a list of concrete activities that deserve an exemption in all circumstances. The veil of ignorance requires a degree of abstraction that precludes such specific legislation. As the government failure analysis demonstrates, such a statute is even less likely as the veil of ignorance begins to lift, since majoritarian legislatures are unlikely to reflect the interest of high-demanding voters, especially in the case of goods for which the public's desire varies widely. As a result, in order for every deserving group in society potentially to benefit from the exemption, we must employ a concept of charity that is open-ended as to subject matter but bounded by a requirement of some demonstrated need for public subsidy. The donative theory of the charitable exemption operates precisely in this fashion by automatically subsidizing whatever activities garner substantial voluntary support from the community.

Once this Rawlsian framework is understood, elitism is not a valid objection because of the reciprocity of the charitable exemption among different donative groups. Using Hansmann's illustration from Chapter 7, rich Met-goers will pay somewhat higher taxes to support the perhaps more provincial interests that happen to attract donations in Peoria. The apparent unfairness exists only when considering a single charity. At a more societal level that evaluates the charitable sector as a whole, all taxpayers are likely to benefit from the donative exemption since those who unwillingly contribute to the charitable causes of others will likewise receive support for their own philanthropic interests. The fact that those able to give the most will tend to receive the larger subsidy is a just inequity because it is necessary in order for those who are least advantaged to receive any subsidy.[15]

This explanation assumes that everyone donates, but, under certain assumptions, it holds up even for those who do not donate to anything. There may be potential donors who desire to support undersupplied public goods, but who do not wish to engage in the "search costs" to determine which, among many competing objects of charity, are the most deserving. For them, the exemption would operate like the United Way: they pay marginally more taxes to be distributed as an implicit tax subsidy according to the donative choices made by others. Such a system benefits all participants inclined to give, even though some participants are not actual donors.

Finally, the apparent regressivity of a donative exemption is countered by observing that the reciprocal support that the rich will provide through the tax system to the favored activities of others will tend to be character- ized by at least an equal degree of progressivity (perhaps more), for the very reason that the rich have more income and property to tax, and it is sometimes taxed at a higher rate. It might be possible to correct further for social inequities by giving less weight to gifts from rich patrons than from poor ones, but this would impose extreme administrative burdens. Also, this would not help those who are the very worst off and therefore unable to donate at all. Indeed, the wealth-neutral approach is likely to benefit the poor more because they are frequent objects of donations and hence of the accompanying tax subsidy.

Thus, properly understood, the charitable exemption has a much stronger moral base than most legislation. Like the principles of justice derived from Rawls' original position, it is blind to individuals' "conception of the good." As Rawls states, "other things equal, one conception of justice is to be preferred to another when it is founded upon markedly simpler general facts, and its choice does not depend upon elaborate calculations in the light of a vast array of theoretically defined possibilities."[16] The donative theory of the exemption, in stark contrast to other tax legislation, partakes remarkably of these qualities of generality.

Nozick's Libertarian Theory of Justice

According to Nozick, any activity of government that goes beyond the role of a "minimal, nightwatchman state" violates the rights of its citizens. The minimal state is "limited to the narrow functions of protection against force, theft, fraud, enforcement of contracts, and so on." Consequently, "the state may not use its coercive apparatus for the purpose of getting some citizens to aid others."[17] In other words, any taxation that accomplishes a redistributive purpose (rather than a protective, policing purpose) is illegitimate.

The illegitimacy of taxation by the welfare state might suggest as a Nozickian justification for the charitable exemption the banality that an absence of taxation, in whatever form, is better than its presence. But generalized tax opposition does nothing to justify the particular form of exemption that applies to charities, or to instruct us what are charities for purposes of the exemption. On surface inspection, a Nozickian appears to have nothing more to contribute to the debate than that all tax exemptions are equally valid, whether they are for charities or for brothels, since Nozick's brand of extreme libertarianism provides no half-way principles for shaping society's laws within an imperfect structure. Although in the ideal state of affairs one might favor private initiative and cooperation as a complete alternative to government, we do not live in a world that even approximates this ideal. Instead, philanthropy exists on a small island surrounded by a sea of government filled with its many funding vessels. It seems of little consequence that this island too might be swamped by taxation.

Indeed, one might expect a Nozickian to argue *against* the charitable exemption on the grounds that, within an impure state where taxation is the norm, an exemption constitutes an implicit subsidy to the exempt activity. Therefore, the failure to tax some institutions might itself be viewed as a form of illegitimate redistribution.

Deeper reflection on Nozick's theory, however, reveals substantial support for a charitable exemption founded on donative principles. Under the libertarian view, philanthropy is not merely residual to the failure of government to supply a good that is not available through the private marketplace; instead, given the libertarian view that government's proper role is limited to preventing citizens from encroaching on each others' rights, philanthropy is the *primary* alternative to market failure.[18] "The only morally legitimate way that will work for society to provide [public] goods is the encouragement of private philanthropy. So there is a major role for private philanthropy in a free democratic society, a role that becomes more and more significant as one becomes stricter and stricter in one's libertarian views."[19]

Still, Nozick can be read as opposed to any form of government subsidy for donations when he devotes several pages to debunking the public goods justification for government spending.[20] In so doing, Nozick maintains that no free-rider disincentive to giving disables voluntary relief of societal ills because the following two options are open to all who are concerned about those ills: (1) donating to specific individuals, which will fully confer to the donor the satisfaction of having solved a discrete portion of the problem; or (2) to the extent the donor is satisfied only by curing the societal ill at a macro level (by wiping out poverty, hunger etc.), those who are like minded are free to band together voluntarily to form a consortium that agrees to give only on the condition that all other members contribute. However, Nozick fails to grapple with the considerable transaction costs that inhibit the formation of such large contractual organizations of contributors, as well as the practical difficulty of ensuring that all who in fact derive psychic gratification from the organization's activity are identified and signed up. Thomas Nagel quips that this reliance on voluntary relief of poverty "is no more plausible coming from Nozick than it was coming from Barry Goldwater."[21] Nozick is willing to overlook these obstacles to philanthropy because, ultimately, he views the alternative of government coercion as illegitimate regardless, unless every single individual who is taxed in fact consents to the tax. Relaxing these demands of extreme libertarianism somewhat, and recognizing the inevitability of free riding, it does not entail a large compromise of Nozick's position to allow room for some government encouragement of voluntary behavior.

The donative theory garners additional support from the libertarian moral outlook by undoing the redistributive characterization that otherwise might apply to an implicit tax subsidy. Under the donative theory, the exemption's implicit subsidy is conferred not on those who are deemed by government to be less advantaged, but instead on those objects that individual donors desire but are unable to purchase in a market transaction. Thus, the donative theory, properly understood, confers a subsidy in order to satisfy the *donor's* desire to rid the world of hunger, not principally to satisfy the appetites of the hungry per se (or in the case of donors who seek only public recognition from their gifts, the subsidy is conferred to those proxied donors whose recognition the actual donor seeks). In rigorous theory, the subsidy benefits the recipients of the charity secondarily only as a means of accomplishing the donors' desires.

This conception of the exemption's subsidy dampens its redistributive quality. Once seen in this light, the purpose of the subsidy is no longer to tax the wealthy in order to support the needy; it is to relieve from government burden those acts of individual initiative that are directed toward satisfying a private desire that can be met only through a public good. The donative theory of the charitable exemption is necessary to save it from the libertarian accusation of being merely another redistributive tool of the welfare state because only this theory judges the needs of the recipients by the desires of voluntary donors. In sum, in a society where illicit taxation exists, libertarians must view the implicit support for philanthropy conferred by the charitable exemption as at least a second-best option. In the libertarian view, if there is any proper governmental role in supporting social causes, it would be this minimal role of conferring a shadow subsidy.

Classic Liberalism and the Value of Pluralism

Rawls and Nozick present very intricate versions of liberal moral theory, but even the most rudimentary form of liberalism supports the donative theory. A fundamental tenet common to all liberal theories of justice is that members of society are autonomous moral agents, each free to pursue his own notion of the good. This elemental freedom constitutes a basic constraint on the political sphere. The charitable exemption partakes of this autonomous tradition. It is said to be born out of the "spirit of classic liberalism," whose "dominant tenets . . . were distrust of government and faith that the progress and well-being of mankind could best be achieved by natural forces, harmonizing the individual actions of men who were left untrammeled."[22] Perhaps the strongest statement of this view is a frequently-quoted explanation from Harvard President Charles Eliot in 1872 of why a system of private educational institutions supported by tax exemptions is superior to one of direct government funding:

> The exemption method fosters public spirit, while the [government] grant method . . . annihilates it . . . . The exemption method fosters the public virtues of self-respect and reliance; the grant method leads straight to an abject dependence upon that superior power—Government. The proximate effects of the two methods of state action are as different as well-being from pauperism, as republicanism from communism.[23]

In order for these liberal, pluralistic benefits to be fully realized, however, it is necessary to formulate the charitable exemption according to the donative theory. Only under this theory is the charitable subsidy distributed automatically based on autonomous decisions by individual donors that determine which activities within the nonprofit sector are socially valued. Fashioning the exemption under the community benefit theory, for instance, would relegate it to merely another mechanism for the government to, in effect, make direct spending decisions by selecting which nonprofit activities confer a sufficient benefit to the community to deserve tax relief. More troubling still, these normative political judgments would be made by revenue agents rather than elected officials or agencies in charge of substantive social policy. We might instead call on the courts to define charitable, as occurs under the approach that draws the exemption's substantive content from the common law of charitable trusts,[24] but it is impossible to promote pluralism and diversity of view by making these judgments through an institution that necessarily reflects collective societal values as seen from the privileged and protected perspective of the judiciary. This conflict would be particularly severe if the court were asked to play the role of social arbiter for the worth of religious organizations.[25]

Those moral theorists who stress the value of pluralism in the third sector thus help us to understand why only the donative theory is compatible with the present structure of the charitable exemption. Whereas any other theory delegates discrete value judgments to government decisionmakers, "the essence of the advantage of th[e donative] system is that it is automatic. The government does not control the flow of funds to the various organizations; the receipts of each organization are determined by the values and the choices of private givers. The donors determine the direction of their own funds, and the distribution of 'tax savings' as well."[26]

One must be careful, though, in relating these noble thoughts to the humble tax exemption, for some exemption advocates would rely on such arguments of moral superiority to extend the exemption to the entire nonprofit sector, contending that, in any of its activities, it offers a valued alternative to markets and government.[27] This position too loosely accounts for the benefits of pluralism and the need for the exemption to promote those benefits. As Professor Gergen has explained, using the exemption simply as an encouragement for "self-expression" is not defensible because self-expression is not unique to nonprofit enterprise. "My purchase of season tickets to see the Texas Longhorns play football is a form of self-expression. Why is it not equally deserving of a tax preference?"[28] Only the donative theory of the charitable exemption successfully identifies the particular acts of self-expression that deserve subsidy, without undermining through excessive government involvement the pluralism that self-expression fosters. We value most the form of pluralism inherent in voluntary support of public causes because this support is the only clear sign that the benefits fostered are not available elsewhere.

The Communitarian Critique of Liberalism

Yet another school of moral and political theory known as communitarian has emerged in recent years. The communitarian critique challenges the assumptions underlying all of the foregoing branches of liberalism by questioning their individualistic orientation. According to this critique, all versions of liberalism—classic, contractarian and libertarian—are flawed by their premise that society is composed of atomistic, autonomous individuals differentiated from the state who form values and preferences independently from each other. The focus of liberal theories of justice is on individual rights as a means to guard against. In the view of communitarians, this a priori separation of the individual from others and from society is false. Instead, individuals have no meaningful identity separate from the constitutive and supporting institutions of family, church, school, clubs, neighborhood, etc. Communitarians believe that the modern liberal theories developed by Rawls and Nozick lose sight of the preeminence of these multiple dimensions of community for shaping individual identities, values, and conflicts.

This still developmental and loosely formed body of thought has potentially revolutionary significance in many realms—political, moral, social, philosophical, psychological, and legal—only some of which relate to our present inquiry.[29] Of particular importance is the concern that modern legal institutions neglect the various forms of community and provide insufficient opportunities to form and strengthen community ties. For instance, the conventional tax-and-spend mode of operation by the welfare state creates the win-lose or us-them mentality that government is taking my money and giving it to others. The welfare state also produces a separation between individuals and their community and an excessive focus on individual rights by distributing its benefits according to defined entitlements that are enforced through legal due process.[30] It is these communitarian concerns in the social and political realms to which the donative theory is most responsive.

In the political realm, organizing the charitable exemption according to donative principles offers an alternative to government provision that is voluntary and benevolent, as opposed to coercive and formalized, without abandoning altogether government support for social problems. Returning social provision to localized private initiative harkens to notions of participatory democracy and civic virtue drawn from classic republicanism, with its Aristotelian and Jeffersonian traditions that lie at the base of our political origins.[31] In contrast with modern, liberal political theory which sees governance as a competitive contest among special interest groups who seek legislative support from the limited public funding trough, the subsidy provided through the donative theory leaves plenty of room for all seekers. Indeed, the more who are exempt, the higher are the subsidies, since the greater is the residual tax from which they are relieved. By choosing its objects of subsidy through means of self-governance rather than representative governance, the donative theory promotes civic virtue. In the words of philosopher and social critic Michael Walzer, "The act of giving is good in itself; it builds a sense of solidarity and communal competence . . . . The connected activities of organizing fund-raising campaigns and deciding how to spend the money will involve ordinary citizens in work that parallels and supplements the work of [government] officials . . . . One might think of the gift relationship as a kind of politics: like the vote, the petition, and the demonstration, the gift is a way of giving concrete meaning to the union of citizens."[32]

In the social realm, the donative theory is broadly consistent with the communitarian critique by promoting the formation of actual communities. Whereas liberalism has been described as "communo-pathic," the charitable exemption administered according to donative theories is "communo-generative."[33] The classic charitable institutions of churches and schools are regarded as paradigms to which communitarian theory applies.[34] The donative theory reveals that, in part, this is due to their donative status. Because the act of giving is altruistic (other-regarding), in this very act is the establishment or connection with a community of interest. Whereas liberalism tends to regard altruism as an anomaly to be explained either by exception to or as a consequence of individualistic desires, altruism is primary in a communitarian outlook. Liberal theory views altruism as a secondary alternative to government provision dictated by self-interested voting patterns. Communitarian theory views altruism as primary and pre-political—as a natural dimension of social behavior and structure. Constructing a shadow subsidy that follows altruistic behavior only further reinforces its primacy.

Drawing together all of these schools of distributive justice, the donative theory provides a partial resolution of the classic dilemma of how the welfare state can perform its regulative and redistributive functions without constraining individual values and invading individual choice. The solution has been expressed by Rawls in terms of liberal pluralism, by Nozick in terms of Utopian societies, and by critics of liberalism in terms of communitarianism. In each of these guises, the essential solution is for people of like-minded concern to form communities of interest to address social problems. The donative theory employs the charitable tax exemption to encourage this result, not just through rhetoric but through implicit financial support. It finds its sense of community from the meaningful expression of actual support rather than from the speculative and self-serving assertions of community benefit that come from all nonprofits. The donative theory is therefore one vehicle for achieving the shared ideal of "society as a social union of social unions."[35]

Notes

1. *See* CHANDRAN KUKATHAS & PHILIP PETTIT, RAWLS: A THEORY OF JUSTICE AND ITS CRITICS (1990) (discussing impact of and contrast between the two works); JOHN PAUL, READING NOZICK 1–2 (1981) (same); THOMAS POGGE, REALIZING RAWLS 15–16 (1989) (same); Jeffrie G. Murphy, *Rights and Borderline Cases*, 19 ARIZ. L. REV. 228, 228 (1977) (these two competing theories of justice "are currently dominating discussion within contemporary Anglo-American moral, social, political, and legal philosophy"); (discussing impact of and contrast between the two works). *See generally* JAMES STERBA, JUSTICE: ALTERNATIVE POLITICAL PERSPECTIVES 2–12 (1980) (outlining modern theories of justice).

2. JOHN RAWLS, A THEORY OF JUSTICE 11–12 (1971).

3. *Id.* at 83, 153.

4. ROBERT NOZICK, ANARCHY, STATE AND UTOPIA 333–34 (1974). *See also id.* at 149–55, 198–204 (responding to Rawls).

5. The leading communitarian works are ALASDAIR MACINTYRE, AFTER VIRTUE (1981); MICHAEL J. SANDEL, LIBERALISM AND THE LIMITS OF JUSTICE (1982); and MICHAEL WALZER, SPHERES OF JUSTICE (1983). *See generally* LIBERALISM AND ITS CRITICS (Michael Sandel ed., 1984); Stephen A. Gardbaum, *Law, Politics, and the Claims of Community*, 90 MICH. L. REV. 685, 689 (1992).

6. CHANDRAN KUKATHAS & PHILLIP PETTIT, A THEORY OF JUSTICE AND ITS CRITICS 36–59 (1990), and ROBERT WOLFF, UNDERSTANDING RAWLS 60–63 (1977) are useful for parsing the essential from the nonessential in Rawls' complex and often dense exegesis.

7. RAWLS, *supra* note 2, at 12. *See also id.* at 136–42.

8. Deborah Merritt, *Communicable Disease and Constitutional Law: Controlling AIDS*, 61 N.Y.U.L. REV. 739, 787 (1986).

9. *Id.* at 786 n.232. *See also* Stephen Griffin, *Reconstructing Rawls' Theory of Justice: Developing a Public Values Philosophy of the Constitution*, 62 N.Y.U.L. REV. 715 (1987) (discussing relevance to legal thought).

10. RAWLS, *supra* note 2, at 196–201, 358. Further elaboration of this point is contained in Rawls' later work, POLITICAL LIBERALISM (1993), especially at 88–129 and 336–40.

11. We have relaxed the unanimity principle, as is appropriate under Rawls' analysis, because as the decisions to be made become more specific and less in the nature of broad principles of justice, more facts about society must be revealed in order to inform the hypothesized decisionmakers, and, as this occurs, it is more likely the decisionmakers will adopt idiosyncratic views. *See* RAWLS, supra note 2, at 200. Nevertheless, we believe the argument is powerful enough that a high degree of consensus can be expected, perhaps even unanimity.

12. *Id.* at 83.

13. *Id.* at 151–57.

14. *See* BRIAN BARRY, THE LIBERAL THEORY OF JUSTICE108–15 (1973) (critique of the maximin rule); KUKATHAS & PETTIT, *supra* note 6, at 39–42 (same).

15. *Cf.* John G. Simon, *The Tax Treatment of Nonprofit Organizations: A Review of Federal and State Policies*, *in* THE NONPROFIT SECTOR: A RESEARCH HANDBOOK 67, 86 (Walter W. Powell ed., 1987) (concluding that the "dynastic" quality of the deduction is an acceptable imperfection in the system).

16. RAWLS, *supra* note 2, at 142.

17. NOZICK, *supra* note 4, at ix.

18. *Id.* at 265.

19. Baruch Brody, *Private Philanthropy and Positive Rights*, 4 SOC. PHIL. & POLICY 79, 85–87 (Spring 1987).

20. NOZICK, *supra* note 4, at 265–68.

21. Steven Nagel, *Libertarianism Without Foundations*, *in* PAUL, *supra* note 1, at 199.

22. Chauncey Belknap, *The Federal Income Tax Exemption of Charitable Organizations: Its History and Underlying Policy*, *in* RESEARCH PAPERS SPONSORED BY THE COMMISSION ON PRIVATE PHILANTHROPY AND PUBLIC NEEDS 2025, 2031 (U.S. Dep't of the Treasury ed., 1977); *see id.* at 2030 (stressing the consistency of the charitable exemption with "the spread of the laissez faire doctrine" which "lent color of philosophic sanction to a process" where "private relief was deemed more efficacious than governmental").

23. CHARLES W. ELIOT, THE MAN AND HIS BELIEFS 667, 675 (William Nielson ed., 1926), *quoted in* Belknap, *supra* note 22, at 2038–39. Further quotes of Eliot and more explanation of the context of his remarks are found in Boris I. Bittker & George K. Rahdert, *The Exemption of Nonprofit Organizations from Federal Income Taxation*, 85 YALE L.J. 299, 332 (1976). *See also* Walz v. Tax Commission, 397 U.S. 664, 674 (1970) (religious groups are exempt because they "enhance a desirable pluralism of viewpoint and enterprise"); Belknap, *supra* note 22, at 2036–37 (the tax exemption "maintain[s] [a] rich diversity of values and abilities, . . . intellectual freedom, multiplicity of viewpoints and interest, and diversity of individual inspiration and action"). *Cf.* JAMES DOUGLAS, WHY CHARITY? THE CASE FOR A THIRD SECTOR VIII-10 (1983) ("It is th[e] ability to tolerate different views

of the public good that the pluralistic philosophy sees as the characteristic of a free society. Voluntary organizations are one of the means—indeed a necessary and essential means—of putting that philosophy into practice.").

24. *Cf.* Stanford v. Kentucky, 109 S. Ct. 2969, 2974–75, 2977 (1989) (Eighth Amendment requires Court to look to "conceptions of decency . . . of modern American society as a whole" and to find a "settled national consensus"); Michael H. v. Gerald D., 109 S. Ct. 2333, 2341–44 (1989 (same, for an asserted liberty interest to be protected by substantive due process).

25. *See* Texas Monthly, Inc. v. Bullock, 489 U.S.1, n.2 (1989) ("inquiry into the particular contributions of each religious group 'would introduce an element of governmental evaluation and standards as to the worth of particular social welfare programs, thus producing a kind of day-to-day relationship which the policy of neutrality seeks to minimize.'").

26. Belknap, *supra* note 22, at 2039.

27. *See, e.g.*, DOUGLAS, *supra* note 23, at *Conclusion* at 17:

> The way the idea of democracy is developed in the western world, [it] contains two different strands, one emphasizing the individual and hence diversity and one emphasizing the majoritarian principle and hence uniformity. . . . The institutions of the Third Sector are one of the principal sources of the flexibility which enables a free society to preserve both strands and thus avoid both the practical injustices and the logical contradictions that would flow from relying too heavily either on self-regarding market forces or on an all embracing role for government.

See also Rob Atkinson, *Altruism in Nonprofit Organizations*, 31 B.C.L. REV. 501, 629 (1990) (Extending the exemption to virtually all nonprofits "would necessarily promote the acknowledged metabenefit of pluralism; [nonprofit] provision of goods and services is an alternative to both market and governmental provision"). Atkinson's analysis of pluralism bears superficial resemblances to ours, for he speaks in terms of the pluralistic benefit of "altruism," but his definition of altruism is so broad as to encompass virtually all nonprofit organizations, regardless of their donative status. For a further discussion of Atkinson's altruism theory, see Chapter 6 at 85-90.

28. Mark Gergen, *The Case for the Charitable Contributions Deduction*, 74 VA. L. REV. 1393, 1395 (1988).

29. For example, we need not concern ourselves with much of the philosophical debate, which has focused on the ontological claims regarding the meaning and identity of self in terms of whether we are "individuated, atomized" selves with identity apart from our histories and values or instead whether we are "situated, encumbered" selves that are unalterably products of our communities. For material explaining and distinguishing these various claims, see Allen E. Buchanan, *Assessing the Communitarian Critique of Liberalism*, 99 ETHICS 852–53 (1989); Stephen A. Gardbaum, *Law, Politics, and the Claims of Community*, 90 MICH. L. REV. 685, 689 (1992).

30. *See generally* MARY ANN GLENDON, RIGHTS TALK (1991).

31. On the revival of participatory, republican democracy, see Suzanna Sherry, *Civic Virtue and the Feminine Voice in Constitutional Adjudication*, 72 VA. L. REV. 543, 544–59 (1986); Frank Michelman, *Law's Republic*, 97 YALE L. J. 1493 (1988); Cass Sunstein, *Beyond the Republican Revival*, 97 YALE L. J. (1988).

32. WALZER, *supra* note 5, at 85.

33. We borrow this terminology from Cynthia A. Ward, *The Limits of "Liberal Republicanism": Why Group-Based Remedies and Republican Citizenship Don't Mix*, 91 COLUM. L. REV. 581, 583–84 (1991).

34. *See* Symposium, *Individualism and Communitarianism in Contemporary Legal Systems: Tensions and Accommodations*, 1993 BRIG. YOUNG U. L. REV. 385; Michael Walzer, *The Communitarian Critique of Liberalism*, 18 POL. THEORY 6, 17 (1990).

35. JOHN RAWLS, POLITICAL LIBERALISM 321 (1993).

10

Evaluating the Donative Theory

The preceding chapters develop the fundamental economic, behavioral and moral principles underlying the donative theory. In this chapter, we subject the theory to the same evaluative criteria as we have other theories. We also illustrate that, unlike other theories, the donative theory explains the major limitations on exempt status imposed by the tax laws and is consistent with prior judicial precedent and historic notions of what constitutes a "charity."

Deservedness

The donative theory offers an elegant and powerful rationale for subsidizing the objects of donative activity, one that fully meets both the worth and need components of the deservedness criterion. Donors' selections of particular objects of philanthropy from the many available alternatives reveal those that the public finds are of special worth. An institution's resort to solicitations evidences that its needs are not being met elsewhere. We can be assured that donations themselves will not fully satisfy this need since donors do not lightly relinquish their assets; in the absence of a quid pro quo return, the free-rider incentive that affects the motivation to give tells us that donors as a whole systematically will give less than the deservedness that they perceive (as measured hypothetically by their willingness to purchase the good if it were capable of being delivered in ordinary market transactions). Hence, the existence of substantial donative support from the public at large signals the need for an additional, shadow subsidy to take up the donative slack.

In broad perspective, the donative theory stands in fundamental contrast to other theories of the charitable exemption in the social engine that it uses to establish the exemption's proper scope. The theory that refers to the law of charitable trusts unsuccessfully employs a common law judicial process to define the subject matter limits of the exemption. Other approaches employ a political process to make ad hoc, normative judgments of which activities deserve the exemption based on intensely empirical inquiries.[1] For instance, the community benefit theory requires taxing authorities to determine which activities are performed better in a nonprofit setting, and Professor Hansmann's capital subsidy theory requires in addition a determination of which such activities suffer a disadvantage in obtaining capital financing. Only the donative theory employs a market-like process that relies on the individual desires of donors who select the objects of charity that deserve public support. Donors "vote" for an indirect subsidy by participating in a "market in altruism" when they have been unsuccessful in obtaining direct provision through actual political or market mechanisms. This mechanism automatically makes the intensely empirical determinations of which among the universe of activities that conceivably deserve support actually earn the exemption by providing services that are not otherwise available. This theory also actively induces those nonprofit firms with sagging support to search out new ways to satisfy public needs.

Proportionality

On first inspection, the donative theory appears to meet the proportionality criterion only roughly. Unlike the charitable deduction which operates in a perfect sliding scale fashion, the exemption does not automatically match donations dollar for dollar by a proportionate amount of tax support. Nevertheless, the exemption fares passably well with respect to the property tax because the amount of property a donative nonprofit holds likely is proportionate to the amount of contributions it receives. Similarly, an exemption from paying sales tax on purchases by donative nonprofits provides a subsidy that is roughly proportionate to the size of a donative institution, in contrast with an exemption from charging sales tax, which would be inversely related to an institution's donative base.

For the income tax, the connection between the size of the subsidy (determined roughly by earned surplus) and the criterion for deservedness (donations) is much more attenuated. Generally, gifts are not considered as income to the recipient by virtue of I.R.C. § 102.[2] Therefore, the value of an income tax exemption with respect to donations alone is zero.[3] Even if donations were considered income, purely donative organizations likely would offset that income by the expenses entailed in the organization's providing its services for free, and therefore an income tax exemption still would not provide any implicit subsidy to these institutions. For mixed donative and commercial nonprofits such as education and the performing arts that potentially earn taxable income, however, the potential subsidy effect is quite large. A random sampling from all medium-to-large 501(c)(3) organizations in 1983 revealed that 86% earned some surplus, that the average surplus was $2.7 million per entity, and that the average operating margin (surplus as a portion of total revenues) was 10%.[4] Significantly, these figures were not markedly different for religious and educational institutions than for more commercial nonprofits such as health care institutions.[5]

Nevertheless, analysis of the proportionality criterion is still complex for profit-earning nonprofits because the relationship between the indicium of deservedness and the level of subsidy may turn on whether donations are devoted to capital or operating costs. A nonprofit that applies its contributions to capital funding needs is likely to generate more revenues from income-producing sales of goods or services. Schools with the largest endowments, for example, are likely to have the most tuition-paying students because they will have the largest facilities. However, there still may not be a positive relationship to taxable income because even donated capital assets generate depreciation expenses to offset the enhanced revenues. Donations applied to operating costs can paradoxically result in less taxable income since funds spent on the organization's revenue-producing activities generally are deductible as business expenses. Stated differently, organizations that need to devote donations to operating expenses probably generate no operating surplus. The fact that they need to solicit donations indicates that, over the long run, their business receipts are less than their expenses.

This mismatch can be minimized to some degree by the manner in which the donative theory is administered. In Chapter 11, we propose a threshold for donative status that requires no more than one-third donative support. The other two-thirds of revenues can come from commercial sales, which provide more of a predictable base for a donative subsidy under the income tax. Still, the objection remains that the size of that subsidy is inversely related to the size of the donative base above the threshold. Those entities with the highest proportion of donations will, all else being equal, receive the least implicit income tax subsidy. Further possible refinements are suggested in Chapter 11, such as multiple levels of charitable status that confer increasing tax benefits to entities with larger proportionate donative bases. But regardless of what is done, donations inherently will always have at best only a rough relationship to the income tax subsidy.

This level of compromise in proportionality seems unsatisfactory until one realizes that the donative theory, despite these imperfections, provides the most accurate measure of deservedness available. This insight comes from Burton Weisbrod's explanation of government failure. We previously have noted that a principal litmus test for proportionality is whether, assuming a given activity deserves subsidy, the exemption is a more sensible means to administer the subsidy than a direct government grant. The "twin failure" rationale underlying the donative theory confronts this inquiry directly. It reveals that where substantial donations exist, direct government aid must be unavailable because it is the failure of the government to serve a high-demanding minority that leaves donors with no other alternative than to make voluntary contributions. In essence, the donative theory is designed to cover only cases where the tax subsidy is necessarily a second best solution because the theory excludes all cases where the government in fact subsidizes production directly in sufficient amount. This observation establishes why the donative theory elegantly satisfies the proportionality criterion: The political stalemate that prevents a direct government subsidy means that, however flawed, an implicit subsidy through the tax system is the only available mechanism for a subsidy. Proportionality is thus satisfied because, intrinsically, no more accurate mechanism for direct government support is available in cases where the donative theory applies.

The objection still remains, however, that among alternate types of implicit tax subsidies, some are more proportional than others. For example, the subsidy provided by the charitable donations deduction appears to be the most proportional, because it exactly matches the level of donative activity (the more donations, the greater the subsidy). One might ask, then, why the donative theory does not require that the charitable deduction be made the sole source of implicit tax support. The resulting loss in total tax subsidies could be made up by multiplying the income-deducting effect of individual donations (that is, deduct $200 for a $100 gift), or by converting the deduction to a tax credit, which would also ease the regressive effect of deductions under a bracketed tax. We do not oppose such refinements in the implicit tax subsidy system as a matter of theory, only as a matter of pragmatics. It is not our purpose to radically reformulate the exemption to perfectly match the proportionality criterion. Doing so would ignore or violate other of our evaluative criteria such as universality and historical consistency that assume the continuation of the exemption in roughly the same form in which it has existed for four centuries. Moreover, even if we were to rely solely on a new version of the charitable deduction, we would still need some mechanism for identifying which entities are eligible to receive such tax-deductible contributions, a job that is now done by the 501(c)(3) concept of charity. Therefore, the donative theory would still be necessary in order to define what is a charity for purposes of the deduction; in other words, a taxpayer could deduct contributions only to entities that receive substantial donative support from other taxpayers. The donative theory is needed in order to explain why this is so, even if the income or other tax exemptions were to be abandoned.

Universality

The earlier discussion observed the complementary aspects of the donative tax subsidy: the charitable *deduction* is directed to the *donor* to stimulate making a gift while the *exemption* goes to the *recipient* to enable the gift to be more productive. This symmetrical aspect of the donative theory provides one of its greatest strengths. Unlike all other theories of the charitable exemption, it satisfies the deservedness criterion for both the income tax exemption and the property tax exemption at the same time that it justifies the charitable deduction. This universality is critical to a successful theory of charity because, under the structure of the federal and most state codes, all three tax benefits follow automatically once the organization is characterized as charitable. Only by defining charities as organizations that receive substantial donative support is it possible to make sense of the unified federal/state, exemption/deduction structure.

A further dimension of the donative theory's universality is its ability to explain the value-added tax exemption that many states confer on sales *to* charities.[6] This exemption from *paying* sales tax provides a form of matching subsidy that assists donations in being more productive by relieving them of the tax that otherwise is imposed when the donations are used to purchase supplies. Notably, the donative theory would not provide strong support for a value-added tax exemption on sales *by* nonprofits since such an exemption would target primarily commercial nonprofits. Consistently, very few states exempt charities from *charging* sales tax.[7]

So far, however, we have not examined whether the donative theory is capable of explaining the major restrictions on exempt status other than by merely accommodating them as side constraints unrelated to the core theory. Professor John Simon, for example, explains these limitations in terms of the tax law's "border patrol function," that is, as necessary "to keep nonprofit organizations from wandering off their reservation into the territory of government and business."[8] This metaphor, although descriptively appealing, is entirely question-begging as a normative explanation. Who is to say these areas are not the territory of nonprofits, other than the border police themselves? Without some explanation that defines the border, the proper metaphor for these restrictions is a border-*creating* function. Simon in fact offers some explanations for how the borders have been drawn, but few relate to the core rationale for exempting charitable entities.

If the donative theory is capable of integrating these limitations as part of its general rationale, the theory's explanatory power would be quite remarkable. We will examine in turn the four major restrictions on eligibility for tax exemption: the requirement of nonprofit status, which includes the prohibition on private inurement; the preclusion of activities judged contrary to the public interest; the limitation on political activity; and the tax on unrelated business income. Although the particular justifications that underlie these disparate components of tax exemption have each generated considerable separate discussion and litigation, the donative theory can be shown to integrate each of these components into a comprehensive theory of charitable taxation.

Nonprofit Status

The various federal and state manifestations of the charitable tax exemption uniformly require that exempt organizations be organized as nonprofit entities. Usually, this restriction is enforced through a prohibition on the distribution of the exempt entity's assets or profits to private individuals (the "private inurement" prohibition).[9] While it is sometimes quite difficult to draw the boundaries between forbidden profit distributions and permitted payments of salaries and expenses,[10] the basic nondistribution requirement is uncontroversial. It simply prevents the entity's economic benefits from being diverted from the charitable class the entity is supposed to serve into the hands of "insiders" such as officers, directors, employees and the like.[11] Examples of prohibited private inurement include excessive salaries paid to a manager or controlling individual, excessive rent paid by the exempt entity to an insider lessor, inadequate rent charged by the entity to an insider, below-market loans made by the exempt entity to an insider, and so on.[12]

Because of the lack of controversy, little thought has been given to why charitable institutions must be nonprofit. One can conceive of a third-party relief organization, similar to the Red Cross, organized on a for-profit basis, contracting with governments and other agencies to provide relief services for a fee. In fact, as we previously have noted, in many sectors of the economy (health care and education, for example), nonprofit institutions co-exist alongside for-profit ones that perform many of the same services. If the donative theory can explain why nonprofit status is a *necessary* part of exemption, as opposed to simply a desirable condition, it would have a considerable explanatory advantage over other theories, which cannot do so. For instance, the relief of government burden theory is unable to explain why the exemption should not extend to profit-making institutions that equally relieve a governmental responsibility—say, a for-profit school that relies entirely on tuition. Because such a school also relieves the burden on government of educating any student who attends that school, no good reason exists not to grant such a school the same economic benefits granted to nonprofit schools that perform the same function.[13] The typical response to these arguments is that the nonprofit restriction is necessary to keep the firm's owners from siphoning off the exemption to their own proprietary advantage, but competitive restraints and shareholder oversight should prevent the owners from earning more than a fair market return on their investment, which return benefits the community by better attracting investment capital.

Under the donative theory, however, this limitation is an inherent part of the donative status of exempt organizations. This connection can be established by examining Henry Hansmann's rationale for the existence of nonprofit enterprise in all of its major manifestations. As we have noted in Chapters 5 and 6, Hansmann posits that nonprofit firms exist in those activities where the private inurement prohibition solves one of a variety of market imperfections that he refers to as "contract failure." Contract failure is any instance in which consumers are unable in normal market transactions to solve effectively a difficulty in monitoring the firm's output. The primary example is the desire of donors to contribute to various forms of public goods production.[14] Such payments suffer from a form of contract failure described as "marginal impact monitoring": donors to a joint product cannot determine whether their small portion of the production costs has been used to enhance the output. Because a public good is not divisible, there is no severable portion that could be said to have been produced only by virtue of a particular donor's contribution. This is precisely the same phenomenon that gives rise to free-riding, and this is the very characteristic of a donation that makes it a gift rather than a purchase.

Because of the monitoring problem, donors require some assurance that their gifts were actually used for the intended purpose, rather than siphoned off by the firm's managers. The nondistribution constraint that defines nonprofit status provides this assurance by denying the firm's managers the legal right to pay the contributions to themselves, other than as fair market value compensation for their services. This limitation enhances donors' trust by creating some greater assurance that nonprofit firms will use their funds to increase output. It is this enhanced trust that explains why donors prefer to give to nonprofits rather than to for-profit businesses.

This positive economic theory for the existence of nonprofits also suggests a normative explanation of why *only* nonprofits should be eligible for the charitable exemption, that is, why giving to for-profit firms, where it might exist, does not contain just as strong a signal of subsidy deservedness. The size of the monitoring problem and the resulting temptation for abuse suggest that a rational donor would always choose a nonprofit over a for-profit recipient, all else being equal. If a person makes a "donation" to a for-profit firm, therefore, some mechanism must have overcome the marginal impact monitoring problem. If no marginal impact monitoring problem exists, this in turn suggests that the "donation" is not a donation at all, but rather a quid pro quo exchange. This in turn indicates the lack of a free-rider disincentive to give. Without this disincentive, there is no case for a tax subsidy since the complete level of public desire is satisfied through the "donation" itself.

To take a concrete example, people typically feed their families by patronizing for-profit grocery stores. Since the transactions between these stores and their patrons are fully quid pro quo exchanges, no free-riding will occur and the private market will function to provide output equal to the level of demand. Hence, no exemption is necessary to further stimulate production. Contrast the situation in which an individual gives money to C.A.R.E. in order to "adopt" a starving child. One might argue that the identifiability of the aid recipient cures the monitoring problem that attends donations (perhaps pictures are sent to the donor each month documenting the child's improvement), and that these "gifts" purchase the exact quantity of relief effort desired by the individual donor, just as one purchases the exact quantity of food one needs from a private grocery store. But if, indeed, what motivates the donor is solely and literally the welfare of this one child, then there is no reason for the donor not to patronize a for-profit firm: the donor can just as easily go to the local grocery store, buy the necessary amount of food, and send it to the child in question (or have a for-profit firm at the child's location do this). In this case, no actual donation would occur since the putative "donor" has every incentive to give to the full extent of benefit derived. More likely, though, "adopting" a child is a marketing gimmick; the child would be fed by C.A.R.E. anyway and the absence of a particular $100 gift would have an undiscernible effect on each member of the bulk of recipients. From the donor's perspective, the gift is likewise probably not motivated solely by the welfare of this one child but at least in part by a more generalized desire to address child starvation worldwide, a desire that is shared by others. Thus, such a gift is most likely a classic public goods donation. The fact that giving to for-profits for hunger relief is unknown signals that this latter motive in fact predominates. If a significant amount of hunger relief support was in fact going to for-profit firms, we would have a strong indication of the absence of free-riding which would undermine the need component of deservedness.

This analysis shows that the nonprofit restriction is intimately related to the donative status of exempt organizations. Because we hypothesize that donations signal the need for the exemption subsidy, and that donations go only to nonprofit entities, nonprofit status is an integral part of explaining exemption under the donative theory.

Activities Contrary to the Public Interest

Current exemption law contains a public policy overlay that allows the IRS to deny exemption to groups that otherwise qualify but that pursue certain goals contrary to established public policy.[15] For example, in *Bob Jones University v. United States*, the Supreme Court held that the exemption may be denied to racially discriminatory private schools, despite the statute's omission of a general public policy requirement, because the Court found such a requirement to exist implicitly in the common law concept of "charity."[16] A potential objection to the donative theory is that it would overturn this public policy screen by blindly exempting any activity that attracts significant donative support from some segment of society. Such a result would force taxpayers to support a subsidy that validates the worst prejudices and meanest spirits of our populace. Of course, we could simply declare that certain donative objects are inconsistent with our core notions of what activities deserve a public subsidy, but this subjective approach to setting the definitional boundaries of the exemption is exactly what we hope to avoid with the donative theory, and so would offer little improvement over other theories.[17]

The donative theory solves this dilemma by offering a much more theoretically satisfactory rationale for the public policy limitation. This rationale derives from the government failure component of the donative theory discussed above. This aspect of the donative theory posits that a subsidy for donative activity is necessary because of the apathy of the majority of the electorate: low demanding voters who could vote for a *direct* government subsidy will not because they do not value the undersupplied good or service enough to incur the entire cost of providing it. These voters, however, are willing to incur the cost of a *partial, indirect* subsidy (exemption) because they are not actively opposed to the subsidized activity per se; they simply do not want as much as high-demanders willing to vote for full government subsidization. Their willingness to participate in the subsidy establishes an implicit social contract: if those who benefit the most from an undersupplied good donate a portion of the costs of additional production, those who benefit the least will agree to the tax burden of an implicit subsidy because they in turn will receive tax support for their favored projects.[18]

If exemption, however, is used to support activities of which the majority of voters disapprove, not due to diminished interest but due to outright distaste, then there is no social mechanism for expressing these negative preferences other than for society to withdraw the exemption. As a consequence, we can have no confidence that the social cost to them of supporting the exempt activity will be paid back through others' support of their causes. In economic jargon, when the donative theory is applied to public goods for which the negative externalities outweigh the positive, the result is neither Pareto optimal nor Kalder-Hicks optimal since, not only would some voters be worse off, but their suffering might exceed the enjoyment fostered by the exemption. The efficiency and fairness of the donative theory, therefore, is enhanced by a public policy screen that attempts to detect those extreme cases where support for an activity entails a substantial social evil, not just an economic cost.

This position is consistent with the Supreme Court's statement in *Bob Jones* that the purpose of a charitable entity may not be "illegal or violate established public policy."[19] Some commentators have complained that the "fundamental public policy" standard is "open-ended and beclouded," leaving far too much discretion in the hands of the IRS.[20] The Court, however, recognized the potential breadth of the public policy limitation, and accordingly cautioned in its opinion that exemption should be denied "only where there can be no doubt that the activity involved is contrary to a fundamental public policy."[21] Most courts, for example, have held that gender discrimination does not adversely affect exemption.[22]

These line-drawing problems are no worse under the donative theory than under existing law. Indeed, the donative theory, by explaining the source of the limitation, may offer a superior means for defining the scope of the public policy limitation. For instance, because the purpose of the doctrine is to limit the exemption to cases of voter apathy rather than voter opposition, the public policy limitation should be asserted only where a large majority of voters have strongly expressed antipathy, such as by enactment of anti-discrimination legislation, not simply in cases of vague uneasiness about a group's activities. Under this analysis, it would be incorrect, for example, to apply the public policy limitation to groups advocating feminist issues or gay rights (an area in which the IRS previously indicated its substantive disapproval).[23]

The Limitations on Political Activity

The federal income tax law contains two separate limitations on the political activities of charities. First, charities lose their eligibility to receive tax-deductible contributions if they engage in legislative lobbying to any substantial degree.[24] Second, the organization cannot to any degree participate in political campaigns on behalf of candidates for public office.[25] State caselaw similarly indicates that excessive political activity will result in a denial of charitable classification for state property and sales tax exemptions.[26] Prior commentators have noted that the rationale for these provisions is muddled, seemingly a conflux of historical accident and political expediency.[27] Although specific abuses have played a role in shaping current law, political activity is not inherently evil; indeed, it is the foundation of our system of government and enjoys a number of legal protections.[28] Moreover, initial impressions suggest that the donative theory would support political activity inasmuch as entities that qualify for exemption under this theory by definition suffer from government failure and therefore are demonstrably in need of more political clout.[29]

Further reflection on the government failure component of the donative theory, however, demonstrates support for at least some limitation on political activity by charitable entities. A case for indirect subsidy through the tax system exists only where the benefitted group is unable to convince the government to provide a direct subsidy. To the extent that an organization is engaged in lobbying or campaigning, we must assume that this activity is directed at improving its legislative fortunes, either by achieving direct government subsidy for its activities or by the passage of favorable legislation making it easier to accomplish its objectives.[30] Therefore, the political activities of such an entity do not demonstrate government failure; they negate it.[31] A tax subsidy for a lobbying or campaigning organization becomes a "double-dip": it subsidizes the activity of attempting to achieve further subsidization, much as if one were to count as donations those funds that are used merely to generate more donations.[32] In contrast, attempts to meet the entity's objectives through litigation or public education are not tainted by their ability to self-correct for government failure because they are outside the political arena.

Political activity tends to undermine the case for a donative subsidy because, where such activity plays a significant part in attracting donations, the donations no longer signal the undersupply of a good through market or government mechanisms. For nonpolitical organizations, donations partially replace purchases or grants by supporting additional production of the undersupplied good, but only partially because of the free-rider disincentive to give. If, instead of supporting increased production, donations are used to negate the government failure, there is no systematic basis for assuming that donations alone are not enough to achieve the optimal level of production.

True, particular groups will continue to claim they are underrepresented, but since all political action groups rely on donations, this is not predictably more true for one group than for another based simply on their donative or nonprofit status. We might conclude that underrepresentation exists for other, external reasons such as the poverty or social status of the members that make up the group, but this is not a characteristic that is shared commonly by all "charities," as that term is conventionally interpreted by the law or as we would interpret it under the donative theory. Because this is so, proposals such as those made by Laura Chisolm to use the tax exemption as a mechanism to correct for political inequality[33] are administratively cumbersome, theoretically inelegant, and have no more foundation than using the tax exemption to correct for other economic and social inequalities. We agree that these inequalities should be addressed; we do not see why the charitable tax exemption is necessarily or even conveniently designed to accomplish this goal.

One might attempt to collapse this analytical distinction between the undersupplied good and the government failure that causes the undersupply by arguing that lobbying and campaigning are themselves public goods, which indeed they are. But this supposes that political activity is an end in itself rather than a means to achieve some personal or social reward. The reward may be "political" in some measure—such as the right to vote—but if the reward is posited to be simply political activity alone, the argument for subsidy becomes nonsensical, or, at best, question-begging. It's as if one argued for a government subsidy to be more litigious.

We do not mean to suggest, however, that *all* political activity by charities should be prohibited, any more than a donative entity should have its exemption revoked for engaging in unrelated business activities. Admittedly, the chance exists that an entity's lobbying efforts will fail, resulting in a corresponding need for subsidization. The need to lobby is particularly acute where the goal of the entity cannot be purchased but must be achieved through legislative reform (e.g., civil rights). So some sort of compromise is necessary. Unfortunately, we do not know in advance where lobbying efforts will be unsuccessful or necessary; organizational goals cannot be neatly compartmentalized. The substance of civil rights might also be achieved through public education or through litigation; pollution control could be achieved through hiring workers to pick up litter as well as by enacting laws against littering. Thus we need some kind of compromise that does not prohibit political activity, but does guard against the "double dipping" effect noted above.

In fact, a compromise is precisely what current law accomplishes. It permits some level of political activity without loss of any tax benefits and only partially withdraws those benefits when the limits are exceeded.[34] Nevertheless, we believe that a better compromise is possible within the confines of the donative theory. Our proposal, which would eliminate the current disparity between legislative lobbying and political campaign activity and at the same time simplify the rules regarding political activity, is discussed in Chapter 11 below along with other aspects of implementing the donative theory. Our only objective at this point is to demonstrate that the donative theory supports a partial restriction on political activity and thus is broadly consistent with both limitations and allowances that have been part of the lore of charitable exemption virtually since the inception of the tax laws.

Unrelated Business Income

Since 1950, the federal government has taxed income of an otherwise exempt organization that is "unrelated" to its charitable purpose. The unrelated business income tax ("UBIT") resulted largely from certain highly-publicized instances of exempt organizations owning businesses completely unrelated to their charitable purpose, such as New York University's ownership of a macaroni factory.[35] Prior to the UBIT, court cases generally had upheld the tax exemption of an entity engaged in such unrelated businesses, as long as the profits from the business were used by the entity for its exempt purpose.[36] This "destination of income" test essentially permitted a tax-exempt charity to operate unrelated businesses tax-free as long as the proceeds from the unrelated business were used to further a charitable purpose. Logically, this old destination of income test made sense under conventional theories of the charitable tax exemption. After all, if charitable status is based upon relief of government burden, aid to the poor, or community benefit, what difference does it make *where* the money to perform these services comes from, as long as the funds are destined to further the worthy goal?

The conventional response to this question is that the UBIT polices "unfair competition" by exempt entities. The UBIT arose from Congressional concern that the tax exemption gave an unfair economic advantage to exempt organizations competing with for-profit firms. This concern led in 1950 to the decision to tax unrelated business income as the best way to "level the playing field."[37] Similarly, most state property exemption laws limit the exemption to property used by the entity only for its exempt purpose. A hospital may be tax-exempt, for example, but an office building for private physicians owned by the hospital would not be, since it is not part of the operation of a hospital.[38] Likewise, a portion of a building owned by a church and used for religious worship is exempt under state law, but not those portions of the building rented to retail stores, or church-owned buildings used as residences for pastors.[39]

Commentators have noted the lack of any coherent rationale for the UBIT. The test for taxing income under the UBIT depends on whether the business is related to charitable activities and not on whether the business competes with for-profit entities.[40] Accordingly, exempt entities may operate businesses whose core activities are considered charitable and still escape UBIT even though they in fact compete with for-profit counterparts in the same markets. This is the case in the health care industry, for instance.[41] Many commentators, moreover, have questioned whether the UBIT is necessary or even desirable to police "unfair competition." A number of commentators reason that a nonprofit firm is no more likely or able to engage in predatory pricing (a common "unfair competition" complaint) than for-profit firms.[42] While some commentators recognize that entry of nonprofit firms into a particular market can create injury to for-profit investors, the remedy proposed by one of these commentators is to repeal the UBIT completely so that business operations of nonprofits will be spread throughout the entire economy, thus creating less havoc in one sector.[43]

In addition, the IRS has often been less than successful in defining the boundaries of relatedness. In the health care field, for example, the IRS has been blatantly inconsistent in its use of the "promotion of health" standard to define the scope of the exemption. Despite professing this as the basis for which nonprofit hospitals are exempt, it refuses to extend the exemption to health-related income that is not strictly *hospital*-related (outpatient care, pharmacy sales, etc.), probably because a number of peripheral health-care activities are undertaken by for-profit entities which might thereby be subjected to unfair competition. But the same is true of the core hospital functions themselves.[44] These difficulties have led Congress to revisit the

UBIT, inquiring whether enforcement can be strengthened and simplified, or instead whether the UBIT should be largely abandoned.[45]

The confusion in federal policy regarding unrelated business income results largely from the failure of the conventional theories of the charitable exemption to justify the UBIT as an integral part of their explanation for the exemption. Therefore, the UBIT exists only as an external constraint, imposed to control what some view as harmful side effects of the exemption. This leaves in dispute how harmful are the effects and how far the UBIT should trespass into the charitable domain to do its job. In contrast, the donative theory itself provides a theoretical rationale for some limits on unrelated activity as well as for allowing some such activity to continue. Because both the relatedness concept and the income destination argument are integral to the donative theory, it is capable of providing a much more satisfactory resolution of these two competing policies that previously have been at war with each other.

According to the donative theory, the tax exemption is a subsidy to correct the undersupply of a good or service that suffers from the concurrence of private market and government failure, as evidenced by donative support. Thus, this subsidy should be limited to the good or service for which twin failure has occurred, that is, the good or service that induces donations. Put more concretely, presumably a person contributes money to NYU because of its educational mission, not because of any undersupply of macaroni. As a result, there is no demonstrated need to facilitate more macaroni production; any such subsidy would be disproportionate to the need for support evidenced by the existing level of donations.

This theoretical argument supporting a "relatedness" limitation on exemption, however, is somewhat at odds with the practicalities of precisely how the income tax exemption creates a subsidy effect. For instance, an exemption for an entity that receives nothing but donations produces no income tax subsidy at all, since, under current definitions of income, a purely donative entity would have no income taxes to pay even absent an exemption.[46] Therefore, in order to create any subsidy from the income tax exemption, we must allow the exempt entity to produce a substantial amount of other, nondonative income.[47] How much other income is appropriate becomes a question of proportionality, that is, matching the subsidy to the level of deservedness demonstrated by donative support. This rough matching of the tax subsidy to the donative base is precisely what we accomplish when, in the following chapter, we suggest a one-third donative threshold that an exempt entity must meet in order to qualify for charitable status.

As we propose to implement the donative theory, there would be no need for the UBIT as a separate check on exempt status. Once we set this threshold of one-third donative support, the source of the other, nondonative income is of no concern. It does not matter whether it is related or unrelated. As long as the tax savings are used to produce the undersupplied good or service, the donative theory would exempt unrelated business income (up to two-thirds of the entity's total operations) in order to overcome the market failure that induced the donations.

For example, assume two museums with similar collections, each of which receives donations of $400,000 per year, and expends $500,000 on museum costs. Museum A gets its extra $100,000 from admission revenues ("related" income) using volunteer workers. However, Museum B charges no admission because it receives $100,000 income from macaroni sales (net of $300,000 of expenses in macaroni production). Both entities meet the one-third donative threshold (Museum A is 80% donative; Museum B is 50% donative ($400,000 out of $800,000).) Since each entity is expending the same amount of money on its museum activities, and those activities are substantially supported by donations, we would give each the same amount of subsidy (an abatement of taxes on the $100,000 of otherwise taxable income).

This assumes, of course, that the exempt entity in fact uses the tax savings to enhance its donative activity, which suggests a troublesome need to assess and police operational spending decisions. Fortunately, the donative theory avoids this difficulty through its threshold requirement of a significant percentage of donative support. If donors are not satisfied with the organization's spending decisions, the operation of the market in altruism will cause donative support to drop off, threatening its exempt status.[48] Even if this does not occur, the mere fact that the organization chooses to invest more in the unrelated business will increase its overall revenues, thus tending to dwarf the donative base that is in place and threaten the organization's exempt status.

This end result of the implementation of the donative theory appears superfically to be nothing more than an adoption of the old destination of income test, and a refutation of the relatedness test. In fact, the donative theory resolves these competing theories through the compromise entailed in setting the donative threshold. Unlike the destination of income test, which would permit exemption of *any* amount of income from unrelated business as long as the money is spent on a purpose that is in any way "charitable," our implementation of the donative theory contains a substantial restriction on the subsidy given to unrelated activity: the receipts from unrelated activity may not exceed by a certain percentage the entity's donative base. Thus, to the extent we retain the requirement of a substantial donative base, we recognize the cross subsidization concerns that form the basis for the UBIT; but to the extent we allow the exemption to extend to other, nondonative activity, we recognize the logic of the income destination argument. In sum, the threshold requirement embodies in theory the idea that the subsidy must be matched to the level of deservedness, while avoiding the practical difficulties of defining relatedness or identifying undue competitive effects.

Historical Consistency

An appealing feature of the donative theory of the charitable exemption is that, while its economic justification is rigorous and elaborate, it leads to a fundamentally intuitive concept of charity—a concept that reaffirms the popular sense of charity as "the impulse to give."[49] The public goods explanation for donative behavior is captured in the concept of altruism that reflects a donor's disregard of the narrow perspective of economic self-interest and in the very etymology of philanthropy, the love of mankind. It is incontrovertible that society has an interest in encouraging giving and supporting the objects of philanthropy.[50] It is thus serendipitous that a more conventional analysis of precedent and history confirms the common sense notion of giving as the archetype of charity.

The Role of Donations in Charitable Trusts

The connection between tax law and trust law, discussed in Chapter 3, emerges as one of the great puzzles of the charitable exemption. Anglo-American law has employed a uniform concept of charity for centuries. Yet even casual examination of these two bodies of law reveals that they serve disparate purposes. Charitable trust law addresses the proper purposes for which the law will relieve a trust from the requirements of having definite beneficiaries, a limited duration, and an achievable purpose. These comparatively minor concerns allow trust law to consider as charitable any purpose that provides a conceivable social benefit; trust law can afford to be lenient because enforcing a benefactor's disposition of his own assets imposes relatively small public costs. It seems absurd, then, to adopt this same sweeping concept of charity—one that encompasses essentially any activity that benefits the public at large in any manner—to justify a tax exemption that costs the public billions of dollars in lost tax revenue each year. Yet this is precisely what virtually every tax law authority ostensibly advocates.

The notion of a uniform concept of charity is so entrenched that a successful theory of the exemption must offer a satisfactory explanation of the relevance of trust law. Only the donative theory connects these two bodies of law in a sensible fashion. It does so by focusing attention on the donative aspect of trust creation to reveal the following, crucial limiting principle contained in charitable trust law: the reason that trust law does not evaluate what purposes are of sufficient public importance to deserve special legal protection is that the self-sacrifice entailed in forming a trust without private benefit provides safe assurance that its founder's motives are worthy. As one early decision explained:

> What is the tribunal which is to decide whether the object is a benefi-
> cent one? It cannot be the individual mind of a Judge . . . . On the other
> hand, it cannot be the *vox populi*, for charities have been upheld for the
> benefit of insignificant sects, and of peculiar people. It occurs to me
> that the answer must be . . . that the benefit must be one which the
> founder believes to be of public advantage.[51]

In other words, the conception of charity embodied in trust law can afford to be essentially boundless because it contains the inherent limitation that a donor must be willing to divert his wealth from himself or his family to support the public purpose in question. Therefore, tax exemption law blunders terribly if it transplants trust law's concept of charity without maintaining this crucial limiting principle—the self-sacrifice entailed in a gift. In effect, the categorical and community benefit tests assert that any activity deserves tax support if it *conceivably* might form the basis for a trust, but without inquiring whether such actual, objective support exists. To avoid this nonsequitor while maintaining the connection with trust law, tax exemption law must define a charitable purpose as one that the public perceives to be sufficiently meritorious to warrant sacrificing a significant amount of personal resources to support it.[52]

This simple observation is made even more apparent by reexamining the foundational trust law authorities with the donative factor in mind. Many of the leading authorities who articulate a boundless public benefit concept of charity qualify their description of charity with the proviso that a gift be devoted to the stated purpose. The listing of charitable purposes in the 1601 Statute of Charitable Uses, the seminal codification of the legal concept of charity, is explicitly premised on giving. The statute's preface stated as its rationale for creating a rigorous enforcement mechanism for charitable trusts that "lands, goods, . . . [and] money . . . have been heretofore *given* . . . by sundry . . . well disposed persons" to these purposes. The seminal American decision defined "a charity, in the legal sense, . . . as a *gift*, to be applied . . . for the benefit of an indefinite number of persons."[53] The leading modern British case that establishes the per se charitable status of hospitals declares that "a *gift* for the purpose of a hospital is prima facie a charitable gift."[54] The element of gift is also fundamental to tort law's former willingness to clothe charities with immunity.[55] Even those authorities that do not speak explicitly in terms of a gift implicitly recognize this element by reminding us that the definition of charitable is in the context of a trust established for the stated purpose.[56]

The donative theory also is consistent with charitable trust precedents in other, less obvious ways. Trust law reinforces the public goods component of the donative theory through the concept of public benefit used to define what objects are charitable. In Chapter 3, we exlained that the public versus private benefit distinction was the only significant limitation on the objects of charity that qualify for trust law protection. A trust is not charitable if its primary purpose is to benefit the donor or a private interest closely related to the donor (such as a trust to maintain a gravesite). This distinction captures the same notion as the economic concept of positive externalities used to describe public goods. Public goods are those for which the benefits to others are much larger than the benefits captured by the price charged to an individual purchaser.[57] These are also the goods for which people are induced to make voluntary contributions. Therefore, limiting the charitable tax exemption to those objects that attract donations accomplishes the same purpose as the public/private distinction in charitable trust law.

The Role of Donations in Tax Exemption Precedents

The donative theory is also confirmed by the central categories of charitable activity established in tax exemption law. Religion and education, the two arenas that uniformly enjoy categorical charitable status, are traditional recipients of large amounts of philanthropy. In 1990, religion received 54% of all gifts, amounting to $65.8 billion. Educational institutions (including arts and cultural organizations) received $17 billion, amounting to 13% of total giving.[58] The example of religion also helps to confirm the government failure component of the donative theory. The charitable exemption has its strongest application to religion, the dominant form of charity throughout the ages. As summarized in Chapter 1, temples were exempt in ancient Egypt, Greece and Rome because it was thought beyond the power of man to tax gods—an extreme form of government failure. The religious exemption carried over into medieval England for the simple reason that there was no centralized government capable of imposing a tax. In the American colonies, which were established as theocracies, churches were not taxed because no government thinks to tax itself. After the constitutional adoption of the separation principle, though, the religious exemption is justified by the constitutional prohibition on government supporting religion's worthwhile activities in any direct manner.[59] The government failure theory is but a weaker version of this modern rationale applied to forms of governmental incapacity other than outright prohibition of direct funding. The Supreme Court captured the germ of this government failure idea when it explained that "charitable exemptions are justified on the basis that the exempt entity confers a public benefit—a benefit which the society or the community may not itself choose or be able to provide, or which supplements and advances the work of public institutions already supported by tax revenues."[60]

One might object that the categorical exemptions conferred on religion and education refute the donative theory because they seem to declare that these activities are eligible for exemption regardless of their donative support. Under existing law, however, the statutory enumeration of religion and education creates only a presumption of exempt status; the enumeration is still subject to residual requirements implicit in the common law concept of charity. In *Bob Jones University v. United States*,[61] for instance, the Supreme Court upheld the authority to deny the charitable exemption on public policy grounds to racially discriminatory private schools, despite the statute's omission to impose a general public policy requirement. The Court reasoned that the public policy screen is one of the "certain common-law standards of charity" drawn from charitable trust law that "under[lie] all relevant parts of the Code."[62] Likewise, the donative aspect of the trust law concept of charity underlies all enumerated categories of charitable organizations. Therefore, it is just as easily applied to all charitable activities, even those that seem to enjoy per se exemption.

The existence of this systemic limitation on the charitable exemption is not left to mere speculation. State court decisions provide significant precedential support for the donative element of the charitable exemption despite their apparent endorsement of a more sweeping per se view of exemption.[63] For example, many of the state court decisions that most liberally extended the exemption to hospitals earlier in this century are, upon closer examination, premised on a donative theory. The court in *City of Richmond v. Richmond Memorial Hospital*,[64] one of the leading cases thought to establish hospitals as categorically exempt regardless of their willingness to treat indigent patients, observed that "these hospitals were built through charitable impulses. Over thirty thousand charitably inclined citizens contributed to the construction."[65]

The donative theory also finds explicit precedential support in the federal sphere. One study of federal tax exemption rulings concluded that "there is a strong tendency on the part of the IRS to require that a charitable organization embody to some degree a donative factor."[66] The court in *Harding Hospital v. United States*, for example, used the lack of charitable donations to support the denial of exempt status for a specialized psychiatric hospital.[67] The lack of contributions was also noted by the Eighth Circuit in denying an exemption to a nonprofit pharmacy.[68] Donations also appeared to play a major part in one of the key cases on propaganda institutions: the D.C. Circuit's reversal of the IRS's denial of exemption in *Big Mama Rag*. There the court noted that the organization in question "has a predominantly volunteer staff and . . . is dependent on contributions, grants and funds raised by benefits for over fifty percent of its income."[69]

More recently, Congress expressed implicit support for the donative theory by denying the federal exemption to certain inherently commercial activities.[70] In 1986, Congress withdrew the charitable exemption from "commercial-type insurance" such as Blue Cross/Blue Shield and the Teacher's Insurance Annuity Association (TIAA).[71] In 1987 Congress held extensive hearings inquiring into the concern that tax-exempt nonprofits are engaged in a vast array of commercial activities that constitute unfair competition with proprietary businesses.[72] The essence of commercial activity is the sale of goods and services on a quid pro quo basis. Commercial nonprofits are thus polar opposites of those that raise their revenues through donations. Therefore, rejection of the exemption for commercial activity can be seen as a tacit endorsement of the donative standard.

Perhaps most impressive is that the donative theory reconciles the deep-seated historical division explored in Chapter 2 between tax-base and subsidy explanations for the charitable exemption. We observed there that historically exemptions arose because of the underlying structure of the then-existing tax base, but because of the modern scope of taxation, it no longer makes sense to say, for example, that property that does not produce income lies outside the modern property tax base. This mismatch between the historical rationale for exemption and modern taxation is what has forced theorists to justify the modern scope of exemption on subsidy grounds. Donative institutions, however, retain the historical link with the tax-base rationales for exemption because many (though certainly not all) donative entities rely on other income only as a secondary source of financing, and because many (again, certainly not all) operate in a sort of "trust" method that does make regressive taxation of beneficiaries an issue. Accordingly, the donative theory we have constructed for the modern subsidy rationale of exemption retains its connections with historical precedent, and largely closes the analytical divide between the tax-base and subsidy camps by restricting exemption to a class of entities that can make a strong claim for it under both theories.

The donative theory, then, not only fares better under our evaluative criteria than any other theory of exemption for charitable organizations, it also has firm grounding in court precedent, economic theory, and common sense. This theory uses the objective conduct of those most interested in the fate of tax dollars—the taxpaying public—as the standard for granting exemption, thus taking out of the hands of tax authorities subjective evaluations of the inherent "goodness" of a particular enterprise and making the granting and supervision of exempt status far more administrable than it is today. Having established the theoretical and public policy grounds for the theory, we now turn to issues of practical implementation.

Notes

1. We do not mean that discrete political judgments *could* or *should* not be made by political bodies with appropriate authority over social policy, as in fact legislatures sometimes do by extending ad hoc exemptions to encourage particular, favored activities. Our point instead is that this is not what *has* been done in defining exempt status for over a century.

2. We note, however, that commentators have questioned the theoretical propriety of § 102: because a gift increases the consumption ability of the donee, an argument can be made that the gift should be included in the income of the donee. *See generally*, UNITED STATES DEPARTMENT OF THE TREASURY, BLUEPRINTS FOR BASIC TAX REFORM 37–41 (1977).

3. An exemption from property tax might still be a major subsidy, however. *See* John G. Simon, *The Tax Treatment of Nonprofit Organizations: A Review of Federal and State Policies*, *in* THE NONPROFIT SECTOR: A RESEARCH HANDBOOK 67, 81 (Walter W. Powell ed., 1987) (income tax exemption would result in minimal consequences to most charities, but state property tax exemption likely is a significant financial benefit).

4. Cyril F. Chang & Howard P. Tuckman, *Why Do Nonprofit Managers Accumulate Surpluses, and How Much Do They Accumulate?*, 1 NONPROFIT MGT. & LEADERSHIP 117, 127 (1990). The sample included only nonprofits that receive more than $25,000 in annual revenues, since only these are required to file IRS forms.

5. Indeed, the former had much higher operating margins (about 13%) than did health care institutions (5%). *Id.*

6. For a survey of state sales tax exemptions, see Janne G. Gallagher, *Sales Tax Exemptions for Charitable, Educational and Religious Nonprofit Organizations*, 7 EXEMPT ORG. TAX REV. 429 (1993). Gallagher's survey indicates that at least 37 states exempt charities from paying sales tax on their purchases.

7. *Id.* at 431. This situation, however, may be due more to the fact that few states historically have imposed a sales tax on services; since most nonprofits operate in a service economy, an exemption from charging sales tax historically may have been moot (although not so today, when many states, such as Florida, are attempting to expand their sales taxes to services).

8. Simon, *supra* note 3 at 89–90.

9. One of the requirements of exempt status under I.R.C. § 501(c)(3) is that "no part of the earnings [of such organization] inures to the benefit of any private shareholder or individual." *See also* Treas. Regs. § 1.501(c)(3)-1(b)(4). *See generally*, BRUCE R. HOPKINS, THE LAW OF TAX-EXEMPT ORGANIZATIONS 264–66 (6th ed. 1992); PAUL E. TREUSCH, TAX-EXEMPT CHARITABLE ORGANIZATIONS 92–95 (3d ed. 1989). State laws uniformly include a prohibition on private inurement either as an express statutory requirement or as part of the common-law interpretation of "charitable." *See* Mark A. Hall & John D. Colombo, *The Charitable Status of Nonprofit Hospitals: Toward a Donative Theory of Tax Exemption*, 66 WASH. L. REV. 307, 330 n.74 (collecting citations). The IRS breaks this doctrine into two parts: the private inurement limitation that is actually part of the statutory language, and a limitation on *private benefit* that is derived from the statutory language and separately stated in the regulations ("an entity must not be operated for the benefit of private interests such as designated individuals"). Treas. Reg. §1.501(c)(3)-1(d)(1)(ii). We treat the private benefit limitation separately as expressing the publicness concept contained in the notion of community benefit. Note that the nonprofit requirement is a prohibition on the *distribution* of profits, not a prohibition on an entity *making* a profit. *See, e.g.*, HOPKINS, *supra*, at 232–34.

10. This has been a particularly vexing problem with health care entities, where the IRS has perhaps gone too far in its zeal to avoid private inurement. *See* John D. Colombo, *Are Associations of Doctors Tax Exempt? Analyzing Inconsistencies in the Tax Exemption of Health Care Providers*, 9 VA. TAX REV. 469 (1990).

11. *E.g.*, BORIS I BITTKER & LAWRENCE LOKKEN, FEDERAL TAXATION OF INCOME, ESTATES AND GIFTS, ¶ 100.4 (2d ed. 1992); HOPKINS, *supra* note 9, at 264–66.

12. *E.g.*, Harding Hosp. v. United States, 505 F.2d 1068, 1078 (6th Cir. 1974); Birmingham Business College v. Commissioner, 276 F.2d 476, 480–81 (5th Cir. 1960); John Marshall Law School v. United States, 81-2 U.S.T.C. (CCH) §9514 (Ct. Cl. 1981); Maynard Hosp. v. Commissioner, 52 T.C. 1006, 1031–32 (1969); Sonora Community Hosp. v. Commissioner, 46 T.C. 519, 526 (1966), *aff'd*, 397 F.2d 814 (9th Cir. 1968). *See, e.g.*, HOPKINS, *supra* note 9, at 276–80.

13. *See, e.g.*, Note, *Religious Nonprofits and the Commercial Manner Test*, 99 YALE L.J. 1631, 1634–39 (1990) (struggling to explain why for-profit religious publishers do not deserve the exemption). Hansmann's capital subsidy theory of the income tax exemption is an exception, for he explains the exemption as a means to overcome the relative disadvantage that nonprofits face in the capital markets. See our discussion of this point in Chapter 6 at pp. 83-86.

14. Hansmann also applies this explanation to commercial nonprofits (those that derive their revenues primarily from sales). As explained in Chapter 5, he reasons that a similar monitoring problem can arise for complex services that are difficult for consumers to evaluate, such as day care and nursing home care. We note in our discussion in Chapter 6 that a number of other nonprofit scholars take issue with whether the trust rationale properly extends to any commercial nonprofit. *See* Chapter 6, *supra*, at 84. But these objections, which essentially go to whether there is a legitimate role for *commercial* nonprofits, are not germane to the present analysis since none of Hansmann's critics disagrees that *donative* nonprofits serve the useful role that he identifies.

15. For a general discussion, see HOPKINS, *supra* note 9, at 65–71. The public policy requirement appears to harken back to charitable trust law. *Id.* at 69; RESTATEMENT OF TRUSTS (2d) § 377, comment c (1959).

16. 461 U.S 574, 586 (1983). The amount of commentary this decision generated is mind-boggling, far exceeding the commentary on the fundamental basis for the exemption. For citations to all 23 articles regarding this decision and the IRS revenue ruling preceding it, see John D. Colombo, *Why is Harvard Tax Exempt? (And Other Mysteries of Tax Exemption for Private Educational Institutions)*, 35 ARIZ. L. REV. 842, 853 n.79 (1993).

17. For example, Atkinson would attach an external public policy constraint to his altruism theory, even though the theory itself does not explain why such a constraint is necessary. *See* Rob Atkinson, *Altruism in Nonprofit Organizations*, 31 B.C.L. REV. 501, 636–37 (1990).

18. For further discussion of this point, see Chapter 7, *supra*, at 108.

19. 461 U.S. at 591.

20. Charles O. Galvin & Neal Devins, *A Tax Policy Analysis of* Bob Jones University v. United States, 36 VAND. L. REV. 1353, 1379 (1983). *See also* David L. Anderson, *Tax Exempt Private Schools Which Discriminate on the Basis of Race: A Proposed Revenue Procedure*, 55 NOTRE DAME LAW. 141 (1980); William A. Drennan, Note, *Bob Jones University v. United States: For Whom Will the Bell Toll?* 29 St. Louis U.L.J. 561, 596 (1985); Galvin & Devins, *supra*, at 1373; Thomas Stephen Neuberger & Thomas C. Crumplar, *Tax Exempt Religious Schools Under Attack: Conflicting Goals of Religious Freedom and Racial Integration*, 28 FORDHAM L. REV. 229, 275 (1979).

21. 461 U.S. at 592.

22. *E.g.*, New York City Jaycees, Inc. v. United States Jaycees, Inc., 512 F.2d 856 (2d Cir. 1975); Junior Chamber of Commerce of Rochester, Inc., v. U.S. Jaycees, 495 F.2d 883 (10th Cir. 1974); McCoy v. Schultz, 73-1 U.S.T.C. (CCH)

¶ 9233 (D.D.C. 1973).

23. *See* Big Mama Rag, Inc. v. United States, 631 F.2d 1030 (D.C. Cir. 1980) (overruling IRS denial of exemption for feminist publication); IRS Gen. Couns. Mem. 37173 (June 21, 1977) (stating that the IRS had a "legitimate" concern that the activities of certain organizations advocating homosexual rights could harm society by encouraging or facilitiating homosexual practices). *See generally* Tommy F. Thompson, *The Availability of the Federal Educational Tax Exemption for Propaganda Organizations*, 18 U. CAL. DAVIS L. REV. 487. A tougher call is presented by National Alliance v. United States, 710 F.2d 868, 875 (D.C. Cir. 1983), which denied an exemption to a group advocating race war on grounds that such advocacy does not constitute an educational activity. One of us (Professor Hall) believes this result would be correct under the public policy limitation following the reasoning employed in *Bob Jones*. The other of us (Professor Colombo) believes that the public policy limitation should be restricted to cases where the precise activity being subsidized is positively illegal. Because this case involved advocacy, not actual conduct , of race wars, the organization probably was not breaking the law (assuming no inciting to riot or the like).

24. I.R.C. § 501(c)(3) states that an entity will be exempt only if "no substantial part of [its] activities . . . is carrying on propaganda or otherwise attempting to influence legislation." Although a violation of this prohibition (repeated in § 170, which specifies those entities to which one can make tax-deductible contributions) can result in loss of exemption, entities that engage in substantial legislative lobbying may be eligible for exemption under other subsections of § 501(c)(3), such as § 501(c)(4). *See generally* HOPKINS, *supra* note 5, at 311–13; Miriam Galston, *Lobbying and the Public Interest: Rethinking the Internal Revenue Code's Treatment of Legislative Activities*, 71 TEX. L. REV. 1269, 1278–80 (1993). Accordingly, the lobbying restriction really translates into a limit on the ability of organizations to qualify for the special tax benefits that are accorded charitable entities under § 501(c)(3), such as the ability to receive tax-deductible contributions and issue tax-exempt bonds under § 145.

I.R.C. § 501(h) contains mechanical tests to determine when expenditures for legislative lobbying have become "substantial," although an entity is not required to use this procedure and can instead rely on sparse common-law interpretations of "substantial." For a general discussion of the lobbying limitations, see HOPKINS, *supra* note 5, at chapter 13; Laura B. Chisolm, *Exempt Organization Advocacy*, 63 IND. L.J. 201 (1987); Galston, *supra* at 1275–80 . The scope of lobbying permitted by § 501(c)(3) also is the subject of very detailed (and highly controversial) regulations. *See generally* James J. McGovern et al., *The Final Lobbying Regulations: A Challenge for Both the IRS and Charities*, TAX NOTES, Sept. 3, 1990 at 1305.

25. I.R.C. § 501(c)(3) states that an entity cannot "participate in, or intervene in (including the publishing or distributing of statements), any political campaign on behalf of (or in opposition to) any candidate for public office." The IRS has indicated that there may be a limited de minimis exception to this rule, *see* Chisolm,

supra note 24, at n.55, but even with this allowance the nearly absolute ban on campaigning is more strenuous than the limitation on legislative lobbying, which clearly contemplates that exempt organizations may engage in lobbying to some (insubstantial) degree. Direct campaign activity also appears to be prohibited under 501(c)(4), *see* HOPKINS, *supra* note 9, at 313, which means that direct participation in campaign activity disqualifies a charity from tax exemption as well as deductible donations and the other benefits attaching to 501(c)(3) status.

26. *See* Pennsylvania v. American Anti-Vivisection Soc'y, 32 Pa. Commw. 70, 377 A.2d 1378 (1977) (organization whose primary activity was lobbying not exempt).

27. *See* Laura B. Chisolm, *Politics and Charity: A Proposal for Peaceful Coexistence*, 58 GEO. WASH. U. L. REV. 337 n. 130 (1990); Elias Clark, *The Limitation on Political Activities: A Discordant Note in the Law of Charities*, 46 VA. L. REV. 439, 466 (1960); Galston, *supra* note 24, at 1282–85.

28. The major one, of course, is the first amendment protection for free speech. *See generally* HOPKINS, *supra* note 9, at 275–80; Chisolm, *Politics and Charity*, *supra* note 27, at 319–26.

29. *See* Chisolm, *Exempt Organization Advocacy*, *supra* note 24, at 277–99. Miram Galston argues that charities should be permitted greater latitude in lobbying because charities help present viewpoints that should be considered by legislators in reaching decisions on legislation. *See* Galston, *supra* note 24, at 1336–38. Other commentators have suggested that the lobbying restrictions be dropped completely, James H. Fogel, *To the IRS 'Tis Better to Give Than to Lobby*, 61 A.B.A.J. 960, 961 (1975); that lobbying restrictions be liberalized through "more flexible" Treasury interpretation but that the restrictions on political activity be kept intact, Clark, *supra* note 27, at 462, 464; or that permissible lobbying be judged by the relationship between the lobbying and the exempt purpose of the entity, Mortimer M. Caplin & Richard E. Timblie, *Legislative Activities of Public Charities*, 39 LAW & CONTEMP. PROBS. 183 (1975).

Critics of lobbying by charities include Jeffrey Hart, *Foundations and Social Activism: A Critical View*, *in* THE FUTURE OF FOUNDATIONS 43 (Fritz F. Heimann ed., 1973); Jerome Kurtz, *Tax Incentives: Their Use and Misuse*, 1968 U. SO. CAL. L. CTR. TAX INST. 1, 8–9; and Lawrence M. Stone, *Federal Tax Support of Charities and Other Exempt Organizations: The Need for a National Policy*, 1968 U. SO. CAL. L. CTR. TAX INST. 27, 55–56.

30. This assumption mirrors the lobbying limitation in current law, which does not include "nonpartisan analysis, study or research" in the definition of impermissible lobbying. I.R.C. § 4911(d)(2)(A). That is, prohibited lobbying occurs only when the organization promotes a specific legislative result favorable to itself. However, the line between permitted nonpartisan activity and prohibited lobbying is not always clear, and IRS enforcement may be variable. *See* Chisolm, *Exempt Organization Advocacy*, *supra* note 24, at 229–33; Galston, *supra* note 24, at 1344. The final lobbying regulations attempt to clarify both the definition of lobbying and what constitutes "nonpartisan analysis". Treas. Reg. § 56.4911–2 (1990). *See*

McGovern et al., *supra* note 24, at 1306–09, 1311–12.

31. *See* Pepper, Hamilton & Sheetz, *Legislative Activities of Charitable Organizations Other Than Private Foundations,* in 5 RESEARCH PAPERS SPONSORED BY THE COMMISSION ON PRIVATE PHILANTHROPY AND PUBLIC NEEDS 2917, 2937 (1977) (hereafter FILER COMMISSION PAPERS) for a similar argument based upon the government burden theory of exemption. These authors observe that the government only *increases* its burden by exempting entities that attempt to squeeze more money out of the government. *See also* Galston, *supra* note 24, at 1325–30 for a summary of these arguments. As Galston notes, it is impossible to verify empirically whether increased lobbying leads to increased government spending. We need not have empirical support for this argument, however; if one agrees that much lobbying is directed at improving the fortunes of the exempt entity, as even Galston appears to do, *see id.* at 1338–43, then under the donative theory lobbying would tend to negate government failure.

32. Accordingly, as discussed in Chapter 11 at 212-14, to determine what percentage of an organization's revenues come from donations we would deduct expenses for fundraising and use only the "net" donation figure. Our rationale is that the proportionality criterion requires that the subsidy provided by tax exemption be aimed at the undersupplied good, not at expenses for achieving donative status. Here, we face an analogous problem of unduly amplifying the subsidy; thus we have suggested in Chapter 11 a similar approach for subtracting lobbying costs from the donative base in order to control the incentive to generate funds to do nothing but lobby.

33. Chisolm, *Exempt Organization Advocacy, supra* note 24.

34. As stated above in note 24, many organizations can retain exempt status even if they lobby, although such organizations are not eligible to receive tax-deductible contributions or to issue tax-exempt bonds.

35. *See* Harvey P. Dale, *About the UBIT . . . ,* 18TH CONF. ON TAX PLANNING FOR 501(C)(3) ORGANIZATIONS §9.02 at 9-5 (1990); Richard L. Kaplan, *Intercollegiate Athletics and the Unrelated Business Income Tax,* 80 COLUM. L. REV. 1430, 1432 (1980).

36. *See generally* Dale, *supra* note 35, at 9-3 to 9-5; Kaplan, *supra* note 35, at 1433.

37. *See* Dale, *supra* note 35, at §9.02.

38. *E.g.,* Mason District Hospital v. Tuttle, 61 Ill. App.3d 1034, 378 N.E.2d 753 (1978).

39. *E.g.,* Pearsall v. Methodist Episcopal Church of Waukegan Station, 315 Ill. 233, 146 N.E. 165 (1924); Carson v. Muldoon, 306 Ill. 234, 137 N.E. 863 (1922); First M.E. Church v. Chicago, 26 Ill. 482 (1889).

40. Dale, *supra* note 35, at 9-5.

41. *See* Chapter 5.

42. Henry B. Hansmann, *Unfair Competition and the Unrelated Business Income Tax,* 75 VA. L. REV. 605, 610–11 (1989); Kaplan, *supra* note 35, at 1465–66; William A. Klein, *Income Taxation and Legal Entities,* 20 UCLA. L. REV. 13,

65–66 (1972); Susan Rose-Ackerman, *Unfair Competition and Corporate Income Taxation*, 34 STAN. L. REV. 1017, 1021 (1982).

43.*See* Rose-Ackerman, *supra* note 42, at 1025–30.

44. Colombo, *supra* note 10, at 516–17.

45. *E.g.*, *Unrelated Business Income Tax, Hearings Before the Subcommittee on Oversight of the House Committee on Ways and Means*, 100th Cong., 1st Sess. (1987) (hereafter *UBIT Hearings*).

46. This point is explained above at page 164.

47. This is not necessarily true of the property tax exemption, since, absent an exemption, property owned by a donative entity would be taxable. Nevertheless, the size of the tax relief may still fall short of the need for a subsidy. Depending, then, on the legislature's assessment of the extent of free-riding behavior with respect to particular entities, see Chapters 7 and 8, states may or may not want to extend the property tax exemption to portions of property that are not donated, that are not supported entirely by donated revenues, or that are not related to activities that receive substantial donative support.

48. *See* Chapter 8 at 128-29 (discussing how market in altruism will adjust donations over time to account for variations in perceived deservedness).

49. John P. Persons et al., *Criteria for Exemption under Section 501(c)(3)*, *in* FILER COMMISSION PAPERS, *supra* note 31, at 1911, 1945.

50. *See* Atkinson, *supra* note 17, at 628–30 (taking the worth of altruism as a given).

51. *In re* Cranston, [1898] 1 I.R. 431, 446 (Ir. H. Ct.).

52. We are not here backtracking on our disagreement with Professor Atkinson that the initial decision by a person to form a nonprofit entity should result in exemption for that entity essentially forever. As we noted in Chapter 7, the formation of an entity may, indeed, entail a gift, such as the initial capital contribution. Since tax exemption provides a continuing annual subsidy, however, we would require evidence of continuing donations to justify continued subsidy. For further discussion of this point, see Chapter 11 at 215-16.

53. Jackson v. Phillips, 96 Mass. (14 Allen) 539, 556 (1867) (emphasis added). *See also* Black's Law Dictionary 212 (5th ed. 1979) (defining "charitable" as "every gift for a general public use").

54. *In re* Resch's Will Trusts, [1969] 1 App. Cas. 514, 540 (P.C.) (emphasis added).

55. "'If an organization for charitable purposes founded upon the bounty of others who supply funds for the purpose of administering relief . . . may have its funds diverted from such kindly purpose, would it not inevitably operate to close the purses of the generous and benevolent who now do much to relieve the suffering of mankind?'" Dille v. St. Luke's Hosp., 196 S.W.2d 615, 617 (Mo. 1946) (quoting Adams v. University Hosp., 122 Mo. App. 675, 99 S.W. 453, 454 (1907)).

56. *E.g.*, RESTATEMENT (SECOND) OF TRUSTS § 372 (1959) ("A trust for the promotion of health is charitable.").

57. *See* JAMES DOUGLAS, WHY CHARITY? THE CASE FOR A THIRD SECTOR 19 (1983).

58. LESTER M. SALAMON, AMERICA'S NONPROFIT SECTOR: A PRIMER 15, Table 2.1 (1992)

59. *See* Walz v. Tax Comm'n, 397 U.S. 664 (1970) (upholding constitutionality of charitable exemption applied to religion).

60. Bob Jones Univ. v. United States, 461 U.S. 574, 591 (1983).

61. 461 U.S. 574 (1983).

62. *Id.* at 586.

63. *See generally* W. HARRISON WELLFORD & JANNE G. GALLAGHER, UNFAIR COMPETITION? THE CHALLENGE TO TAX EXEMPTION 134 (1988) ("Many states take into account the level of charitable support an organization receives in determining whether it is charitable.").

64. 202 Va. 86, 116 S.E.2d 79 (1960).

65. *See id.* at 80 ("[S]ome 33,000 individuals and businesses contribut[ed] approximately $4,000,000 in the fund-raising campaign."). *See also* Fredericka Home for the Aged v. San Diego County, 35 Cal. 2d 789, 221 P.2d 68, 71 (1950); Southern Methodist Hosp. v. Wilson, 51 Ariz. 424, 77 P.2d 458, 460–461 (1938); *In re* Prange's Will, 208 Wis. 404, 243 N.W. 488, 491 (1932); St. Elizabeth Hosp. v. Lancaster County, 109 Neb. 104, 189 N.W. 981 (1922).

66. Persons et al., *supra* note 49, at 1947–48. *See also* Easter House v. United States, 12 Ct. Cl. 476 (1987); EST of Hawaii v. Commissioner, 71 T.C. 1067, 1081 (1979); B.S.W. Group v. Commissioner, 70 T.C. 352, 359 (1978); Fides Publishers Ass'n v. United States, 263 F.Supp. 924 (N.D. Ind. 1967); WELLFORD & GALLAGHER, *supra* note 63, at 97 (1988) (noting a number of federal cases outside the health care field in which lack of charitable donations was a contributing factor to denial of exemption).

67. 505 F.2d 1068, 1077 (6th Cir. 1974).

68. Federation Pharmacy Servs. v. Comm'r, 625 F.2d 804, 808 (8th Cir. 1980).

69. Big Mama Rag, Inc. v. U.S., 631 F.2d 1030, 1032 (D.C. Cir. 1980).

70. *See* WELLFORD & GALLAGHER, *supra* note 63, at 95–97; Note, *Religious Nonprofits and the Commercial Manner Test*, 99 YALE L.J. 1631, 1632, 1640 (1990).

71. I.R.C. § 501(m) (1989); Tax Reform Act of 1985, H.R. Rep. No. 426, 99th Cong., 1st Sess., at 663 (1985).

72. *UBIT Hearings*, *supra* note 45.

11

Implementing the Donative Theory

The donative theory is theoretically superior to other theories of the charitable tax exemption in explaining not only the core concept of what is a charity but also the major limits on the charitable status under both federal and state tax law. Nevertheless, the most theoretically elegant theories can fail in the face of insurmountable problems of practical implementation.[1] Fortunately, most of the mechanisms necessary to implement the donative theory already exist in the Internal Revenue Code and Treasury Regulations. Our analysis in this part establishes the administrative feasibility of the donative theory in two stages. First, we present an overview of the current regulatory scheme that distinguishes publicly-supported charities from private foundations. As noted below, this regulatory scheme is not aimed at granting exemption, but rather at controlling the amount of deductible contributions to different entities and guarding against abusive use of those contributions. We then compare this existing law with the donative theory and suggest how the current regulatory system can be adapted to the task of granting exemption under the donative theory.

Determining Donative Status

Defining a Publicly Supported Entity Under Current Law

Since 1954, the Internal Revenue Code has distinguished between certain types of charitable entities for purposes of limiting the deductibility of charitable gifts. As originally enacted, § 170 generally limited the deduction for charitable donations to 20% of the taxpayer's adjusted gross income; however, donations to churches, certain educational institutions, and hospitals were permitted up to 30%.[2] In 1964, Congress added certain publicly-supported organizations to the higher contribution limit,[3] but it wanted to make sure that these benefits were available only to organizations with broad-based public support, as opposed to "private foundations," which typically are funded by large contributions from a single donor.[4] Accordingly, the 1964 law limits the availability of the higher contribution limit to those organizations that receive a "substantial part" of their support from the government or general public.[5]

A parallel provision emerged from the Tax Reform Act of 1969, which enacted a comprehensive set of rules to regulate the conduct of "private foundations." The classic private foundation is a trust funded by a single family (for example, the Fords) which uses its funds to make contributions to other charities. Throughout the late 1950s and 1960s, tax policy analysts became increasingly concerned that the general retention of control over family funds represented by the private foundation device created a potential for self-dealing between the foundation and its managers/founders.[6] In order to define those entities potentially subject to abuse, § 509 creates a presumption that all § 501(c)(3) organizations are private foundations, then excepts from private foundation status those entities already subject to the higher contribution limits of § 170 and certain other entities that demonstrate broad-based public support.[7] The new class of publicly-supported organizations is then given the benefit of the higher contribution limits by virtue of a cross reference in § 170.[8] The result of the 1969 legislation is two sets of rules designed by Congress to differentiate charities that are broadly supported by the public from charities that are not.[9]

Since many of the rules already in place under § 170 and § 509 can be adapted to implement the donative theory, a somewhat detailed introduction to these rules is in order. We begin with § 509. In order to be classified as a publicly-supported organization under the private foundation provision, an entity must meet two tests. First, it must "normally" receive more than one-third of its total support from a combination of: (1) gifts, grants, contributions, and membership fees; or (2) gross receipts from admissions, sales of merchandise, performance of services or rental of facilities, provided that such gross receipts do not constitute an unrelated trade or business.[10] Two limits exist on counting support for purposes of this test. Gross receipts from sales or admissions (category (2)) from any one source are counted only to the extent of $5000 or, if higher, 1% of the entity's total support for the year.[11] In addition, by virtue of a complex cross reference,[12] donations, grants, contributions, and membership fees (category (1)) will count toward the one-third support test only if the item does not exceed the greater of $5000 or 2% of the total contributions received by the organization since its inception. This limitation differs from the $5000/1% limit in a number of ways. First, the $5000/1% limit applies only to gross receipts from sales, admissions, etc. (items often referred to as "exempt function income") and not to contributions, grants or membership fees. The $5000/2% limit, however, applies to everything, including contributions, grants and membership fees. Moreover, the $5000/1% limit is based upon support (as defined in § 509) *for the year in question*; the $5000/2% limit is based upon total contributions *for all prior years* of the entity. Grants or contributions from government or other publicly-supported organizations generally are not subject to either limitation.

The second test for publicly-supported status under § 509(a)(2) is that the organization may not receive more than one-third of its annual support from a combination of investment income and net unrelated business income. In short, these tests require calculation of two fractions: under the first test, the denominator is total support and the numerator consists of donations, grants, contributions, membership fees and gross sales receipts as limited by the previous rules. This fraction must be more than one-third. The second fraction also uses total support as the denominator, but the numerator consists of gross investment income and net unrelated business income. This fraction must be one-third or less.

"Support" for these purposes is defined in § 509(d), and generally includes all types of gross receipts other than gains from the sale of capital assets.[13] In addition, the regulations interpret the word "normally" by averaging the preceding four taxable years, and special rules are provided for excluding from both the denominator and numerator of the relevant fraction unusual gifts which might unfavorably skew average numbers.[14]

The tests used by the IRS to identify publicly-supported organizations under § 170 are similar, but differ in material respects. Although the § 170 regulations also use a one-third-of-support threshold, they apply different limits on what counts as support. First, per statutory directive, gross sales receipts from activities related to the entity's exempt function are eliminated from support.[15] Thus admission charges by an exempt symphony orchestra society would not count either in the denominator or numerator of the support fraction.[16] Second, individual donations count in the numerator of the support fraction only to the extent they do not exceed 2% of the total support for the year. As with the tests under § 509, however, government grants and donations from other public charities generally count in full toward the threshold. The § 170 regulations also provide an alternative test for organizations that fail the one-third safe harbor. In such a case, the regulations provide that an organization can still meet the "substantial part" test of § 170(b)(1)(A)(vi) as long as at least 10% of its total support comes from government grants or donations, and the organization meets a "facts and circumstances" test which identifies other factors that indicate broad-based community support.

While these rules are complicated, they provide an outline of two similar approaches to the problem of identifying organizations receiving broad-based donative support, which is the essential practical problem in implementing the donative theory. Moreover, as noted below, we believe that the key provisions of these rules integrate well with the donative theory and, subject to the changes and suggestions noted below, can be used as the basis for a system implementing the donative theory.

Setting the Donative Threshold

Our analysis of the practical aspects of implementing the donative theory must begin with the relationship between the tax exemption and the level of public support necessary to invoke exemption. As noted above, private philanthropy indicates a twin failure of government and private markets to supply a good or service at optimal levels and, because of the free-riding disincentive to donate, a need for an additional, indirect government subsidy to correct this undersupply. The question of an appropriate donation threshold essentially asks for a line beyond which we believe that a tax subsidy is both worthy and needed. Obviously, the best case for exemption is one in which the entity in question receives all its support from private donations, but very few, if any, organizations would meet this test.[17] Even churches, which empirical studies show are most dependent on philanthropy for their existence, engage in bake sales, raffles and that most ubiquitous nondonative activity: bingo. In any event, an income tax exemption tied to complete donative support would be no exemption at all since such entities earn no income to begin with. Accordingly, what we need is a level of giving that signifies a great enough market failure that subsidization through the tax system is warranted, yet not so high that the effect of the subsidy is nil.

The discussion of a threshold, however, requires as a prerequisite a base against which to measure the threshold. The relevant inquiry is the significance of the aggregate level of giving relative to the entity's output capacity. Put another way, we desire to measure the importance of donations to the amount of money an entity *could* spend to produce the undersupplied good or service. The simplest measure of the significance of giving is the entity's total revenues.[18] The portion of such revenues from donations, as opposed to other sources such as sales, investment income or government grants, will indicate the extent to which the entity's production is still suboptimal due to the free-riding disinclination to give. Moreover, the entity's entire operation is what will receive the benefit of the exemption and will produce the subsidy effect. Accordingly, the base against which to measure donations is simply the gross revenue of the organization.

Section 509(d) conveniently provides a good definition of the gross revenue base, with two exceptions. We see no reason to eliminate receipts from the sale or exchange of capital assets from the base against which to measure the importance of donations. This exclusion is not explained in the legislative history to the 1969 Tax Reform Act and such receipts represent funds available to the entity to supply goods and services.[19] Second, we would include in full the receipts from unrelated businesses, rather than only the net income of such business. As noted above, we would not keep the tax on unrelated income as part of the administrative machinery of the tax exemption because we believe the use of a donative threshold properly controls for unduly extending tax benefits beyond the core exempt activity. Thus we would not treat receipts from an unrelated business any differently than receipts from a related business.[20]

In adapting the § 509(d) test, we expressly reject the notion contained in the § 170 regulations that exempt-function income (that is, income from sales related to the performance of the entity's exempt purpose) should be excluded both from the support base and the threshold. Excluding exempt-function income from the base and threshold potentially permits an entity to qualify as publicly-supported with a minor amount of donations. For example, one could envision a museum that earns $1,000,000 in admissions receipts, and $10,000 in donations. Although donations constitute only 1% of the total revenues in this case, excluding exempt-function income from the test base would leave us with an entity that received 100% of its base from donations. The current regulations under § 170 handle this problem by stating that an organization will not meet the tests of public support if the entity receives "almost all" its support from gross receipts from exempt functions.[21] We believe, however, that the simpler approach, as well as the better measure of the importance of donations to the entity, is to include all receipts in the measuring base.

Having defined the base, we can now move to the threshold—that is, the percentage of the base of gross revenues that needs to come from donations in order to qualify as a "charity." The difficulty we encounter is that, for the income tax deduction, the two relevant considerations point in opposite directions. The more donations (as a percentage of revenues) that an organization attracts, the better is its case for subsidy since the higher donation level indicates a more highly valued service and a more serious market/government failure. On the other hand, the higher the threshold, the *less* help the income tax exemption is in correcting this failure. Because donations themselves are not considered income even in the absence of an exemption (and, if they were, they would likely be offset by the "business" expenses entailed in spending the donations), the value of an income tax exemption per dollar of donation declines as donations increase. For instance, as between two organizations that produce and distribute religious literature, both with $1 million in gross revenues but one that receives $100,000 in donations and the other that has a $900,000 donative base, the subsidy effect created by exempting the nondonative income is 81 times *greater* for the *less* deserving of the two.[22]

The same dilemma does not present itself so starkly with respect to the property tax exemption, for there the value of the exemption will not vary according to the threshold, only according to the size of its property holdings. Drawing from the example just given, assuming both organizations have the same property holdings (a reasonable assumption since they each spend the same amount—$1 million per year—on distributing religious literature), the subsidy effect per dollar of donation from a property tax exemption would be 9 times less disproportionate than from an income tax exemption (9-fold discrepancy versus 81-fold). Nevertheless, since we assume that both income and property tax exemptions will be determined by the same threshold, setting a threshold still involves compromising these two competing considerations of deservedness and proportionality.

While this basic value judgment ultimately must be resolved in the political arena, historical experience suggests a threshold in the vicinity of one-third of gross revenues. First, the pioneering work on the economics of nonprofit institutions done by Burton Weisbrod indicates that the traditional "charitable" institutions—religious, cultural and social welfare organizations—all receive more than one-third of their revenues in the form of donations. Based on data taken from 1973-1975, Weisbrod calculated for various classes of entities the following percentage of total revenues that consisted of donations. Weisbrod refers to this calculation as the "Collectiveness Index."[23]

Cultural (museums, orchestral societies, etc.) 90
Religious   71
Public Affairs   47
Social Welfare   41

Agricultural	41
Educational	34
* * * * *	
Health	2

Weisbrod's original data is largely supported by more recent studies of the revenues of nonprofit organizations. Data from 1989, for example, shows that private contributions accounted for over 84% of the total revenues of religious organizations; 62.5% of the revenues of arts and cultural organizations (museums, symphony societies and the like); and 33% of the revenues of social and legal services organizations.[24] Health care institutions reported donations of about 5.5% of total revenues. Thus the one-third threshold appears supported by history.

The only doubtful case is education. The same 1989 data listed education/research organizations as receiving only 14.6% of their revenues from private contributions, and as noted below in Chapter 12, later data collected by the authors indicate that many private colleges and universities would not meet the one-third threshold, although most private primary schools would.

A one-third threshold also exists in Code § 509(a)(2) and the Treasury Regulations under § 170 and therefore already has been approved by the political process and tax administrators to differentiate between levels of public support relevant to determining the level of tax subsidy. Another factor in favor of this threshold is that, in contrast with the extreme disproportionality noted above for a hypothesized 1/10 threshold, the difference in subsidy effect per dollar of donation between a one-third donative organization and a two-thirds donative organization would be only four-fold under the income tax exemption and two-fold under the property tax exemption, using the assumptions we stated earlier. Accordingly, one-third appears to be at least a good starting point for the threshold.

If one-third appears to be too demanding on some portions of the nonprofit sector, we note that considerable flexibility exists in designing the threshold while still taking into account the basic elements of the donative theory. The following modifications are possible. First, the one-third test could be applied to a *portion* of the entity seeking tax exemption. This would invite exempt entities to segregate their operations into units that meet the threshold. As long as such units meet the one-third threshold, no reason exists not to permit a subsidy *to that unit*. An example might be a hospital children's ward that receives substantial donative support as a stand-alone unit, even though the hospital as a whole does not. Such segregation avoids the possibility of cross-subsidizing activities which do not need a subsidy, while permitting a subsidy for those activities that do.

Second, one might want to relax the one-third threshold to 10% or 20% for certain categories of historically-exempt organizations such as schools and hospitals, according to the reasoning that there is already some measure of confidence that these institutions are deserving and therefore they should be under less of a burden to demonstrate their worthiness and neediness for a subsidy. This is suggested by the regulations under § 170, which contain a "facts and circumstances" test that permits an entity to be classified as a public charity if it both receives 10% of its support from donations and demonstrates certain factors designed to show that the entity is responsive to public needs.[25] Many other areas of tax law use 10% as the dividing line between a significant and insignificant amount.[26] Thus, plausible cases can be made for donative percentage ranging from as high as 33% to as low as 10% for the income tax exemption. Conversely, for state property tax exemptions it is possible to argue for a threshold even higher than one-third. A rather large percentage of nondonative revenue is necessary to create a significant subsidy effect under the income tax exemption because of the fact that donations do not count as taxable revenues, but this is not the case for the property tax exemption since donated property counts as property. Also, a higher threshold might be warranted for activities that experience less free-riding and therefore historically receive more donative support. For instance, a 50% threshold for religious organizations might be in order.

Third, it is possible to treat differently under a single threshold gifts of a different nature. A single threshold assumes that all donations signal about the same level of worth and need, based on our analysis in Chapter 8 that the motive for donations is not relevant to whether they deserve *any* subsidy, since some level of free-riding attends all giving. We observed there, however, that motive might matter for purposes of determining the *amount* of subsidy. One way to accommodate predictable variations (those that do not average out over donations and institutions generally) is to give less weight to donations that systematically suffer from less free-riding.

This can be done by discounting these donations in the numerator of the one-third threshold. For instance, there is good reason to believe that, as between two equally-sized gifts, one from a rich donor is more easily given than from a poor donor. If so, an argument could be made for differential accounting according to the wealth of donors, but this would be a rather complex and controversial proposition to implement. Similarly, one might demonstrate that, for a given activity, donors are more willing to give to capital than to operating expenditures because, with the former, there is more of a lasting, tangible embodiment of one's altruism and therefore more psychic ("act utility") gratification. (This is just speculation; we have no evidence.) Also, one might imagine that there is more willingness to give at death (or in contemplation of death) than during life since the donor does not have the alternative of personal consumption. On the other hand, we have no confirmation for this speculation, and it may well be that legatees value as strongly the desire to leave their wealth to their families as they value consuming it during life; indeed, spending on one's own family is usually considered a form of personal consumption.

The final way in which to depart from a uniform threshold is to adopt a tiered or sliding scale approach to subsidizing charities, whereby varying degrees of tax benefit are conferred according to the level of donative support they demonstrate. This is already suggested by the present structure of the Code, which distinguishes between 501(c)(3) charitable organizations eligible to receive both an income tax exemption and tax deductible contributions, and 501(c)(4) "social welfare organizations," which are still tax exempt but lose their eligibility to receive deductible contributions and issue tax-exempt bonds. This tiered effect also exists under the charitable deduction. Federal law allows individuals to deduct contributions up to 50% of their adjusted gross income (AGI) for donations to "public charities" such as churches, schools, hospitals, medical research entities, and any other entity which receives a "substantial part of its support" from public contributions or the government.[27] In contrast, the maximum deduction for contributions to "private foundations" is limited to 30% of AGI. The dividing line between these, moreover, is whether the entity in question meets the one-third of receipts tests discussed above.[28]

Combining this observation with those just preceding, we might gingerly suggest a system in which different subsidies "kick in" at different donation levels as illustrated in Figure 11.1: at 10%, an entity qualifies for income tax exemption, but not donation-deductibility or property tax exemption; deductibility of donations and the other "charitable" income tax benefits could kick in at the 33%, but not property tax benefits; while full exemption (income, property and deduction) might be limited to organizations with over 50% donative support. We stress, however, that each potential variation adds a considerable level of administrative complexity. Whether the trade-off is worth it is a value choice we leave to those in charge of setting and implementing public policy.

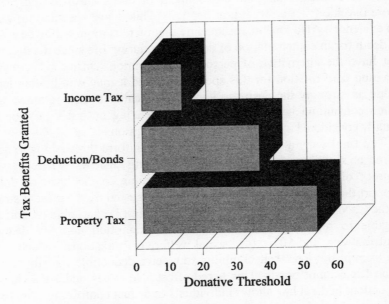

FIGURE 11.1 Possible Tiered Exemption System

Measuring Donations

The second practical issue of implementation is how to define exactly what counts as a donation for purposes of computing the threshold. This overall issue breaks into a number of subcomponents each of which we examine separately.

As noted in Chapter 8, a large body of case law in federal taxation has examined what constitutes a donation for purposes of the charitable contribution deduction under § 170 of the Code. Although court decisions sometimes vary in their exact rationale, the key attribute of a donation is that no direct quid pro quo exists for the payment. As we previously have explained, this common-law definition of donation fits well with our donative theory. The quid pro quo definition obviously excludes from the threshold payments for goods or services rendered by the entity in question. Similarly, it would exclude membership dues, since such payments are in direct exchange for valuable membership privileges.[29] As a result, our measurement of the donation threshold would more closely track that used by Code § 170 (which excludes sales and dues income) than that used by § 509 (which includes this income).

Nevertheless, even the § 170 regulations include in the donation base certain items that we would exclude, such as government grants,[30] and they exclude certain items that we would include, such as donated labor. In addition, other aspects of calculating the donation threshold, such as whether to require breadth in donations and whether to differentiate capital gifts from gifts for operations, must be examined.

Donated Labor

The reasons for the exclusion of donated labor from the definition of a publicly-supported entity under § 170 are unclear. Although the tax laws have long prohibited a *deduction* for contributed services, the reason for this is that allowing a tax write-off for personal services without imputing the value of such services as income to the donor would give a taxpayer a double tax benefit.[31] The exclusion of donated labor from the definition of a publicly-supported entity under § 170 or § 509, therefore, may simply have been out of a desire for statutory symmetry. The donative theory, however, would require inclusion of donated labor, in both the support base and the calculation of the donation threshold, for the simple reason that donation of services worth $100 is as indicative of the need for subsidy as is the donation of $100 in cash used to purchase the same services. Moreover, donated labor constitutes a very large percentage of the total value of private gifts to nonprofit institutions. Data from a 1990 Gallup survey of donations and volunteering in the United States estimated that the value of donated labor was $170 *billion*, as opposed to $123 billion of cash contributions for the same year.[32]

The obvious difficulty is how to place a monetary value on donated time. One could value donated labor at a rate that equals the volunteer's own salary, such that the time of bankers would carry much more weight than the time of bank tellers. But this would create administrative and accounting nightmares as well as ethical objections. The only feasible option is to value labor according to what it would cost the recipient in the labor market. This measure is also a fair proxy for the donative value of labor, since the organization is free to spend the savings in labor costs to increase its output. In addition, it is fair to estimate the value of a volunteer's time by what the same services would have brought if they had been sold.

Nevertheless, significant administrative burdens still exist in measuring donated labor since this is an open invitation to abusive overvaluing of those services in order to meet the contribution threshold. For example, an entity straddling the donative threshold would be tempted to call for far more volunteers than it actually needs to staff the litter pick-up for the local park, since all the volunteers' time could be counted, regardless whether they were working a hard eight-hour day or picking up litter between conversations about the weather. To ease the administrative problems, taxing authorities could adopt a standard valuation system, much as the IRS already has standard mileage rates for deduction of automobiles used for charity.[33] For instance, academic studies have valued donated labor by assuming that each worker could earn the average hourly wage of nonagricultural workers, plus 12% for fringe benefits.[34] While this is a relatively crude measure, it indicates the possibility of constructing a standard valuation system, both for hourly rates and for whole jobs.

Government and Private Grants

The donative theory dictates that government grants not be counted toward meeting the donative threshold. While an entity dependent upon government grants for operational revenue clearly has experienced private market failure, government grants *negate* the existence of the second prong of the donative theory, government failure, since by definition a grant occurs because the democratic process already has provided a mechanism for direct funding of the particular activity. Accordingly, government grants do not indicate a need for additional indirect subsidization through the tax system. Government grants would be included, however, in the denominator of the threshold fraction (gross revenues), since, like other revenues, government grants provide funds to increase output.

We recognize that elimination of government grants from the calculation of the donation threshold would cause many research organizations currently exempt from tax under § 501(c)(3) to fail our test of exemption. The loss of charitable status, however, does not eliminate the possibility of of exemption on other grounds. As noted above, we have no objection to the government deciding to found exemptions on bases other than the charitable status of the organization. One such separate basis for a noncharitable exemption is that the government should not tax itself. By extension, the government might well decide to exclude grantees from the tax base, since it makes little sense for the government to tax the very money it pays out. Such an exclusion could be crafted simply by excluding grants from income (which is not presently done).[35] Another possibility is to add such organizations to the list of entities in § 501(c)(4)-(26) that are granted exemption on some noncharitable basis.[36]

Finally, one could exclude government grants from *both* the numerator and denominator of the donation threshold, thus permitting such organizations to meet the donation threshold independently of grants. Assume, for example, a research organization that receives $900,000 in government grants and $100,000 in private donations. While donations account for only 10% of total revenues of this organization, if the government grants are excluded from gross revenues, donations make up 100% of the narrowed revenue base. The argument for this treatment proceeds from a combination of the donative theory and the theory that the government should not tax its own money. This hybrid approach attempts to avoid the "penalty" that occurs when an organization falls partly under both theories, but qualifies under neither.

In contrast with government grants, we would count as donations grants from other *private* entities since they do signal government and market failure. One might object that these private gifts suffer from no free-rider disincentive because they are often made by private foundations organized under terms that require them to make gifts to certain causes.[37] But grants by private foundations are not entirely lacking in the ability to signal deservedness because, like the case for reputation-driven giving discussed in Chapter 8, there are fewer such funds than the recipients who seek them. Therefore, a market in altruism is at work that assures us that such grants go to worthy causes and to those that the grantor perceives as being the most needy. Still, there is a valid argument that gifts by private foundations suffer from less free-riding, and therefore signal less neediness, than do other private gifts. This concern is offset by observing that most private foundations themselves receive the vast majority of their assets from gifts, typically a single large donor. Therefore, they serve as donative conduits and the signaling quality of the original gift should pass through to the foundation's distribution of that gift.

Large versus Small Gifts

Earlier, we suggested the possibility of altering the measurement of donations to depart from a system that counts all donations equally in favor of one that weights some donations more than others. The suggested rationale was that such an adjustment might be advisable to account for predictable variations in the degree of free-riding that attends different types of gifts. The one area where we think the case for this adjustment is most compelling concerns the minimum number of donors necessary to achieve charitable status. A donative threshold that does not require a minimum breadth of support suffers under both the worth and the need criteria. The aberrational, idiosyncratic desires of a single individual may not reflect the desires of any significant portion of society and thus may not be worthy of a public subsidy. The same point can be made in less absolute terms under the proportionality criterion. Even if a very large gift signals an activity valued by others, an idiosyncratic large donor may place a far greater value on the activity than do others. Therefore, even if the entity should be exempt to some extent, using that person's gift to form the entity's donative base would allow it to obtain a disproportionate subsidy by founding a much larger commercial, nondonative enterprise on the larger donative base. Moreover, as the number of donors decreases, the risk of significant free-riding, which in turn causes undersupply of the good or service, declines because factors such as peer pressure, group cohesiveness, implicit reciprocity and other external inducements likely play a larger role in motivating the donation. Thus the smaller the donative pool, the greater the probability that an additional government subsidy is not needed to provide the optimal level of goods and services.

On the other hand, the donative theory by definition primarily assists insular groups in society, since a widespread interest group presumably is better able to achieve direct government subsidy through the political system. Hence requiring too great a number of donors would undermine the very purpose of the exemption to correct for government failure. Moreover, the donative theory creates no objections to large gifts per se. There is no basis at present for assuming that the absolute size of a gift bears any predictable relation to a free-rider disincentive to give. As for worth, one might argue that a donative subsidy gives disproportionate weight to the hobbies of the rich, who obviously tend to make larger gifts. But, as discussed in Chapters 7 and 9, the reciprocity inherent in the charitable exemption means that rich taxpayers will provide proportionally more tax support (in part due to the progressive tax rates, but even under a flat tax) for the favored activities of the poor. As for need, obviously, all things being equal, a large gift "hurts" more than a small one. However, one might speculate that larger gifts come from wealthier donors who are therefore more inclined to give, but, then again, they are giving more, so these two speculative possibilities tend to cancel out.

Consequently, the only legitimate concern under the donative theory is with a very few gifts being the virtual sole source of donative support for a single entity. We should have no more concern that an entity receives 100% of its $100 million in revenues from only twenty $5 million gifts as that another entity receives $1000 from only twenty $50 gifts. The concern is not with the absolute size of gifts but their size relative to the exempt entity's overall operations.

These considerations lead us to adopt some minimal "screening" device to weed out aberrational giving. A simple numerical test (such as requiring fifteen separate donors), however, does not serve the purpose, because it could be met with one $20 million gift and fourteen $1 gifts. Obviously, such a situation is so close to a single-donor that worth and need concerns (or, at least proportionality concerns) are still present. Instead, a preferable system is one that both requires a minimum number of donations and guards against disproportionate gifts.

Fortunately, § 170 already contains such a system, including donations in the numerator of the threshold calculation only to the extent they do not exceed 2% of total support for the year.[38] This limitation effectively requires at least seventeen roughly-equal donations in any one year to satisfy the threshold limitation.[39] Such a limitation appears well-suited to the purposes of the donative theory, with one important exception. The effect of excluding most of such gifts from the numerator but not the denominator is to, in effect, penalize a charity for receiving a single large gift, since it is then more difficult for the remaining gifts to satisfy the one-third threshold.

Assume, for example, that a rich alumnus donates $10,000,000 in a single year for a new university building, and that other donations (all less than $10,000 each) equal $500,000. Under our definitional scheme, the revenue base would be $10,500,000 and the donations would count toward the threshold only to the extent of 2% of the base, or $210,000. The total amount included in the threshold for this year, therefore, would consist of the small gifts totalling $500,000 plus $210,000 of the $10,000,000 grant, for a total of $710,000, well below the one-third threshold. While this problem is ameliorated to some extent by the four-year average test of donative status used by current statutory provisions (discussed below), it may not cure it altogether.

A superior approach to accounting for large gifts would be to exclude them from both halves of the fraction, thereby avoiding a penalty effect while also not counting them toward satisfying the threshold. In fact, the current regulations adopt this bifurcated approach, distinguishing between what might be called "innocent" disproportionate gifts and those that are "suspect," according to criteria such as whether the donor is related to the organization's management, whether the gift is only tangentially relevant to its operations, and whether the organization would have met the threshold in the absence of the large gift.[40]

This bifurcation in the remedy for disproportionate gifts is well suited to the donative theory.[41] An "innocent" gift deserves more lenient treatment because it appears to be a true donation; therefore there is some level of neediness, and some indication of worthiness comes from the fact that there are a sufficient number of other, smaller gifts supporting the activity to qualify it for donative status absent the gift. Consequently, we would not want a rule that revoked an entity's charitable status merely because it happened to receive a very large gift one year. The only concern is one of proportionality—that we do not wish a single, aberrational gift to determine the *size* of the subsidy by setting the donative base on which the organization might found a commercial, nondonative enterprise.

Assume, for example, that an entity receives one $1 million gift and 16 $100 gifts. If the large gift were counted in full in both the revenue base and in the donation threshold, the one-third threshold would allow the entity to use such a gift to receive an exemption on $2 million of other income. On the other hand, if this gift is included in the revenue base but limited in counting toward the threshold, the entity will fail the exemption test even though it received nothing but donations. If the large gift were excluded from both the revenue base and the donation calculation, however, the entity is not penalized for having the large gift and also is not permitted to use the large gift to shield nondonative income. In the example, the entity could not have other income of more than $3200 (in which case, total revenue would be $4800, and it would just meet the one-third test).

However, a "suspicious" gift is one that either lacks entirely an independent indication of worthiness, or for which there are doubts about its neediness because of indications that there might be a hidden quid pro quo. Such gifts therefore should be given the status of nondonative income rather than being simply ignored. Nevertheless, disqualifying such gifts almost entirely based on these concerns is in tension with the analysis in Chapter 8 that demonstrates that motive is irrelevant to whether donations deserve a tax subsidy. This tension can be resolved by observing that the prior analysis acknowledged possible doubts in its conclusions, which we set aside because of their minor nature in the run of donations and the administrative inconvenience of isolating the doubtful cases. Here, though, we have defined a class of doubtful cases for which the correct outcome is quite important (because of the size and determinative status of disproportionate gifts). Therefore, it is justifiable to, in effect, reverse the benefit of the doubt by disqualifying these gifts absent a demonstration that they are in fact "innocent." If this still seems to treat large gifts unduly, a compromise might be struck that counts such gifts entirely in the denominator but only to a discounted extent in the numerator (although more than the 2% allowed by § 170), much as we suggest elsewhere the possibility of discounting other categories of gifts.

We also would keep two other exceptions to the breadth limitation that are part of current law. First, we would credit donations or grants from other donative entities, but only in proportion to that entity's donative status (for instance, recipients of gifts from 80% donative institutions would be counted in the numerator at 80% of their value). This implements a conduit theory that attaches to gifts from tax-exempt donors the same deservedness-signalling qualities they possessed when they were originally given to the exempt donor for redistribution.

Second, under what might be called a reverse conduit theory or a reflected worthiness test, we would exempt from the breadth limitations organizations that expend most of their income for the year as grants to donative entities. This exception would be similar to the current law's treatment of private operating foundations (those foundations that expend virtually all their income each year in making grants to public charities),[42] and is based upon our view that an entity that gives all its income each year to other organizations that have already established their deservedness does not itself need an independent check on worth and need. Since the donor institution is not itself engaging in any supply of an end good or service, it can be viewed simply as a holding tank for money and therefore engaged in the same activities as the donee institution(s).

Finally, the current statutory and regulatory schemes contain a number of "backup" rules which we would keep to avoid abuse. The regulations under § 170 and § 509(a)(2), for example, both state that "earmarked" gifts (i.e., gifts given to one entity which are earmarked for redistribution to a second entity) will be treated as having come from the original donor, and thus are not excepted from the breadth limitations. We would keep this rule under the donative theory to avoid end-runs around the breadth limitation through use of a donative entity conduit.

Capital Assets versus Operating Expenses

Another important aspect of measuring the donative base is whether donations for capital projects, such as a new hospital wing, should count the same as donations to cover operating expenses, and, related to this issue, whether capital gifts should be credited over some time period (say, the depreciation period of the asset they purchase) since presumably they are not "used up" during the current year. Our starting assumption is that each type of gift is equally worthy. Typically, an organization must have both a capital base and a means of meeting operating expenditures in order to produce goods and services. No significance should attach to the fact that a donation is used to purchase a building for Local U. rather than defraying the electric bill, because both are integral parts of the delivery by Local U. of its educational services. In fact, one can surmise that any given entity will target solicitations for donations to those areas in which the entity most needs help to continue its production of goods and services. As we have stated before, however, empirical or other evidence might show that a given class of gifts, such as gifts to capital campaigns, suffers proportionately less free-riding than other classes of gifts and therefore is less in need of an additional tax subsidy. The donative theory obviously can accommodate such modulations by using separate thresholds for different classes of gifts, or by "weighting" such gifts in the calculation of the donation threshold differently.

Another difficulty created by capital gifts is created by the fact that we favor an implementation of the donative theory that tests donative status on a periodic basis; therefore, proper measurement of the importance of donations to the output capacity of an entity in any one year suggests that some type of amortization system for capital gifts is appropriate. In effect, such a system attempts to match the portion of the donation used in a particular year for production of the undersupplied good or service to other revenues available that year. Moreover, because of the 2% limitation on counting gifts, simply including gifts for capital purchases entirely in the year the donation is made might unfairly skew the donation threshold calculation for a year in which the entity receives a very large capital donation.[43] We do not want a system which forces entities to structure donations to eliminate such skewing, such as by having the gift made in portions over a number of years.[44]

Amortizing capital gifts into the donation threshold fraction (both numerator and denominator) over some predefined period, such as the depreciation period for the assets purchased with the capital gift, solves each of these concerns.[45] This approach would avoid undue pressure to structure the donation as a series of several smaller gifts. It also is a better fit with the donative theory: to the extent that the amortization period approximates the economic useful life of the asset purchased, the tax subsidy is made more proportionate by being applied as the asset is expended in producing the undersupplied good or service rather than all in one year. Finally, common intuition suggests that donors to capital campaigns view their gifts as having some measure of lasting effect—the current gift of $1 million to the children's hospital wing is prompted by the long-term nature of the asset purchased with the gift. Amortizing the gift into the donation threshold calculation would more closely align the tax effect of the gift with this donor motivation.

A third facet of this issue is how to count contributions made to endowment funds and how to count the interest earned on those funds. A case can be made to treat gifts to endowment similarly to capital gifts and to amortize them into the donation threshold calculation over some period of time. Donors to endowment funds, like donors to capital campaigns, probably believe their gifts have a lasting quality. Moreover, like capital items, endowment funds are not "used up" in the current year. However, such an approach would present far more difficult issues of administration than amortizing capital gifts. Whereas accounting for capital assets gifts easily plugs into depreciation schedules that exempt entities already keep for financial accounting purposes, amortization of endowment gifts would require creating new accounting systems that apply the amortization schedule to each year's gifts. This kind of annual segregation requirement could become an administrative nightmare. Moreover, an amortization system would have to account for what happens when endowment funds are used to meet extraordinary operating expenses: presumably, the unamortized amount of the gift would be immediately included in the denominator and numerator of the donation threshold calculation, but determining which funds are immediately included would require tracing the funds used or adoption of some accounting convention such as first-in/first-out. Therefore, we would count gifts to endowment in full in the year received. Under this system, interest from endowment funds would be part of the gross revenue denominator of the threshold fraction, but would not be counted in the donation numerator (any more than rental income on a donated building would be).

However, this presents the possibility of unduly penalizing recipients of large gifts to endowment—those that violate the 2% rule set forth above. Like capital gifts, the penalty effect will be larger than the actual economic benefit of the gift in the time-span in which the penalty is felt. Therefore, there is a good case for modifying the approach just outlined in text to allow amortization of disproportionately large gifts to endowment that exceed the 2% limit. Observe, though, that this is an issue only for such gifts that are classified as "suspect," which is more likely for the donation of capital assets than for the donation of cash. Thus, there are likely to be few such exceptions. However, if the leader of a local Boy Scout troop donates his limited partnership interest in a highly-depreciated Texas oil well and the troop sells the interest to create an endowment, then it might be unfair to impose the entire penalty effect from this gift in a single year.

Fundraising Abuse and Political Activity

Two final issues of practical implementation that affect how donative status is measured are fundraising abuse and political activity. This section demonstrates that these misuses of the exemption can be effectively controlled by determining how gross revenues and net donations are accounted for under the donative theory.

Controlling Fundraising Abuse

Obviously, a system that keys tax exemption to a specific level of donative support encourages aggressive fundraising campaigns. We do not intend in this space to address the legal aspects of regulation of fundraising by charitable organizations, a subject that has been examined by economists and legal commentators.[46] We note, however, that the abuse that has engendered the most legislative action and critical commentary is the problem of excessive costs of fundraising—that is, a charitable entity that spends a very small portion of a donation on delivery of charitable services, with the lion's share covering the costs of fundraising itself.[47] A donative system that counted donations toward the threshold regardless of the associated costs clearly would exacerbate the excessive cost problem, since there would be every incentive to spend up to 100% of receipts on fundraising. In fact, one can hypothesize situations in which fundraising costs *exceeding* 100% of donations would be rational, since the gross donations so generated might trigger the donative threshold and result in tax savings that exceed the fundraising costs.

Assume, for example, that an entity has gross revenues of $1000, none of which are from donations, and has taxable income after expenses of $100. The entity owes federal tax of $35 under the current maximum corporate tax rate of 35%. Donations to the entity of $500 under our system would invoke charitable status and a tax exemption, saving the entity $35 in taxes. If the gross donations counted toward the one-third threshold, presumably the entity would pay up to $535 for successful fundraising services. That is, at a cost of $535, the fundraising campaign "breaks even" producing zero net return (a cost of $535, offset by additional revenues of $500 and a tax savings of $35).

Professor Espinoza notes a number of other situations in which charities may engage in fundraising campaigns where costs exceed the amount raised. For example, a charity may want to present a "successful image" by raising as much money as possible regardless of cost. Or a charity might rationally engage in a donor acquisition program where costs exceed the actual donations.[48] In the latter case, the charity presumably believes that once the donor is "hooked," future contributions will offset the current excess expenses.

The obvious solution to this problem is to count only net donations in the threshold amount—that is, gift receipts less fundraising expenses. A system that counts only the net donation better matches the level of tax subsidy to the level of deservedness by insuring that the tax subsidy is not provided to entities whose primary activity is fundraising.[49] Classifying expenditures of an entity as fundraising costs versus expenditures on charitable programs raises an inherently difficult, but, as Professor Espinoza has pointed out, not insurmountable, problem of classification and accounting.[50]

A net system also provides incentives for the entity to engage in the most cost-effective fundraising, since gross donations will be included in the total revenue base and will cause a "gross-up" effect that makes meeting the threshold harder as proportionate fundraising costs rise. Taking the previous example, assume that fundraising costs are 50% of donations. In order to meet the one-third threshold, gross donations would have to be at least $2000 (the gross donations would increase total revenues to $3000, one third of which is $1000, which is the net donation amount in the example). If fundraising costs are only 10%, then the gross donations needed to meet the threshold would go down to $590 (gross revenues are now $1590, one third of which equals $530, and net donations are $531).[51] While this system probably would not eradicate the excess cost problem, at least it insures that the donative theory does not erode the general economic incentive to control costs in order to maximize revenues.

The donative theory is also open to the objection that making huge tax subsidies turn on the amount of fundraising will aggravate fundraising abuses by prompting charities to engage in false or misleading claims to the public about their activities. We witness regular news reports or prosecutions of outright fraudulent fundraising, and even respected charities are attacked for playing into mere "popularity contests" when they approach the public for support. Naturally, we do not deny that these abuses and irrationalities exist; we can only observe that they are no worse, and could be less worse, than the equivalent behavior the exists in the political and market sectors. The donative theory cannot be judged in isolation but only in comparison with its principal contenders, which are to distribute tax support through the administrative decisions of tax bureaucrats or the

judicial rulings drawn from anachronistic trust law. Each of these competing systems suffers from its own severe flaws. If consumer ignorance or
gullibility were an absolute objection, then we would also have to abandon
our market economy for a planned economy. Distributing tax subsidies
according to the collective wishes of hundreds of millions of donors is
much more consistent with our political and cultural heritage. Efforts to
expose abuses and educate donors should be encouraged, and adopting the
donative theory would only underscore the need for this social activism.

Limiting Political Activity

As noted earlier, political activities by exempt organizations raise many
of the same issues as fundraising expenses.[52] In a sense, political activity is
a form of fundraising, since much, if not all, such activity will be directed
toward improving the financial fortunes of the entity. While the current
federal scheme provides a type of compromise on political activity,
permitting some types of legislative lobbying to some degree, but prohibit-
ing political campaign activity, the donative theory permits a simpler
mechanism for checking political expenditures. As with fundraising costs,
the donation threshold could be calculated by deducting political activity
costs from donations for purposes of computing the donative threshold.
This netting calculation produces the same incentive to limit lobbying costs
as it does to limit fundraising costs, while avoiding substance-based
regulation. Obviously, determining what costs are attributable to political
activity will require some administrative definition, but current law already
requires identifying certain such expenditures for purposes of the I.R.C.
§ 501(h) safe-harbor rule regarding lobbying.[53]

Timing and Identification Issues

So far we have outlined the basic system for identifying donations and
measuring them against an entity's revenue base. What remain are some
general issues of implementation, such as whether the classification of
donative entities should proceed on an individual or industry-wide basis,
when the measurement of donative status should occur, and how to deal
with start-up entities that have no support history.

Implementing the Classification: Entity versus Industry

An industry-wide measurement has the advantage of the administrative
simplicity of a one-for-all decision. What statistical compilations exist on
donations generally are assembled on an industry-wide basis, permitting

fairly easy implementation of such a system. Nevertheless, we believe that an entity-by-entity system is preferable.

To be valid, industry-wide data would have to come from reports by all or most of the individual industry participants; if each entity has to report its position for purposes of an industry-wide survey anyway, little administrative advantage is gained by avoiding scrutiny of specific entities. In addition, organizations may not be amenable to convenient pigeonholing: exactly what sector is the United Way associated with, for example? Perhaps most important, however, is the fact that a given organization's support base may vary widely from the norm depending on its exact activities and geographic location. The statistics for an entire industry say little about what funding situation a particular entity faces. For example, the hospital industry as a whole does not receive high levels of donative support, but a particular institution, or a particular service within many institutions, may be fully deserving of charitable status. For instance, Shriners hospitals, which care for children, rely almost entirely on donations, and cancer treatment for children seems to attract significant donative support for conventional hospitals.[54] Finally, an entity-by-entity approach is already used in classifying publicly-supported organizations under the Code. The administrative machinery for individual decision-making, therefore, already exists in current law.

When Is Donative Status Tested?

The donative theory requires that entities justify their exemption on some regular basis. The fact that a charity received substantial donative support in one prior period does not preclude social conditions from changing in the future. For example, the history of nonprofit hospitals recounted in the next chapter illustrates a dramatic shift from an industry reliant on donations to an industry reliant primarily on direct government subsidies and income from sale of services. Accordingly, some mechanism is necessary to recheck entities periodically to ensure that they still meet the donative standard.

On the other hand, donation levels can vary for a given year, and it is perfectly possible that an entity can miss the threshold requirement in any one year but still meet it on an average basis over a number of years. Requiring an entity to meet the donation threshold every year would create undue pressure to structure donations so that little yearly variation occurs. Moreover, such a system would be unwieldy from the standpoint of yearly budgeting for managers of exempt entities: since in any given year an entity could "go taxable," managers would have to plan for the possibility of tax payments which might or might not be due that year.

Some level of compromise between the necessity of periodic retesting and unwieldy "flip-flopping" is already a part of the Code scheme, however. The regulations under § 170 and § 509 both use a four-year rolling average for the calculation of the public support threshold.[55] Moreover, once an entity meets this threshold, it is presumed to satisfy the public support test for the succeeding two years. This system appears consistent with the donative theory.

Start-up Entities

The final timing issue deals with the mechanism for handling start-up enterprises. Since by definition these entities have no operating history, they cannot demonstrate that they meet the donative threshold requirements. One method for handling such situations, of course, is simply to withhold tax-exempt status until the entity satisfies the donation threshold based upon past operations. Most studies of charitable contributions concede, however, that the tax deduction for contributions is critical to attracting donations;[56] accordingly, withholding exempt status and the corresponding deduction for contributions would put the entity at an unfair disadvantage in the market in altruism.

As a result, we favor a system that permits exemption on a trial basis, after which an entity would be required to meet the donation threshold on the basis of actual operations. Once again, we are guided by current law. The regulations under § 170 and § 509 permit newly-created organizations to apply for an advance ruling which essentially permits the entity to be classified as a public charity for a two- or five-year test period.[57] The test period ruling is granted on the basis of a facts and circumstances test which attempts to determine whether the entity's "organizational structure, proposed programs or activities, and intended method of operation are such as to attract the type of broadly based support from the general public"[58] that is necessary to meet the test of publicly-supported organizations. The regulations list a number of factors to guide the decision, including breadth of public representation on the governing board of the entity, breadth of initial funding, size of initial endowment, plans for fundraising solicitation and the like.[59] At the end of the test period, the entity must demonstrate that it meets the regular tests for publicly-supported status. This procedure can be adapted wholesale to the donative theory.

Summary of Practical Implementation

To summarize, we would apply the donative test on an entity-by-entity basis, using a donation threshold of from one-tenth to one-third of total revenues (and perhaps higher for some purposes) to classify charitable organizations eligible for tax-exemption. We would also adopt the four-year average approach of current law to even out fluctuations in gifts that could adversely affect the calculation of the donation threshold, and we would adopt the advance ruling procedure of current law for start-up entities. This is essentially the same procedure and threshold tests used by current law in defining publicly-supported organizations.

We would define total revenues in generally the same manner as is already done in Code § 509(d) to include almost all sources of revenue, but we would also include gains from capital asset sales. The donation threshold calculations would include all those items currently included for purposes of § 170(b) other than government grants, and would continue to limit the amount any one donation counted in the threshold to 2% of the gross revenues for the year. Moreover, to help control fund-raising abuses and political activity, we would calculate the threshold with reference to the net donations (that is, the excess of donations over fundraising expenses and political activity expenses). Because of the overall importance of donated labor to judging the level of public support of an organization, we would add labor to the donation threshold calculation (both numerator and denominator) using a standard valuation system. Unlike current law, we would amortize gifts for capital purchases into both numerator and denominator over a predefined time period, such as the asset's depreciation period. We also suggest a number of other possible refinements that could be adopted, depending on the results from further empirical inquiry into altruistic behavior and depending on regulators' appetites for accuracy over simplicity.

Given the amount of material that can be adapted from current statutes and regulatory procedures, implementing the donative theory would not require a major overhaul of the tax administrative system. Although our proposed system borrows heavily from federal tax law, states could piggyback on the system by either copying the federal statutes or by conferring charitable status automatically on anyone that receives federal approval, as is already the case with most state income tax laws. The significance of this change, however, should not be minimized: the proposed system would completely replace the current system of administering exemptions under § 501(c)(3), by eliminating activity-specific judgments of community benefit, commercial manner, relatedness and the like in favor of more bright-line, quantitative tests for donative status that would not permit any categories of presumptively donative entities. Individual churches, nonprofit hospitals and nonprofit educational institutions each would have to prove their case for the exemption. The final chapter explores how likely they are to be able to meet this burden.

Notes

1. We note, however, that critics of new theories too frequently overstress the impossibility of perfect implementation while downplaying the imperfections of the status quo. As Professors Surrey and McDaniel have noted, the taxing system can be as simple or as complicated as one desires. *See* STANLEY S. SURREY & PAUL R. MCDANIEL, TAX EXPENDITURES (1988) 101–102.

2. I.R.C. § 170 (1954). The stated reason for the differentiation was "to aid these institutions in obtaining the additional funds they need, in view of their rising costs and the relatively low rate of return they are receiving on endowment funds." Senate Finance Committee Report to H.R. 8300, *reprinted in* 1954 U.S.C.C.A.N. 4660.

3. Pub. L. No. 88-272, § 209(a), 78 Stat.19, 43. The specific reason for this addition was Congressional recognition of the "many beneficial activities carried on by various philanthropic organizations not now eligible for the [higher deduction limit]." S. REP. NO. 830, 88th Cong., 2d Sess., *reprinted in* 1964-1 Cum. Bull. 562 (part 2).

4. *Id.* at 563–64.

5. I.R.C. § 170 (1964).

6. *See generally* Council on Foundations, *Private Foundations and the 1969 Tax Reform Act*, in RESEARCH PAPERS SPONSORED BY THE COMMISSION ON PRIVATE PHILANTHROPY AND PUBLIC NEEDS 1557, 1557–59 (U.S. Dept. of the Treasury ed., 1977) (hereafter FILER COMMISSION PAPERS).

7. I.R.C. § 509(a).

8. I.R.C. § 170(b)(1)(A)(viii).

9. One set, contained largely in the regulations under § 170(b)(1)(A)(vi), derives from the 1964 legislation adding certain publicly-supported organizations to the higher contribution limit enacted in 1954. The second set, which is a combination of statutory tests set forth in Code § 509(a)(2) and the regulations thereunder, drew on the IRS regulations under § 170 to further refine the difference between organizations that received broad-based public support and those that did not.

10. I.R.C. §509(a)(2)(A).

11. *Id.*

12. I.R.C. § 509(a)(2)(A)(ii) states that items will count toward meeting the one-third of support test only if they are not from "disqualified persons" as defined in Code § 4946. Section 4946(a)(2) includes in "disqualified persons" a person who is a "substantial contributor," which § 507(d)(2) defines as explained in text.

13. I.R.C. § 509(d) defines "support" as the sum of
   (1)   gifts, grants, contributions, or membership fees;
   (2)   *gross receipts* (not gross income) from admissions, sales of merchandise, performance of services and the like;
   (3)   net income from unrelated business activities;
   (4)   gross investment income;
   (5)   tax revenues levied for an organization and expended on its behalf; and
   (6)   the value of any services or facilities furnished by government to the entity free of charge.

14. Treas. Regs. § 1.509(a)-3(c)(1) & (3).

15. I.R.C. § 170(b)(1)(A)(vi); Treas. Regs. § 170A-9(e)(7)(i)(a). The statute states that support is "exclusive of income received in the exercise or performance by such organization of its charitable . . . function . . . ."

16. Treas. Regs. § 1.170A-9(e)(9), example (4).

17. *See* BURTON A. WEISBROD, THE NONPROFIT ECONOMY 197, Table C.4 (1988).

18. *See generally,* WEISBROD, *supra* note 17, at 75; Burton A. Weisbrod, *Private Goods, Collective Goods: The Role of the Nonprofit Sector, in* THE ECONOMICS OF NONPROPRIETARY ORGANIZATIONS (Kenneth W. Clarkson & Donald L. Martin eds., 1980) at 150 (both using gross revenues as a measure of various types of goods output). Obviously, one could choose other measuring sticks, such as net worth, net revenues or some modification of these or other measurements. None of these other yardsticks, however, seems as relevant as gross receipts to the issue at hand: whether the undersupply of a good or service is significant enough to warrant subsidization through the tax system. *Net* revenues means nothing in this equation, since an exempt organization may (perhaps ideally would) spend all its receipts on delivery of goods and services to its market and be left with zero net revenues. While a comparison of total donated assets to total net worth might have some bearing on the importance of donations to an entity's overall operation, the major problem with using a net worth comparison is that it says little about the importance of donations to an organization's delivery of goods and services *in the current year*. As set forth below in the text, we would require periodic retesting of an entity's donative status, whereas an entity's net worth may have resulted entirely from a large donation made generations ago. Such an entity should not automatically be exempt today.

19. Note that current law exempts "gains" from such transactions. We would continue to include just the gain, rather than the total receipt, since only the gain represents new revenues. The amount previously invested in the property (its basis, in tax jargon) has already been accounted for in the donative measurement, and hence should not be counted again. To illustrate, assume an entity received $100 in donations in year 1, and invested the money in stocks. In this year, the entity is 100% donative—that is, all its current output capability arose from donations. In year 2, the entity receives $1 in donations, but sells the stock for $100. In this year, the entity has $101 of output capability, but only $1 of "new" money. The other

$100 was already counted in year 1, and should be excluded from the year 2 calculation.

20. In fact, including only *net* income from an unrelated business would run counter to the proportionality criterion. Assume, for example, two entities, one which receives $1000 from donations and expends that $1000 on, say, famine relief, and another which has $100 in donations and $900 in receipts from an unrelated business as against $850 of expenses for that business and as a result spends only $150 on famine relief. Obviously, the first entity is producing a far greater output of famine relief, and because that greater output is funded totally by donations, it is in greater need of subsidization. If the measuring base included only net income from the unrelated business, both these entities would be substantially donative (100% vs. 67%); by including gross receipts from the unrelated business in the measurement base, we can see that in fact the second entity is far less deserving.

21. Treas. Regs. § 1.170A-9(e)(7)(ii).

22. To see this, suppose the nondonative receipts of each organization are produced by selling their literature at a net return of 10% of sales revenue. The first organization has $900,000 of sales revenue and a resulting $90,000 profit which is otherwise taxable income; the second has $10,000 of profit. If the corporate income tax rate were 30%, exempting the first would produce a subsidy of 27 cents per dollar of donation ($27,000 of forgiven taxes versus $100,000 of donations), whereas exempting the second would produce a subsidy of only one-third of a cent ($0.0033) per dollar of donation ($3,000 versus $900,000).

23. Weisbrod, *Private Goods*, *supra* note 18, at 151–60. We note that Weisbrod's Collectiveness Index includes government grants but does not include the value of donated labor. As explained below, we would exclude government grants from the donation threshold, but we would include the value of donated labor. Making these offsetting adjustments is not likely to fundamentally change Weisbrod's observations that those organizations most associated with public goods receive more than 33% of their revenues from donations.

24. VIRGINIA A. HODGKINSON ET AL., NONPROFIT ALMANAC 1992–1993 at 147–52, Tables 4.2 and 4.3 (1992).

25. Treas. Regs. § 1.170A-9(e)(3).

26. Several tax provisions, for example, raise the issue whether "substantially all" the assets or revenue of an entity comes from one source or another. In these cases, the IRS generally has interpreted the phrase to mean at least 90%—or put positively, that more than 10% from the wrong source is significant. *E.g.*, Rev. Proc. 77-37, 1977-2 C.B. 568 (interpreting "substantially all the assets" in a reorganization context as 90% of the net assets); I.R.C. § 141(b) (defining a private activity bond as one in which "more than 10%" of the proceeds are used in private business activity); I.R.C. § 145 (using 90% as the cut-off for determining whether a tax-exempt bond is used entirely for hospital purposes).

27. I.R.C. § 170(b)(1)(A)(vi) (1989).

28. Treas. Reg. § 1.170A-9(e)(2) (1973).

29. It would be appropriate, however, to bifurcate membership dues when there clearly are both quid pro quo and donative elements to the "membership." For example, one becomes a "member" of the Metropolitan Opera Society by making a $100 payment. This payment entitles a member to a biweekly magazine (Opera News) which otherwise would cost $35 per year, and discounts on certain other merchandise. Clearly, a substantial portion of the dues are nothing more than a donation. *See also* Treas. Reg. § 1.170A-9(e)(7)(iii) (support includes membership fees unless fees are for the purpose of purchasing goods, services, access to facilities or the like).

30. Treas. Reg. § 1.170A-9(e)(7)(i)(b).

31. BORIS I. BITTKER & LAWRENCE LOKKEN, FEDERAL TAXATION OF INCOME, ESTATES AND GIFTS ¶ 35.2.1 at 35-17 (2d ed. 1992); MICHAEL J. GRAETZ, FEDERAL INCOME TAXATION: PRINCIPLES AND POLICIES 487 (2d ed. 1988).

32. VIRGINIA A. HODGKINSON & MURRAY S. WEITZMAN, GIVING AND VOLUNTEERING IN THE UNITED STATES 16 (1990). The authors used a figure of $10.82 per hour, which was the 1989 average nonagricultural wage, multiplied this number by the estimated 15.7 billion hours of volunteer time, and then increased the product by 12% to take into account fringe benefit values. The cash donation figure comes from HODGKINSON ET AL., *supra* note 24, at 59, Table 2.1.

33. I.R.C. § 170(i) (12 cents per mile).

34. WEISBROD, NONPROFIT ECONOMY, *supra* note 17, at 132.

35. *See, e.g.*, I.R.C. §§ 102, 117. *See generally* BITTKER & LOKKEN, *supra* note 31, at chs. 10 and 11.

36. *Cf.* I.R.C. § 170(b)(1)(A)(iii) (singling out medical research organizations as qualifying for the higher deductibility limit).

37. This requirement might come not only from the trust instrument but also from tax law itself, which prohibits private foundations from engaging in excessive accumulation of earnings. I.R.C. § 4942 (excise tax on failure of private foundation to make minimum distributions). *See generally* PAUL R. TREUSCH, TAX-EXEMPT CHARITABLE ORGANIZATIONS 497–509 (3d ed. 1988).

38. Treas. Regs. § 1.170A-9(e)(6).

39. Mathematically, the § 170 threshold will always require at least 17 gifts. Under this section, the threshold is more than 33% of the total revenue base, or 33% of 100%. Since each donation "counts" only up to 2% of the revenue base, a minimum of 17 2%-gifts are needed to meet the threshold (17 x 2 = 34). The 2% limitation also guards against cases in which one gift is a disproportionate percentage of total donations. For example, assume an entity with $1 million in total revenues. The 33% threshold will be met with seventeen $20,000 gifts. The threshold will also be met with sixteen $20,000 gifts and one $500,000 gift. Suppose, however, that there is one gift of $500,000 and 16 gifts of $100. In this case, the entity fails the threshold (33% of $1 million is $333,333. The $500,000 gift counts in the numerator up to 2% of $1 million, or $20,000. The total numerator, therefore, is $21,600, far less than the required one third). Of course, the threshold also can be met with 320,000 $1 gifts and one $500,000 gift, but in this

situation, the $500,000 is not as disproportionate a percentage of total donations as it is in the case of the 16 $100 gifts.

We prefer this approach to the limit contained indirectly in § 509(a)(2), which credits donations to the extent of the greater of $5000 or 2% of total donations over the life of the entity. Under the § 509(a)(2) system, an entity that had "built-up" a donation record could meet the threshold with very few large gifts in later years. Suppose, for example, that total donations to an entity for years 1–20 were $20 million, and that in year 21 total revenues are $1,200,000. The one-third test would be met in year 21 with a single donation of $400,000, since such a donation would be one third of total support and would "count" in full since the donation does not exceed 2% of total donations for all years. In our view, an entity ought to demonstrate its need for subsidization on a regular basis and not be able to use prior donations to obtain an exemption forever.

40. Treas. Regs. § 1.509(a)-3(c)(3).

41. However, we would adopt somewhat different indicia for "innocent" versus "suspect" gifts. For instance, we would not give more credit to gifts by bequest than to inter vivos gifts, and we would add additional factors that attempt to ferret out hidden quid pro quos for a gift.

42. I.R.C. § 170(b)(1)(A)(vii) and 170(b)(1)(E) gives preferred status to "private operating foundations" as defined in I.R.C. § 4942(j)(3). To highly simplify an incredibly complex statute, private operating foundations are those foundations which expend virtually all their income each year in making grants to public charities. The statute provides exceptions to the general rule of mandatory distribution, such as permitting income accumulations for special projects. I.R.C. § 4942(g)(2). For a short general discussion of private operating foundations, see TREUSCH, *supra* note 37, at 567–72.

43. This skewing, however, exists only for gifts that are classified as "suspect," under the criteria discussed in text at 207-09, since "innocent" large gifts are excluded from both numerator and denominator. Thus, one might respond to the skewing concern that this effect is precisely what is intended for these kinds of gifts. However, the *degree* of skewing is unfair if it all occurs in a single year rather than being spread out over the economic life of the gift. The amortization remedy we adopt does not avoid all such skewing since even the amortized portion of a large capital gift could exceed the 2% threshold. If so, and if the gift fell into the "suspect" category, the amortized portion would still be treated under the rules set out above. Observe also that the concern over unfair skewing does not exist for disproportionate gifts used for operating expenses (say, to pay off a whopping lawyer's bill), since in such cases the entity in fact receives the full economic benefit of the gift in a single year.

44. Under § 509, items are included in the support denominator and the donation numerator for the threshold fraction under the cash method of accounting. Treas. Regs. § 1.509(a)-3(k). Thus a pledge for a contribution, even if legally binding, is not counted until actually received. *Id.* This permits an entity to spread one large contribution over a number of years, and we would presume that entities would

choose this route as a matter of course if exempt status depended on it.

45. The tax depreciation period is one obvious choice, although we are mindful that the tax depreciation system only rarely attempts to approximate economic useful life. The ADR system in place prior to ACRS (and still used for certain definitional purposes) might be a good starting point, since that system attempts to define an economic useful life. *See generally,* BITTKER & LOKKEN, *supra* note 17, at ¶ 23.6.4. GAAP (generally accepted accounting principles) depreciation lives might be another starting point, although again we must consider the trade-off between administrative simplicity and theoretical purity. Some accommodation would need to be made for assets that are not depreciable, such as land. Perhaps the cost of such capital items would be amortized over the longest available depreciation period.

46. A recent comprehensive treatment of the legal aspects of charitable fundraising is that of Leslie Espinoza, *Straining the Quality of Mercy: Abandoning the Quest for Informed Charitable Giving,* 64 S. CAL. L. REV. 605 (1991). Other discussions include Susan Rose-Ackerman, *Charitable Giving and "Excessive" Fundraising,* 97 Q. J. ECON. 193 (1982); Note, *Regulation of Charitable Fundraising: Riley v. National Federation of the Blind of North Carolina,* 24 U. SAN. FRAN. L. REV. 205 (1989); Note, *Charitable Fraud in New York: The Role of the Professional Fund Raiser,* 33 N.Y.L.S. L. REV. 409 (1988); Note, *Secretary of State v. Joseph H. Munson Co.: State Regulation of Fundraising Costs,* 5 PACE L. REV. 489 (1985).

47. Espinoza, *supra* note 46; *See Organized Charities Pass Off Mailing Costs As "Public Education,"* WALL ST. J., October 29, 1990, at A1 (noting that 90% of money raised by the Doris Day Animal League raises is used for further fundraising, specifically for direct mail campaigns). *See generally Abuses in Charitable and Nonprofit Giving: Hearings Before the Subcomm. on Antitrust, Monopolies and Business Rights of the Senate Judiciary Comm.,* 101st Cong., 1st Sess. (1989). These abuses, however bad, do not defeat the case for the donative theory because they are no worse than those that afflict market and government mechanisms, which are the primary alternatives. Moreover, the donative theory may help focus attention on the need for further reforms.

48. Espinoza, *supra* note 46, at 653.

49. *Cf. id.* at 672–73 ("Congress could declare that fundraising, like lobbying, while a legitimate charitable activity, is of such low public benefit that it should not be subsidized through the tax exemption and deductibility system.").

50. *Id.* at 656–663.

51. Algebraically, the gross donations needed to meet the threshold can be calculated using the formula:

$$1/3(GR + D) = FRC \times D$$

where GR is the gross revenues not including donations, D is the gross donation amount, and FRC is the fundraising cost expressed as a percentage of donations.

52. As noted earlier, we can see no reason to treat political activity such as campaigning differently from lobbying, inasmuch as both are methods for accomplishing a given goal: improvement of the fortunes of the entity engaged in the political activity. One of the strengths of the donative theory is that normative judgments regarding "good" and "bad" activities for a charity, such as "good" and "bad" political activity, can be eliminated.

53. *See generally* James J. McGovern et al., *The Final Lobbying Regulations: A Challenge for Both the IRS and Charities*, TAX NOTES, Sept. 3, 1990, at 1305.

54. *See* Mark A. Hall & John D. Colombo, *The Charitable Status of Nonprofit Hospitals: Toward a Donative Theory of Tax Exemption*, 66 WASH. L. REV. 307, 410.

55. Treas. Regs. § 1.170A-9(e)(4); 1.509(a)-3(c)(1). In each system whether an entity has met the threshold is determined on the basis of the aggregate revenue base and donation total for the previous four years.

56. *See, e.g.*, WEISBROD, NONPROFIT ECONOMY, *supra* note 17, at 93–95 and sources cited therein.

57. Treas. Regs. § 1.170A-9(e)(5); § 1.509(a)-3(d).

58. *Id.*

59. Treas. Regs. § 1.170A-9(e)(5)(ii); § 1.509(a)-3(d)(2).

12

Effect on Traditional Charities

In this chapter, we survey a collection of quintessential charitable institutions to determine how they would fare under the donative theory. For this purpose, we have selected religious, educational (including performing arts and cultural), research and health care organizations. Our omission of several other important categories does not denigrate their significance in the sphere of charitable activities. Instead, space limitations force us to select those areas that are likely to produce the sharpest disputes, and to pass over areas such as social welfare organizations discussed in earlier chapters. Social welfare organizations such as the Red Cross, United Way and Salvation Army are obviously paradigm donative organizations that help the disadvantaged, and hence there is little dispute regarding their entitlement to exemption under any theory. We also do not discuss activities such as social clubs and other mutual benefit organizations that qualify for exemption under theories that do not relate to charitable status. As we explain in the introduction, our purpose is to map the contours of the generic charitable exemption, not to cover exhaustively every ad hoc instance of legislative largesse.

Religious Organizations

Exempting Religious Organizations Under Current Law

As the Supreme Court explained in *Walz v. Tax Commission*, tax exemptions for churches are the product of an "unbroken" history that "covers our entire national existence and indeed predates it."[1] One commentator has noted there was "no time before which churches were taxed and in which we can seek the reason for exemption."[2] Priests and temples were exempt in ancient Babylon and Egypt, with recorded instances of exemption as early as 2169 B.C.[3] British common law held as early as 1639 that trusts for the advancement of religion were charitable, and churches there were eligible for a variety of different exemptions depending on their orthodox status. This differential exemption practice carried over to the Colonies, but the exemption was then generalized to all religions with the Constitutional adoption of the separation principle.

Because of this long history and the freedom of religious exercise guaranteed by the First Amendment concerns, the core rationale for religious exemption has seldom been questioned. The religious exemption originated from the tax-base notion that the state should not tax its own supported religion, and it has carried over into modern era under the subsidy notion that churches provide community services and relieve government burdens.[4] Nevertheless, controversy surrounds precisely what constitutes a religion or church and when the exemption is being abused.

Federal tax law has been extremely reluctant to define what constitutes a "religious" organization for tax exemption purposes, although both the IRS and the Supreme Court insist that whatever religious belief is asserted must be sincerely held.[5] The IRS has developed a list of fourteen factors that it uses in assessing whether a particular institution can validly claim to be a "church" (which is a subset of religious organizations, not co-extensive with it). These factors include (1) whether the entity has called itself a church since its inception, (2) a distinct legal existence, (3) a recognized creed and form of worship, (4) a definite and distinct ecclesiastical government, (5) a formal code of doctrine and discipline, (6) a distinct religious history, (7) a membership not associated with any other church or denomination, (8) a complete organization of ordained ministers, (9) a literature of its own, (10) established places of worship, (11) regular congregations, (12) regular services, (13) religious instruction for members and (14) schools for preparation of ministers.[6] The federal courts also have focused on some of these criteria in assessing whether an organization is a church for exemption purposes, particularly the notion of a regular congregation, religious services and ministers.[7]

This multi-factor criteria approach presents formidable administration problems. Even the IRS admits that "few, if any, religious organizations—conventional or unconventional—could satisfy all these criteria,"[8] so the IRS has considerable leeway in how demanding to be in applying these criteria. The result of providing so little guidance, however, has been an administrative crisis. By the late 1970's the IRS was faced with a series of "mail-order church" cases in which individuals formed so-called churches, transferred their personal assets to the church, deducted the transfer as a charitable contribution, and then claimed exempt status for their former personal assets as church property. One commentator reports that at one time, 88% of the residents of Hardenburgh, New York, became ordained ministers of the Universal Life Church in order to take advantage of this scheme.[9] The ULC and similar entities spawned over 100 litigated tax court cases in the early 1980s and resulted in the IRS placing such entities on its abusive tax shelter list.[10]

Similar chaos has occurred at the state level. Professor John Witte surveyed the multitude of state cases examining the property tax exemption for nontraditional and sometimes fraudulent churches and discerned four distinct tests for genuine religious status, which have generated "widely divergent results."[11] State courts sometimes approve sincere but offbeat, "new-age" religions,[12] and other times reject them because of their unorthodoxy.[13] Only when the church appears to be nothing more than the formalization of a distinct lifestyle (such as a "hippie commune") do the courts consistently reject exempt status.[14]

Limitations on Religious Exemption

Because of these difficulties in defining "religious" for tax purposes, tax collectors more often use the private inurement and the "commerciality" doctrines to police religious exemptions.[15] The IRS virtually never argues that an organization is not religious; instead, the agency claims that the organization in effect siphons off economic benefits to church insiders or else that the claimed "church" is really nothing more than a private business enterprise and hence is not exempt. For example, the IRS initially denied exempt status to the Founding Church of Scientology not because of any objection to its status as a true religious organization, but because the church provided the founder and his wife with a residence, vehicles, salaries, commission, royalties, and various unexplained payments that in total constituted private inurement.[16] Similarly, the IRS denied exemption to a religious publishing house on the grounds that its activities were nothing more than a commercial publishing business.[17] State and local taxing authorities likewise tend to focus their attacks on the use to which allegedly religious property is put rather than on underlying religious sincerity. For instance, litigation is common in the states over whether property should be exempt that is not used directly in and strictly for religious worship.[18]

The result of the inability to define a religious organization and uncertainty over how to apply the ancillary policing doctrines has been administrative chaos. Bruce Hopkins observes that the difficulties in determining when organizations qualify for a religious tax exemption "have become nearly overwhelming" and that the issue imposes "probably unresolvable burdens on regulatory officials and judges."[19] A classic example is the IRS's recently-concluded litigation regarding the Church of Scientology, which spanned some three decades and dozens of litigated cases, ending with a consent settlement in which the IRS essentially conceded defeat. Previously, the Service had argued that Scientology was a front to enrich its founder and not a true religion, and the Supreme Court in *Hernandez v. Commissioner*[20] had sustained its position that many of the members' contributions were not tax-deductible. Because of the protracted litigation and the difficulties in applying these rulings to millions of individual transactions, however, the IRS conceded Scientology's exempt status and apparently permitted deductions for some of the payments that the Supreme Court had declared nondeductible.[21]

The Donative Theory and Religious Exemption

The donative theory would solve many of the most difficult of these administrative issues, although a few admittedly would remain. In contrast with current law, the donative theory does not need to define religion or church because it does not apply a categorical approach, nor does it attempt to assess the substantive worth of the entity's activities. Instead, the donative theory grants exemption on the basis of objective, measurable demonstrations of perceived value by individual donors. Thus under the donative theory, there is no need to consider whether the exemption is deserved more by the outward-looking social activities of churches or by their inward-looking spiritual development, nor is there any need for elusive distinctions between religious and secular. Any organization that in fact meets the donative tests is exempt, whether it is a church, a school, or a commune.

By all accounts, traditional churches are highly donative entities. Data collected by a 1990 Gallup poll on giving and volunteering in the United States showed that religious organizations receive the lion's share of both donated dollars and volunteer time: some 64.5% of total donations go to religious organizations and nearly 18% of all volunteer time.[22] More importantly for the donative theory, however, is that estimates consistently show that donations constitute over two-thirds of the revenues of churches and over one-third of the revenue of non-church religious organizations.[23] This result is consistent with the economic bases for the donative theory. Casual observation will confirm the market-failure hypothesis: not everyone present gives when the collection plate or basket is passed. Thus some part of every church congregation free-rides on the donations of others.

Furthermore, because of the constitutional separation of church and state, the religious sector suffers from complete government failure.

The donative theory also provides a convenient screen for the "bogus church" problem without discriminating against unorthodox faiths. As we observed above, the traditional mail-order church scam involves a single person or family transferring assets to an entity designated a "church," having that person become a "minister" of the "church," then having the "church" provide housing, food, clothing, and other personal expenditures for the minister. These mail-order church systems generally do not involve any significant contributions by third parties; even where they do, to the extent that the "contributions" are recouped in personal living expenses, they may not involve any significant donations at all because the contributions would actually be nothing more than a quid pro quo exchange of money for food, housing, and other personal expenses. Thus these entities would fail both our minimum number of donors test and the one-third threshold.

On the other hand, the donative theory does not solve the perennial problem of defining when something is a donation. This issue has been particularly troublesome with respect to churches and other religious organizations, as discussed in Chapter 8. In *Hernandez v. Commissioner*,[24] the Supreme Court held that fixed payments for "spiritual auditing sessions" by members of the Church of Scientology were quid pro quo exchanges rather than deductible contributions. But in *Powell v. United States*,[25] the Eleventh Circuit noted that the payments made by members of the Church of Scientology did not differ all that much from similar payments made by Catholics for commemorative masses, Jews for "tickets" to High Holy Day ceremonies, and Protestant pew rental fees, which the IRS by longstanding administrative practice permits as deductions. As we noted in Chapter 8, we do not agree with all the IRS precedents, but we acknowledge the difficulty in knowing precisely where to draw the line. Nevertheless, this problem is no worse under the donative theory than under current tax law, given its current import under § 170 of the Code (defining deductible contributions).

Moreover, our analysis provides some additional theoretical guidance for determining when payments in fact should be considered in the nature of quid pro quo exchanges. Since the case for an implicit tax subsidy rests on the free-rider hypothesis, contributions have a weaker claim to donative status when they are less likely to suffer from free-rider slack. Empirical and theoretical work discussed in Chapter 8 reveals that free-riding is reduced the more the benefits are personal to the donor and the smaller the group in which the donations are shared. Therefore, we should be more suspicious of contributions to churches that are used within the congregation than those directed outward to social programs for nonmembers. This distinction might also be captured by setting differential donative thresholds according to how much of a church's receipts are spent on social programs.[26] Naturally, this refinement introduces the complexity of defining and accounting for social for sacramental activities, but, as we have noted throughout the book, regulators are constantly confronted with the choice between greater nuance and accuracy at the cost of greater administrative burden.

Educational and Cultural Organizations

Exempting Educational and Cultural Organizations Under Current Law

Like exemption for religious institutions, tax exemption for private educational institutions has been virtually unquestioned since colonial times and remains so. In fact, several colonies even extended local tax exemption to the professors who taught in colleges or universities as well as their students.[27] Like so much else in the exemption landscape, the seeds of tax exemption for private schools can be traced to the 1601 Statute of Charitable Uses, which included "schools of learning, free schools and scholars in universities."[28] In the modern era, the educational exemption appears to have been connected to the historic exemption for churches and religious institutions, since virtually all educational institutions of the time had the training of ministers as a primary objective.[29] Moreover, many of these institutions began life as quasi-public schools and therefore were exempt under the tax-base rationale that it makes no sense for government to tax its own institutions. Harvard, for example, was chartered with a grant of public funds, as were Yale, Brown, Dartmouth and William & Mary.[30] These exemptions set the pattern followed later in state constitutions and statutes, which virtually all exempt educational institutions from state and local property and income taxes.[31]

Unlike religious institutions, however, the IRS in fact has attempted to define what constitutes "education." The current Treasury regulations include in the definition of education "instruction or training of the individual for the purpose of improving or developing his capabilities" as well as "instruction of the public on subjects useful to the individual and beneficial to the community."[32] Within this definition fall "schools" as one might colloquially think of them: institutions with a regularly scheduled curriculum, a regular faculty and a regularly enrolled body of students, including primary and secondary schools, colleges, professional schools and trade schools.[33] Also falling within this definition are a number of entities that one would not immediately classify as schools, such as entities presenting public discussion groups, forums, panels or lectures, entities providing correspondence courses through radio or television, and nonprofit academic presses. Finally, the federal law has expanded the educational category to include cultural and arts institutions such as museums, zoos, planetariums, and symphony orchestras.[34]

As a result of this breadth, the educational exemption has been applied to activities as diverse as continuing legal education and other professional skills training, university book stores, a jazz festival, various counseling services, research organizations, and a number of organizations whose stated purpose was to disseminate information to the public.[35] Even the IRS, however, has its limits: a dog obedience school was held not exempt since it neither trains individuals nor educates the public.[36]

Limitations on Educational Exemption

The breadth of the federal tax definition of an "educational institution" has resulted in administrative problems akin to those faced by the IRS and the courts in the religious institution area. One has the intuitive sense, for example, that "Hamburger U" ought not to receive tax exemption given that its sole purpose is to teach McDonald's employees the art of hamburger making and serving. Nevertheless, such an institution arguably falls within the "instruction or training of the individual" part of the 501(c)(3) definition of education. Another perennial problem for the IRS has been the perceived need to distinguish between educational institutions and "propaganda" organizations—that is, organizations that espouse particular ideas or viewpoints. Finally, there is the issue of exemption for racially-segregated schools that nevertheless clearly meet the regulations' definition of an educational institution. These problems have led the IRS and courts to search, mostly unsuccessfully, for ancillary limitations on the regulatory concept of education.

Again, as with the religious institution area, the IRS has turned to the private inurement and commerciality principles as its primary tools for denying exemption, producing similar confusion and controversy over the appropriateness of the distinctions being made. Thus the Service has denied exemption to religious publishing houses that it claimed operated like commercial businesses,[37] and in *Est of Hawaii v. Commissioner*,[38] the Tax Court held that a franchise system for training in personal awareness is not exempt because it is "taint[ed] with a substantial commercial purpose."

On the private inurement/benefit front, the Tax Court in *American Campaign Academy v. Commissioner*[39] held that a school for training political campaign professionals was not exempt despite its clear educational purpose ("training the individual") because nearly all of the school's graduates were employed by the Republican Party. Similarly, an organization operated to protect the financial stability of a teachers' retirement system by disseminating information through a newsletter and engaging in litigation when necessary was held not exempt because it served primarily the private interests of its teacher-members.[40]

In addition to the commerciality and private inurement doctrines, however, the IRS also has used an "advocacy group" rule, in which it denies exemption to organizations that advocate a particular viewpoint but do not present "a sufficiently full and fair exposition of the pertinent facts to permit an individual or the public to form an independent opinion or conclusion."[41] The D.C. Circuit, however, held the "full and fair exposition" test unconstitutionally vague in *Big Mama Rag, Inc. v. United States*.[42] The taxpayer in this case published a newspaper dedicated to feminist issues, and the IRS had denied an exemption because of the "political and legislative commentary" in the paper, as well as articles and editorials "promoting lesbianism."[43] The court noted that according to the Internal Revenue Manual, whether an organization was an "advocacy" organization subject to the "full and fair exposition" test was a question of whether its position was "controversial." As a result, the IRS had no objective standard by which to judge which organizations were subject to the test, and no standards by which to judge when the test was met.

In response to *Big Mama Rag*, the IRS adopted a four-part "methodology test" that purports to decide educational status based upon the methodology used by the organization in promoting its viewpoint, rather than on the viewpoint itself. The four factors identified by the IRS in this test are (1) whether the presentation of viewpoints or positions unsupported by facts is a significant portion of the organization's communications; (2) whether the facts that purport to support the viewpoints or positions are distorted; (3) whether the organization's presentations make substantial use of inflammatory and disparaging terms, expressing conclusions based more on strong emotional feelings than on objective evaluations; and (4) whether or not the approach used in the organization's presentations is aimed at developing an understanding on the part of the intended audience or readership by considering their background or training in the subject matter.[44] Using this test, the IRS denied exemption to an organization that openly advocated race war, and the denial was upheld by the D.C. Circuit in *National Alliance v. United States*, a decision rendered three years after *Big Mama Rag*.[45] The court, however, refused to specifically approve the methodology test in its opinion, relying instead on a mostly unsupported conclusion that the publication in question could not fit the definition of "educational" as used in Section 501(c)(3).[46]

The problem with these ancillary limitations is that they fail to distinguish in any substantively meaningful way those entities that should be exempt from those that should not. For example, with respect to the commerciality doctrine, many classically exempt educational institutions "sell" instruction much the same way Microsoft sells software, and their "customers" (students) certainly pay for the product.[47] While Harvard has yet to advertise at half-time of the Superbowl, the slick brochures put out by virtually every private educational institution rival those from Microsoft touting the latest version of their Windows software. Daniel Levy noted the trend in 1986: "Many private colleges and universities have taken to increasingly direct invidious comparisons with competitors (private and public), while even public counterparts sell themselves through media and other campaigns in ways once thought unbecoming. The same can now be said of many private schools as they launch major media efforts, often drawing on seminars run by for-profit concerns."[48] In fact, recent data indicates that more than 60% of the annual gross revenues of private universities come from student tuition and sales.[49]

If the commerciality test is meant to exclude activities in a market that is traditionally dominated by commercial firms, then it is still not wholly consistent. For-profit schools certainly exist. Recent data indicate that for-profit firms dominate vocational training, for example, constituting over 75% of both the number of schools and the revenues.[50] For-profit institutions also populate in higher education and, albeit to a much lesser degree, primary education.[51]

The private benefit limitation as applied to the educational exemption suffers the same problem as the commerciality doctrine: no obvious line exists for deciding when the benefits conferred by an organization otherwise clearly engaged in "training the individual" are too private. For example, the IRS apparently has no problem with exempting organizations that conduct professional seminars or training, such as continuing legal education.[52] Clearly, the benefits of these organizations are limited to a fairly narrow group. Why then are organizations that give seminars only to IBM employees too private? How about to both IBM and Apple employees? IBM, Apple and Microsoft? All computer hardware employees? All employees of the computer industry? Obviously, the private benefit limitation, whatever it may be, leaves entirely too much discretion to the IRS and courts to decide when an exemption is warranted with virtually no guidelines for exercising it.

Similarly, written commentary on the IRS's "advocacy group" limitations generally agrees with the D.C. Circuit that the "full and fair exposition" test places too much discretion in the hands of the IRS without adequate objective guidelines for exercising it (a theme that should now be familiar).[53] Nor have commentators found the methodology test much of an improvement.[54]

The Treasury has never articulated any precise reason for the propaganda limitation. The history of the educational definition in the regulations, however, supports two potential concerns. The first is that propaganda organizations are not "charitable" because they advance the specific viewpoints of their founders—they are, in a sense, selfish rather than charitable.[55] Second, certain propaganda may be deemed harmful to the public.[56] Neither of these concerns, however, explains the scope of the propaganda limitation. Charitable institutions invariably reflect the views of their founders and even traditional educational institutions such as universities engage in a considerable amount of viewpoint-pushing.[57] More than a few educators, in fact, view the noblest purpose of universities as nurturing unpopular ideas that may, at least in the beginning, have little factual foundation. Having embraced the position that "educational institutions" extend beyond traditional schools, the IRS is very hard-pressed to distinguish between propaganda activities of schools and those of other organizations. As to the second potential concern, the legal and political tradition of the United States strongly encourages propagation of doctrine—"propaganda"—and debate over viewpoints as an inherent part of the democratic process. One should view very suspiciously any tax doctrine that in effect permits the IRS to be censor based upon viewpoint, a practice that apparently has occurred with respect to homosexual rights groups.[58] Accordingly, the propaganda limitation appears to suffer the same malady as the commerciality and private benefit doctrines: too much discretion and the lack of objective criteria for exercising that discretion stemming from a lack of clear theoretical underpinning for the limitation.

Educational and Cultural Organizations Under the Donative Theory

Educational institutions are often cited by commentators as paradigm donative entities.[59] The statistical truth, however, is that educational insitutions depend far less on donations than one might think, and for some of them the importance of donations is virtually nil. The critical issue, then, is where the donative threshold is set. As discussed in Chapter 11, we argue for a threshold that ranges between 33% and 10%, depending in part on historical and political factors, and in part on an objective assessment of the degree to which the particular sector suffers from free- riding in its donative support.

With respect to traditional schools, a donative threshold toward the lower end of that range may be justified, based on indications that free-riding is rampant, particularly for colleges and universities. Commentators have observed that private colleges and universities keep tuition artificially low to expand the number of students who can afford to attend, and then impress upon their alumni the "moral obligation" to make donations post-graduation in order to make up the difference between the true value of the education received and the amount actually charged as tuition.[60] Because this payment is a purely moral obligation, however, and the pressure to make it comes after one has garnered the benefit of one's degree, free-riding on the donations of other alumni is likely to be high. Statistical evidence supports this view. During the period 1986–1988, only approximately 28.3% of the alumni of four-year private colleges and universities made contributions.[61]

Since this issue can only be resolved in the political arena, we examine educational institutions under both the highest and the lowest conceivable thresholds. We subdivide our discussion into four parts: colleges and universities, primary and secondary schools, arts and cultural organizations, and other institutions currently exempt under the educational rubric such as professional training seminars and academic presses. While the donative theory would make exemption judgments on an entity-specific basis, rather than by groups or by industry, examining group data will help establish the potential boundaries for exemption under the theory.

Colleges and Universities. The most comprehensive data regarding sources of funding for educational institutions exist in the realm of higher education, due to annual surveys conducted by the Council for Aid to Education. For the years 1986–88, four-year private nonprofit institutions as a group derived only approximately 18.8% of their total education and general revenues from private donations,[62] as opposed to 51.9% from tuition, fees and other charges, and another 13.8% from government grants and contracts.[63] At first glance, therefore, it appears that *as a group* the private nonprofit college/university sector fails the one-third of support benchmark by a fairly wide margin, although such institutions would generally pass the minimum 10% mark. Closer inspection of available data, however, generates several important qualifications.

First, donations played a much larger role for private liberal arts colleges than for either research institutions or private comprehensive institutions.[64] The overall percentage of revenues derived from donations for private liberal arts colleges was 27.12%, while the number for doctoral/research institutions was approximately 17.5% and for private general education colleges was approximately 15%.[65] These numbers appear to correspond generally to the economic basis for the donative theory. As noted below, research institutions depend far more heavily on government appropriations and grants for funding than do liberal arts institutions, and, as a result, they suffer much less government failure.[66]

Second, as might be expected, donations as a percentage of revenues varied widely among institutions. During the period in question, for example, in the research category St. John's University reported donations over the three-year period 1986–88 of about 2.2% of revenues, while Notre Dame reported donations equal to 47.4% of revenues and Cal Tech garnered donations of over 40% of revenues.[67] Except for these two, however, all of the other 63 research institutions fell below a 33% donation threshold while all but nine of the surveyed institutions reported donations in excess of 10% of revenues. This indicates that the lower donative threshold better fits with the historical precedent of exempting private colleges and universities. Similar institutional variations occurred in the other categories. In the comprehensive category comprising 176 institutions, only 13 reported donations above 33% of revenues, while 53 reported donations below 10% of revenues for the period.[68] Of the 301 institutions in the liberal arts category, 98 reported donations in excess of 33% of revenues, while only 18 reported donations below 10% of revenues.[69]

One anomaly in these donative percentages is that while the revenue numbers (the denominator in the donative fraction) include government grants, the donative base we propose (the numerator) does not. As we noted in Chapter 11, a more exact donative percentage would result if government grants were excluded from both the numerator and denominator, that is, not counted either as donations or as revenues. As a theoretical matter, such exclusion is justified by the fact that an entity supported by government grants should be exempt in any event because the government should not tax itself. Eliminating government grants from the revenue base results in donations constituting 23.57% of remaining revenues for all private four-year institutions, still below the one-third threshold, but closer than the

18.8% of all revenues. Once again the results vary widely in importance depending on type of institution.[70]

Finally, the numbers discussed so far do not include the value of donated labor. Because donated labor serves as just as much an indicator of twin failure as actual cash or property donations, the donative percentage of an institution should be measured taking donated labor into account. A recent report on volunteering indicated that in 1987, volunteer labor in the educational sector was worth in excess of $4.6 billion.[71] However, much of this labor should not count in any event because it probably goes mostly to fund-raising rather than instructional programs. As a result, we would not expect donated labor to be a major factor at the college/university level. Accordingly, a significant number of colleges and universities would probably fail the 33% test, but most would pass the 10%, and a substantial majority would pass an intermediate 20% test.

Private Elementary/Secondary Schools. Data regarding donations as a percentage of revenues for private elementary and secondary schools are more difficult to come by. In general, these schools break into two broad categories: religious-affiliated schools, such as the Catholic school system, and nonsectarian schools. As a group, religious-affiliated schools appear to surpass the suggested donative thresholds, largely because of the support they receive from their sponsoring churches. As a group these schools tend to rely on tuition and fees for less than half their revenues.[72] A 1988 report on the financing of Catholic elementary schools indicated that such schools receive approximately 39.6% of their revenues as a subsidy from general parish revenues, another 1.9% from diocesan subsidies, and another 7.5% from private fundraising for an overall donative percentage of 49%.[73] Earlier surveys of Lutheran schools reported an even higher percentage—62.2%—of support from the church.[74]

While not as dependent on donations as religious schools, nonsectarian private schools still receive significant donations, and as a group rank on par with private research universities in total donative support as a percentage of education revenues. The 1985–88 surveys on voluntary support of education by the Council for Aid to Education reported that surveyed independent elementary and secondary schools had total donations in excess of $1.361 million for the two-year period, amounting to approximately 26% of total estimated education and general revenues of such institutions.[75] Moreover, as was the case with private universities, this donative percentage does not include the value of donated labor. Unlike private universities, however, the value of donated labor at the primary and secondary school level is likely to be quite significant since many parents are directly involved in the instructional and supportive programs, particularly at private schools. For example, if one apportions donated labor value to these schools in proportion to their cash donation receipts, the donative percentage would rise to 41%, in excess of even the one-third threshold.[76]

Arts and Cultural Organizations. Arts and cultural organizations are sometimes used to attack the "dynastic" and establishment orientation of the charitable sector, which is accused of being dominated by causes that interest mostly old rich Europeans, to the neglect of more daring or counter-cultural tastes. One nonprofit scholar facetiously accused the Chicago Symphony of basically recycling a tired 18th Century German repertoire, and these authors have seen very little in private, tax-exempt museums that would offend the standards of Sen. Jesse Helms. But it is hardly the place of tax collectors to serve as artistic critics. The donative theory relieves them from these disputes by declaring cultural organizations exempt if they attract sufficient donative support. As discussed in Chapters 7, 8 and 9, the social inequity that results from greater support by the wealthy is only mildly amplified by the donative subsidy, and it is offset by the reciprocal support the wealthy provide implicitly to other causes whose exemptions raise their taxes. At most, these concerns might lead to setting a somewhat higher donative threshold under the hypothesis (which, to our knowledge, is unproven) that those with more money engage in less free-riding.

In any event, artistic and cultural institutions such as museums, symphony societies, opera societies and the like tend to be highly donative entities. Data from 1989 indicates that private contributions constituted some 62.5% of the total revenues for these organizations, well in excess of any of the suggested donative thresholds.[77] These results track the economic notion that donative entities operate at the conjunction of private market and government failure: ticket sales would not sustain many local symphonies, and the government (thankfully) does not run many orchestras.[78] The donative theory also neatly explains why a symphony society, supported in large part by donations, should be exempt, but the local jazz club, supported by admission fees and drink profits, should not. In the former case, the donations signal a failure of both government and the private market to supply symphony music at an appropriate level, while the lack of donations for the jazz club indicates that the private market supplies jazz at the appropriate level.

Other Educational Institutions. One can only speculate with respect to other educational organizations, since no systematic data regarding their donative status is available.[79] We expect that organizations advocating various causes would rely to a significant extent on donations and donated labor. Some indirect support for this assumption exists in the case law: in *Big Mama Rag* the D.C. Circuit noted in the course of its opinion that the organization at issue "has a predominantly volunteer staff and . . . is dependent on contributions, grants and funds raised by benefits for over fifty percent of its income."[80] Exempting these organizations is fully consistent with the twin failure theory: because these groups are usually political minorities, direct government aid is unlikely, and the overall product (representation of the group's view) is not one that can easily be sold in a private market.

On the other hand, one also would expect that organizations offering update seminars to bankers, CLE programs to lawyers, or personal enrichment sessions for new-age Yuppies rely little, if at all, on donations, being primarily fee-for-service enterprises.[81] As a result, such entities probably would not be exempt under the donative theory—without, we might add, any apparent disaster to society, inasmuch as lawyers, bankers, and Yuppies certainly do not need a government subsidy to stay current or achieve self-actualization. We would also shed few tears if nonprofit academic presses were to lose their educational exempt status; these presses should be taxed as any commercial publisher if, in fact, they make a profit.

Border Policing via the Donative Theory. The donative theory is vastly superior to the principles currently used by the IRS to circumscribe the educational exemption. Under this theory, the level of donative support is an objective test for commerciality, since the level of donations indicate whether the services of a particular institution suffer from market failure.[82] The donative theory also allows for a mix of commercial and noncommercial characterizations, which nicely fits the situation of institutions like schools that participate in a three-sector economy (for-profit, nonprofit, and governmental). A substantial donative base signals a partial market failure, while significant commercial sales is necessary to generate a subsidy effect from the income tax exemption. The only situation in which commerciality disqualifies an educational institution is if its sales income is high enough that its donative support falls below the threshold. In short, the level of donative support, not vague standards regarding how a good or service is delivered, marks the dividing line between commercial and noncommercial enterprises.

A similar explanation applies to the "private benefit" limit. The concern that an educational institution serves the narrow interests of only a few users is addressed by the numerosity requirement in the donative threshold, which we explain in Chapter 11. This requirement demonstrates that more than a de minimis portion of the public desires the institution's services, thereby eliminating the need to make intricate inquiries and ad hoc rulings based on visceral reactions.

The donative theory also allows the Service to lay to rest the "full and fair exposition" or "methodology" tests for propaganda institutions. To the extent the concern behind this limitation is to avoid subsidizing the viewpoint of a single individual, the donative theory provides an answer by requiring a minimum breadth of donations to qualify. If an advocacy organization attracts significant donative support, its viewpoint must be one that the donors believe is underrepresented and hence is as deserving—and perhaps more deserving—of subsidy as one espousing a widely held belief.[83] Consistent with the First Amendment, we need inquire into the potential harm done only in the extreme case of organizations that practice (or, more controversially, that profess) actions that are illegal or clearly contrary to public policy.

Scientific Research Organizations

Research organizations obviously span a host of categories. Many major universities engage in significant funded research (some might even say too much), as do some health care institutions and other entities. To the extent research is undertaken by these entities, we would not judge their research activities any differently from, say, their macaroni sales. As we have noted previously, some remunerative nondonative activity is necessary if an income tax exemption is to generate any subsidy effect.

Independent nonprofit research organizations that rely on outside funding, however, present a different issue. Depending on the form the funding takes, it may be difficult to distinguish a donation to these organizations from a mere purchase of research services. Interestingly, the IRS uses the same concepts of private inurement and commerciality to police exempt independent research organizations as it does to police religious and educational organizations. Thus Treasury Regulations under § 501(c)(3) state that exempt research "does not include activities of a type ordinarily carried on as an incident to commercial or industrial operations" such as testing or inspection of materials.[84] Moreover, to be exempt, research must be carried on "in the public interest," rather than for private commercial gain.[85] The result of these tests is a rather tortured set of examples in the regulations and rulings attempting to define what constitutes permitted research. For example, the IRS denied exemption to a nonprofit organization that carried on clinical testing of drugs for FDA approval purposes, claiming that such testing was a normal part of ordinary commercial operations (e.g., drug manufacturers developing and marketing new products); in another ruling, however, the IRS approved research directed at developing new biotechnology products and processes that could broaden the local industrial base and provide jobs.[86]

As with religious and educational organizations, the donative theory would eliminate the focus on what an entity does, again eliminating the need for such fine distinctions. On the other hand, we suspect that without refinement, the donative theory would prohibit exemption for most research organizations, because those organizations likely are funded primarily by government research grants, not by private donations. Some support for this speculation comes from the fact that in 1989, private foundations made grants of approximately $357 million to various exempt science organizations,[87] but in fiscal 1990, the federal government budgeted $ 11.2 billion for basic scientific research.[88]

As we noted in Chapter 11, we would not count government grants in the donative base for purposes of the donative theory, because such grants negate the government failure prong of the twin-failure hypothesis that forms the theoretical basis for exempting donative entities. On the other hand, we also noted that it does not make much sense for the government to tax its own money; accordingly, government grants might still be excluded from the income tax base simply by legislating that result. In addition, we suggested that in assessing the donative status of certain institutions, we would support excluding government grants from *both* the donative base (the numerator of the donative fraction) and the revenue base (the denominator) to obtain a truer picture of the donative status of particular organizations, much as we suggest the same for colleges and universities in our discussion above. Under this approach, an organization that, for example, had $900,000 in revenues, $850,000 from government grants and $50,000 from private donations, would be exempt essentially under a combination of the donative theory and the fact that government should not tax itself.

The outcome is more complex for research organizations that rely primarily on private funding. So far, we have referred to private donations, suggesting that research institutions receive pure, no-strings-attached contributions to use however they see fit. Certainly this is the case for many donations to science, but much private support for scientific research probably comes in the form of research grants from various private grant-making foundations. Often, these research grants are awarded on the basis of competitive applications for specified research, thus raising the question of whether private grants count as donations at all or instead constitute the purchase of research services. Unfortunately, the quid pro quo test explained in Chapter 8 does not neatly resolve this problem. Many forms of classic gifts have strings attached that, for instance, restrict their use to building certain structures named after specified donors. Despite the element of a quid pro quo exchange, we still classify these as donations because the reputational benefits that motivate the gift indicate the presence of a true public good and therefore some continuing free rider slack that justifies a shadow subsidy. We would adopt a similar resolution for research grants. Despite the element of a bargained-for exchange in these grants, the research services "purchased" are usually intended entirely (or largely) for broad public benefit. This absence of a strong private motivation signals the likelihood of underprovision of these research services, and therefore these grants properly qualify as gifts.

This analysis concedes, however, that some research grants indeed might purchase entirely (or mostly) private benefits. An example is the common practice of drug manufacturers paying a university medical center to conduct safety and efficacy testing for a new pharmaceutical product. Therefore, the IRS is partially correct in evaluating the extent of public benefit that results from the activities of particular research organizations. The IRS is incorrect, however, in making this evaluation under the public benefit and private inurement doctrines, since these in theory would disqualify an organization that provides any amount of private benefit through its research activities. An otherwise primarily public-oriented institution, such as a university medical school, should be allowed to sell some of its research capacity to private industry without jeopardizing its exempt status. The IRS in fact recognizes this point, since, to our knowledge, these types of transactions have never been the basis for questioning the status of an entity that is otherwise exempt. The donative theory, however, provides a more principled basis for leavening enforcement of the private inurement/benefit rules. Under the donative theory, the private benefit in industry grants goes to whether the grant counts as a donation. Therefore, the only effect of private classification is to lower the percentage of receipts that count towards meeting the donative threshold. We would allow a research organization, then, to obtain at least two-thirds of its funding from doing private research work under contract with industry.

This test raises the prospect, however, that even the minimum one-third of true donations might be made up entirely of gifts from a single industry, thereby using the exemption to support the private interests of an insular but well-heeled group. We address this concern through our numerosity test, which requires at least 17 approximately equal sources of donations. It is true that this test would in theory allow industries with more than 17 firms to farm out their R & D departments into independent, tax-exempt entities, thereby sheltering a portion of their operations from property tax. This result is very unlikely, however, since competitive pressures within the industry would make firms unwilling to sink substantial funding into research that does not yield a proprietary advantage.[89] Strict application of the quid-pro-quo test would demand that any industry gifts have no strings attached as to their use and no restrictions placed on who has access to the resulting information. It is only in the unusual case where all firms have a common, nonrivalrous stake in a joint research enterprise—in other words, where a nearly pure public good exists—that industry-wide cooperation is plausible. If, for whatever reason, an industry-wide nonprofit research organization in fact were to meet this numerosity screen, in our judgment it would deserve exempt status despite what may appear to be a private purpose. Supporting narrowly held causes that suffer from government and market failure is the central purpose of the charitable exemption under the donative theory.

Health Care Organizations

Exempting Health Care Organizations Under Current Law

Nonprofit hospitals nicely illustrate the full dimension of the donative theory. Frequently termed "voluntary hospitals," they have come to epitomize the type of activity encompassed by the generic concept of charity. In about half of the states they are specifically enumerated along with churches and schools, and hospitals have long been recognized as a classic object for charitable trusts.[90] Nonprofit hospitals have been characterized as voluntary since the nineteenth century, when they were organized by religious societies, heavily funded by donations, and staffed by doctors who worked without compensation and nurses who worked for room and board as part of their lifetime commitment to a religious order devoted to caring for the poor.[91] The role of hospitals as "almshouses for the poor" changed rapidly during the first half of the twentieth century with developments in anesthesia, surgical technique and other aspects of medical science that suddenly transformed hospitals from the dumping ground of humanity to the pinnacle establishment of the health care delivery system. Still, nonprofit hospitals continued in their voluntary tradition, despite opening their doors to paying patients and a secular staff, by maintaining their commitment to treat all patients regardless of their ability to pay and by their continued, if partial, reliance on volunteer labor.[92]

The voluntary nature of nonprofit hospitals, however, has steadily abated over the past generation as a consequence of widespread employer-provided health insurance and massive governmental programs such as Medicare (for the elderly and disabled) and Medicaid (for the poor). The advent of third-party payors transformed the character of the nonprofit hospital sector. Pressured by the emerging competition of investor-owned hospitals, nonprofit hospitals have increasingly taken on the appearance of business enterprises by serving mostly paying patients, decreasing their reliance on donations or volunteer labor, and striving to generate as much surplus revenue as possible through commercial transactions.[93]

These shifts in the character of the voluntary hospital sector are mirrored in the shift of the I RS's position concerning the exempt status of nonprofit hospitals.[94] A 1956 ruling reflected traditional notions of charity by requiring exempt hospitals to treat indigent patients "to the extent of their financial ability."[95] In 1969, three years after the implementation of Medicare and Medicaid, the IRS altered its position regarding the standards for exemption in response to the hospital industry's complaint that these public programs had greatly reduced the demand for charity care and rendered the existing standard for exemption an anachronism.[96] In Revenue Ruling 69-545,[97] the IRS abandoned the charity care requirement imposed in 1956 and adopted the community benefit approach to hospital exemption: an entity engaged in the "promotion of health" for the general benefit of the community is pursuing a charitable purpose, even though a portion of the community, such as indigents, is excluded from participation. This move away from free care for the poor as the traditional standard of exemption was further entrenched by a 1983 ruling establishing that even hospitals with limited services and no open emergency room, such as cancer hospitals, could qualify for exemption merely by treating all patients able to pay.[98]

Public interest advocates mounted an aggressive challenge to this ruling in *Eastern Kentucky Welfare Rights Association v. Simon*,[99] but they lost on the merits at the court of appeals and then before the Supreme Court on technical grounds. The D.C. Circuit's opinion on the merits reasoned that "the rationale upon which the [free care] definition of 'charitable' was predicated has largely disappeared," and that "[t]o continue to base the 'charitable' status of a hospital strictly on the relief it provides for the poor fails to account for these major changes in the area of health care [such as Medicare and Medicaid]."[100] In essence, the court held that nonprofit hospitals are charitable even if they do not provide free care because the concept of what constitutes a charity must change "to recognize the changing economic, social and technological" environment in which hospitals now function.[101]

Much the same pattern has played out in the states, with some notable exceptions. Hospitals were originally exempt based on their free care of indigents, but as funding became more widespread, most state and local taxing authorities, backed by their courts, continued to afford charitable status. They accepted the circular logic that insists on reshaping the concept of charity however necessary to fit the predominant pattern of what most nonprofit hospitals are currently doing, never asking whether the change in hospitals justifies revoking the exemption.[102] The Utah Supreme Court issued the only decision to squarely buck this trend. As it explained, hospitals "argue that . . . the universal availability of insurance . . . make[s] the idea of a hospital solely supported by philanthropy an anachronism. We believe this argument itself exposes the weakness in the [hospitals'] position. It is precisely because such a vast system of third-party payers has developed . . . that the historical distinction between for-profit and nonprofit hospitals has eroded."[103] Nevertheless, most other states have rejected the Utah analysis. Only Pennsylvania courts have shown significant resistance, but they still have not firmly imposed charity care requirements, and only a small handful of states have taken legislative action to do the same (Texas and Alabama were the first).

The strong presumption in favor of hospital exemption resurfaced again in the context of federal health care reform. Just as in 1969 following the passage of Medicare and Medicaid, again in 1993 nonprofit hospitals asserted that enacting universal health insurance coverage would deprive them of the opportunity to earn charitable status by eliminating the demand for uncompensated care. Therefore, the Clinton administration included in its Health Security Act a provision that extends exemption to hospitals and certain HMOs upon a showing only that they attempt to assess and meet unspecified community needs.[104] The driving force behind this proposal was the largely unspoken assumption that hospitals are categorically eligible for exemption despite a fundamental change in the prevailing social circumstances. Thus, hospitals have successfully sought to maintain exemption on each of the conventional theories of exemption: categorical, relief of poverty, and community benefit.

Limitations on Health Care Exemption

Almost immediately after the publication of Rev. Rul. 69-545, the IRS faced numerous claims for exemption by health care entities other than traditional hospitals. Health maintenance organizations (HMOs), for example, sought exemption on the grounds that they, too, "promoted health" for the benefit of the general community even if they did not engage in signficant charity care; nonprofit pharmacies, nursing homes, and even associations of doctors affiliated with medical schools soon followed suit.[105]

Faced with its stated exemption standard based upon charitable trust concepts that contain no limiting principle, the Service soon turned to some familiar tools to deny exemption to these non-hospital health care providers. Primary among these were the commerciality and private benefit doctrines discussed above. Thus the Service successfully denied exemption to a nonprofit pharmacy on the grounds that it was inherently a commercial enterprise, and the IRS subjected outpatient (as opposed to inpatient) pharmacy sales and laboratory testing by hospitals to the unrelated business income tax.[106] At the same time, the IRS resisted exemption for HMOs by claiming they primarily serve the private interests of their members and thus are not sufficiently public to be charitable.[107] Very few physician groups, in fact, have survived the challenge of showing that their clinics do not operate for their private benefit. (The Mayo and Cleveland Clinics are notable exceptions.)

As in the education arena, however, these ancillary limitations are largely unconvincing. If "inherently commercial enterprises" such as pharmacies are not charitable, then why are nonprofit hospitals, which routinely compete with for-profit counterparts in major markets? No one can seriously deny that the sale of drugs and medicines is as inherent a part of providing health care as providing hospital beds and operating rooms. If the promotion of health for the general benefit of the community is a charitable purpose, then why deny exemption to an HMO that serves over 70,000 people, many of whom live in medically underserved areas? The problem, of course, is distinguishing an exempt HMO from mere health insurance, which is not exempt. But to do this, the IRS draws arcane distinctions among HMOs that contract for services with "captive" physician practice associations (associations that perform nearly all their services for the HMO)—considered exempt, those that pay physicians under a capitated payment method—also considered exempt, and those that use a fee-for-service payment method, which are considered too much like private insurance to be exempt.[108]

The Donative Theory and Health Care Institutions

Once again, the donative theory resolves much of the confusion surrounding the rationale for exempting health care entities and which ones qualify as charitable. In this case, however, the theory produces dramatically different result than under current law. To be exempt under the donative theory, a health care provider would be required to demonstrate ongoing social worth and need by attracting a substantial level of donative support in the market for philanthropy. Although health care providers, particularly hospitals, appear on first inspection to be good candidates for the receipt of charity because many of their services have strong public good characteristics, they receive sufficient government funding that they have almost no need to solicit donations. Thus, while they display many of the classic incidents of *market* failure, they are not affected by severe *government* failure.

Hospital services primarily consist of patient care sold through ordinary commercial transactions. Nevertheless, several hospital services are candidates for classic public good characterization. Indeed, Burton Weisbrod uses the hospital industry as one of the principal confirmations of his public goods rationale for the existence of nonprofit enterprise by demonstrating that most hospital services with public good characteristics—research, physician education, and the treatment of indigent patients—exist disproportionately in voluntary hospitals.[109] These are also precisely the services that nonprofit hospitals use to justify the exemption under the conventional government burden and community benefit theories.

But it is not enough to demonstrate the existence of substantial public good production to justify a tax subsidy. The subsidy is deserved only if the government is supplying these goods at a suboptimal level, as demonstrated by actual public contributions to make up the difference. Today, nonprofit hospitals receive in proportionate terms only negligible support from public donations.[110] This was not always the case. At the turn of the century, hospitals depended on philanthropy for roughly one-quarter to one-third of their operating budget and for the bulk of their capital funds.[111] Tracing the history of the deterioration of hospital giving and the changing characteristics of the nonprofit hospital sector over time helps to confirm the rationale for supporting only donative institutions.

The primary impetus for the growth of the voluntary hospital sector prior to World War II was the desire of diverse ethnic and religious groups to create institutions that would cater to their distinct treatment needs without discrimination. The early growth of voluntary hospitals after the turn of the century, "reflected the idiosyncratic qualities of the community they served."[112] Thus, Catholics desired a hospital where last rites would be administered and Jews desired one where the staff spoke Yiddish and served kosher food.[113] These distinctive characteristics allowed voluntary hospitals to appeal to defined interest groups for strong philanthropic support to ensure that treatment would be available when the need arose.[114] This association between heterogeneity in demand for hospital services and the strength of donative support confirms the role public choice theory plays in explaining the existence of philanthropy as a response to government failure.

As a result of the widespread system of third-party reimbursement that developed after World War II, hospitals no longer suffer significantly from government or market failure. Private insurance spread rapidly during the 1950s and the government began directly funding a substantial portion of hospital operations through Medicare and Medicaid in the 1960s. The government also increased direct subsidies to specific public good activities, such as hospital construction, medical research and education. As a consequence, nonprofit hospitals no longer depended on donative support to expand. This displacement of charitable giving caused hospital philanthropy to decay rapidly since 1968, with a half-life of about five years.[115] By 1981, philanthropic contributions to hospitals were less than one-fourth of the level when Medicare began.[116] On average, hospitals now receive 2% or less of their operating budgets and construction budgets from donations.[117]

Either hospitals have felt little need to solicit philanthropic support, or if they have sought it, the public has seen comparatively little need to contribute.[118] Coincident with these changes, the character of nonprofit hospitals has become remarkably homogeneous. One noted medical historian comments that "[b]y the mid-1960s, . . . the notion of an institution closely connected to its community seemed like a romantic remnant of a 'pre-scientific' era."[119]

Hospitals complain that this government generosity is quickly ending, eliminating their ability to cross-subsidize many underfunded but desirable services from the ample surplus previously generated by insured patients. But until the pinch becomes severe enough to motivate hospitals to enter the philanthropy market more aggressively, and donors to respond with more enthusiasm, these assertions are irrelevant under the donative theory. At present, the lack of donative support is evidence either that nonprofit hospitals do not provide a service materially different from that otherwise available, or that if they do, they are sufficiently supported in more direct ways. Accordingly, there is a weak case for supplementing this support with a tax subsidy.

Despite the presently low level of proportionate donative support for hospitals, it is misleading to represent that hospitals as receive no such support. In fact, the aggregate level of donations is quite large. The 1,425 member hospitals of the National Association of Hospital Development received $1.90 billion cash donations in fiscal 1987–88, an average of $1.3 million each. While donative support may not be sufficient to qualify all of the nonprofit hospital sector's holdings and earnings for property and income tax exemption, it also seems unfair to disregard this support simply because it represents a small portion of the nonprofit operation. Fortunately, the donative theory is capable of fine-tuning its application to account for degrees of support. First, as discussed in Chapter 11, the threshold can be adjusted to a level commensurate with historical levels of donative support. For hospitals, during the post-war era until 1968, philanthropy provided from 20% to 30% of hospital construction funding.[120] Second, hospitals that fail to meet this threshold for their overall operations may qualify for the exemption if they are capable of segregating into separate corporate entities those activities that attract the most donative support. For instance, oncology and pediatric services are popular objects of hospital giving, particularly when combined into children's cancer units. Moreover, a taxing authority may make the same accounting adjustment even without formal corporate segregation.[121] As a consequence, it is still possible for a substantial portion of nonprofit hospital assets and income to qualify for at least a limited form of charitable exemption under the donative theory.

Conclusion

This analysis demonstrates both the powerful explanatory force of the donative theory and its relative ease of administration. The theory gains force from its broad historical consistency since most or all churches, schools, social welfare, cultural, and research organizations would continue to be exempt. Hospitals are the only major category of historically-exempt entities that would fare poorly under our donative tests. (Alas, some major research universities and nonprofit university presses would also suffer.) The donative theory also is remarkable for its ability to internalize the explanation for various restrictions on exempt entities to the core justification of the exemption, rather than maintaining these restrictions based on ad hoc, external concerns. The donative theory eases the burdens of administration by employing a market-like mechanism to measure the social worth and need of various organizations automatically, without the intervention of social value judgments made by revenue agents. The designation of donative thresholds and the measurement of actual donations entail several complexities, but they can be just as easily handled as the designation and measurement problems present under the conventional conception of the exemption; indeed, most aspects of the existing regulations are remarkably adaptable to this task.

Adoption of the donative theory—or, more accurately, its recognition, since it can be revealed to be in place already—will solve all of the major pending controversies surrounding the charitable exemption. The donative theory avoids the need to define what is a true religion, it eliminates the difficult and inconsistent commerciality test, and it incorporates the private benefit concern that has plagued many charitable categories. The most recent controversy is over the tax-exempt status of nonprofit hospitals. This skirmish has unmasked a more elemental unease about the fundamental basis for the exemption, why it is tied to charitable status, and what constitutes a charity. The donative theory readily provides the following, long-awaited answers: An organization is a charity if its services are sufficiently valued by the public to attract substantial donative support. Such an entity deserves exemption as a partial subsidy to correct for the market and political defects that produced the need to rely on donations. In sum, the charitable exemption is a means for providing a shadow subsidy to activities that donations signal are socially worthy and in need of further support.

This is not to say that the donative theory is the only plausible basis on which a tax exemption might be conferred, or that society necessarily must confer an exemption at all. We would not stand in opposition if our legislators chose explicitly to restrict the charitable exemption to organizations that assist the poor, or if they chose to repeal the exemption altogether in favor of a more direct form of social subsidy. To this extent, the donative theory is not a "strong" justification for the exemption that precludes all other possibilities. We have meant only to demonstrate that, among plausible accounts, the donative theory makes the most sense of the form of tax exemption that our legislators have in fact chosen. No other theory as successfully explains: (1) what charities are, consistent with common sense understandings and the 400 years of legal history that lie behind this concept; and (2) why they are (a) eligible to receive tax exempt donations, and (b) exempt from both (i) property and (ii) income taxation, but (c) only to the extent of their related income and property, and (d) only if they (i) are nonprofit, (ii) do not violate public policy, and (iii) do not engage in excessive political activity. A theory that can provide a convincing, integrated explanation for each of these components of the present scheme of tax exemption is too compelling to ignore unless we are willing to abandon altogether the concept of a charitable exemption.

Notes

1. Walz v. Tax Commission, 397 U.S. 664, 678 (1970).

2. DEAN M. KELLY, WHY CHURCHES SHOULD NOT PAY TAXES 5 (1977).

3. John W. Whitehead, *Tax Exemption and Churches: A Historical and Constitutional Analysis*, 22 CUMB. L. REV. 521, 524 (1992).

4. John Witte, *Tax Exemption of Church Property: Historical Anomaly or Valid Constitutional Practice?*, 64 SO. CAL. L. REV. 363 (1991).

5. BRUCE R. HOPKINS, THE LAW OF TAX-EXEMPT ORGANIZATIONS 205 (6th ed. 1992); Terry L. Slye, *Rendering Unto Caesar: Defining "Religion" for Purposes of Administering Religion-Based Tax Exemptions*, 6 HARV. J. L. & PUB. POL. 219, 258 (1983).

6. HOPKINS, *supra* note 5, at 222–23.

7. *E.g.*, Pusch v. Commissioner, 39 T.C.M. (CCH) 838 (1980), *aff'd*, 628 F.2d 1353 (5th Cir. 1980). *See generally*, HOPKINS, *supra* note 5, at 224–225.

8. Jerome Kurtz, *Difficult Definitional Problems in Tax Administration: Religion and Race*, remarks before the Practising Law Institute Seventh Biennial Conference on Tax Planning for Foundations, Tax-Exempt Status and Charitable Contributions, *reprinted in* BNA DAILY EXECUTIVE REPORT, Jan. 11, 1977 at J-8. These remarks were made while Kurtz was Commissioner of the IRS.

9. Ira M. Ellman, *Driven from the Tribunal: Judicial Resolution of Internal Church Disputes*, 69 MICH. L. REV. 1378, 1442 (1981). For a general discussion of the mail-order church phenomenon, see HOPKINS, *supra* note 5, at 213–20; Slye, *supra* note 5, at 222.

10. HOPKINS, *supra* note 5, at 217–18. For a complete list of case citations, see *id. See generally* Brian G. Petkanics & Sandra R. Petkanics, *Mail Order Ministries, The Religious Purpose Exemption, and the Constitution*, 33 TAX LAW. 959 (1980); Slye, *supra* note 5, at 222.

11. John Witte, *supra* note 4, at 407. *See also*, Slye, *supra* note 5, at 219.

12. *E.g.*, Roberts v. Ravenwood Church of Wicca, 392 S.E.2d 657 (Ga. 1982) (approving exemption for church operated out of a house that believed in a "primordial, supernatural force" that created the world and sustained its creatures in a "karmic circle"); Holy Spirit Association for Unification of World Christianity v. Tax Commission, 435 N.E.2d 662 (N.Y. 1982) (reversing several lower courts to approve exemption for "Moonies").

13. Religious Society of Families v. Assessor, 343 N.Y.S.2d 159 (Misc. 1973) (denying exemption for society devoted to a variety of ecological, political, and social causes); Ideal Life Church of Lake Elmo v. County of Washington, 304 N.W.2d 308 (Minn. 1981) (denying exemption to group with a theistic orientation but that professed no formal religious doctrine).

14. *E.g.*, Golden Writ of God v. Department of Revenue, 713 P.2d 605 (Or. 1986).

15. For a discussion of the prohibition on private inurement and its relationship to exempt status, see Chapter 10, *supra*, at 168–70.

16. Founding Church of Scientology v. United States, 412 F.2d 1197 (Ct. Cl. 1969), *cert. denied*, 397 U.S. 1009 (1969). *See generally* HOPKINS, *supra* note 5 at 209–220; Slye, *supra* note 5, at 267–73.

17. Scripture Press Foundation v. United States, 285 F.2d 800 (Ct. Cl. 1961), *cert. denied*, 368 U.S. 985 (1962).

18. For a summary of the caselaw, see John Witte, *supra* note 4, at 396–401.

19. HOPKINS, *supra* note 5, at 213, 216.

20. 490 U.S. 680 (1989).

21. *See* Paul Streckfus, *Recap—What We Know About the Scientology Closing Agreement*, 9 EXEMPT ORG. TAX REV. 247 (1994).

22. VIRGINIA A. HODGKINSON AND MURRAY A. WEITZMAN, GIVING AND VOLUNTEERING IN THE UNITED STATES 26, 31 (1990). In terms of the percentage of total donations, the next closest sector to religious organizations was social service organizations, garnering 8.1% of total donated dollars. With respect to volunteers, education came in second with 10.1% of volunteer time.

23. VIRGINIA A. HODGKINSON ET AL., NONPROFIT ALMANAC 1992–1993 at 147, Table 4.2 (1992) (showing private contributions constituting over 84% of revenues of religious organizations); Interfaith Research Committee, *A Study of Religious Receipts and Expenditures in the United States*, in RESEARCH PAPERS SPONSORED BY THE COMMISSION ON PRIVATE PHILANTHROPY AND PUBLIC NEEDS 365, 400, 402, 422, 429, 431 (U.S. Dept. of the Treasury ed., 1977) (hereafter FILER COMMISSION PAPERS) (based on 1970's data, private donations accounted for over 90% of revenues of Protestant and Catholic churches and Jewish synagogues (excluding revenues for Jewish day schools), 60% of the revenues of the Jewish Federation, and 36% of certain non-church Protestant religious institutions such as hospitals, colleges, etc.); BURTON A. WEISBROD, THE NONPROFIT ECONOMY 197 at Table C.4. (1988) (using 1980 data, religious organizations receive over 90% of revenues from donations); Burton A. Weisbrod, *Private Goods, Collective Goods: The Role of the Nonprofit Sector*, in THE ECONOMICS OF NONPROPRIETARY ORGANIZATIONS 150, 151–60 (1980) (data from 1973–75 showed donations accounting for 71% of religious organization revenues). Systematic data on religious institutions is difficult to come by, inasmuch as most such institutions are not required to file informational returns (Form 990) with the IRS.

24. 490 U.S. 680 (1989).

25. 945 F.2d 374 (11th Cir. 1993).

26. *See* John Witte, *supra* note 4 (suggesting that eligibility for religious exemption be judged by social programs in addition to sincerity of religious devotion).

27. The Massachusetts Bay Province Laws of 1706–07, for example, provided exemption from local property and poll taxes for "the president, fellows and students of Harvard Colledge [sic]". Province Laws 1706–07, Ch 6, sect. 2, *quoted in* Chauncey Belknap, *The Federal Income Tax Exemption of Charitable Organizations: Its History and Underlying Policy, in* FILER COMMISSION PAPERS, *supra* note 23, at 2025, 2028. Rhode Island also originally exempted the professors of Brown University from local property taxation. *Id.* at 2029.

28. John P. Persons et al., *Criteria for Exemption Under Section 501(c)(3), in* FILER COMMISSION PAPERS, *supra* note 23, at 1909, 1913. *See also, id.* at 1963.

29. Belknap, *supra* note 27, at 2028.

30. Earl F. Cheit and Theodore E. Lobman, III, *Private Philanthropy and Higher Education: History, Current Impact and Public Policy Considerations, in* FILER COMMISSION PAPERS, *supra* note 23, at 453.

31. Persons et al., *supra* note 28, at 1923. *See also*, William R. Ginsberg, The *Real Property Tax Exemption of Nonprofit Organizations: A Perspective*, 53 TEMPLE L.Q. 291, 292 (1980); Mark A. Hall & John D. Colombo, *The Charitable Status of Nonprofit Hospitals: Toward a Donative Theory of Tax Exemption* 66 WASH. L. REV. 307, 323–24 (1991) and sources cited therein.

32. Treas. Reg. 1.501(c)(3)-1(d)(3).

33. Treas. Reg. 1.501(c)(3)-1(d)(3)(ii), example 1.

34. Treas. Reg. 1.501(c)(3)-1(d)(3)(ii), examples 2 through 4.

35. E.g., Kentucky Bar Foundation, Inc. v. Comm'r, 78 T.C. 921, 924 (1982) (IRS conceded continuing legal education was an educational activity entitled to exemption); Rev. Rul. 78-99, 1978-1 C.B. 152 (counseling for widows and widowers); Rev. Rul. 74-615, 1974-2 C.B. 165 (accuracy of news coverage by newspapers); Rev. Rul. 74-595, 1974-2 C.B. 164 (counseling men on sterilization methods); Rev. Rul. 74-16, 1974-1 C.B. 126 (managing credit unions); Rev. Rul. 73-569, 1973-2 C.B. 178 (counseling women on resolving unwanted pregnancies); Rev. Rul. 70-640, 1970-2 C.B. 117 (marriage counseling); Rev. Rul. 69-538, 1969-2 C.B. 116 (bookstore operated on a cooperative system, refunding excess earnings to students and faculty members in proportion to patronage); Rev. Rul. 69-441, 1969-2 C.B. 115 (personal financial counseling); Rev. Rul. 68-504, 1968-2 C.B. 211 (update seminars for banking); Rev. Rul. 68-17, 1968-1 C.B. 247 (information on model housing programs); Rev. Rul. 68-16, 1968-1 C.B. 246 (instruction in securities management); Rev. Rul. 68-14, 1968-1 C.B. 243 (information on street planning); Rev. Rul. 67-342, 1967-2 C.B. 187 (dissemination of information on the need for international cooperation); Rev. Rul. 67-4, 1967-1 C.B. 121 (research and dissemination of information on medical and physical disorders); Rev. Rul. 65-298, 1965-2 C.B. 163 (update seminars for physicians); Rev. Rul. 65-271, 1965-2 C.B. 161 (jazz festival); Rev. Rul. 65-270, 1965-2 C.B. 160 (dancing); Rev. Rul. 64-275, 1964-2 C.B. 142 (drag racing instruction). There are countless others. *See generally* BORIS I. BITTKER & LAWRENCE LOKKEN, FEDERAL TAXATION OF INCOME, ESTATES AND GIFTS ¶ 100.3.4 nn. 63, 70 (2d ed. 1992); HOPKINS, *supra* note 5, at 185. *See also* National Alliance v. U.S., 710 F.2d 868, 873 (D.C. Cir. 1983) ("We recognize

the inherently general nature of the term 'educational' and the wide range of meanings Congress may have intended to convey."); Weyl v. Commissioner, 48 F.2d 811, 812 (2d Cir. 1931) ("In absence of a specific definition, the words are to be given their usual and accepted meaning . . . . 'Education' has been defined by the encyclopedia and dictionaries as 'imparting or acquisition of knowledge; mental and moral training; cultivation of the mind, feelings and manners.'"); Tommy F. Thompson, *The Availability of the Federal Educational Tax Exemption for Propaganda Organizations*, 18 U. CAL. DAVIS L. REV. 487, 496, 513 (1985).

36. Rev. Rul. 71-421, 1971-2 C.B. 229. *See* Ann Arbor Dog Training Club, Inc., v. Comm'r, 74 T.C. 207 (1980).

37. Scripture Press Found. v. United States, 285 F.2d 800 (Ct. Cl. 1961), *cert. denied*, 368 U.S. 985 (1962). *Contra* Presbyterian & Reformed Publishing Co. v. Comm'r, 743 F.2d 148 (3d Cir. 1984) (religious publishing house exempt religious and educational institution).

38. 71 T.C. 1067 (1979), *aff'd*, 647 F.2d 170 (9th Cir. 1981).

39. 92 T.C. 1053 (1989).

40. Retired Teachers Legal Defense Fund, Inc. v. Comm'r, 78 T.C. 280 (1982).

41. Treas. Reg. § 1.501(c)(3)-1(d)(3)(i).

42. 631 F.2d 1030 (D.C. Cir. 1980). *See generally*, BITTKER & LOKKEN, *supra* note 35, at ¶ 100.3.4; HOPKINS, *supra* note 5, at 195–96.

43. 631 F.2d at 1033. The IRS also claimed that the organization was nothing more than a commercial newspaper publisher.

44. Rev. Proc. 86-43, 1986-2 C.B. 729.

45. 710 F.2d 868 (D.C. Cir. 1983).

46. In a distinctly "I know education when I see it and this is not it" vein, the court concluded "The material may express the emotions felt by a number of people, but it cannot reasonably be considered intellectual exposition." *Id.* at 873, 876.

47. According to latest college handbooks, the tab for four years at Harvard runs approximately $94,000, including annual tuition of $17,674 and annual room and board charges of $5,840. Peterson's Index to Four-Year Colleges 1994 at 522 (24th ed. 1993).

48. Daniel C. Levy, *Private Choice and Public Policy in Nonprofit Education*, *in* PRIVATE EDUCATION: STUDIES IN CHOICE AND PUBLIC POLICY 18 (Daniel C. Levy ed., 1986).

49. NATIONAL CENTER FOR EDUCATION STATISTICS, CURRENT FUND REVENUES AND EXPENDITURES OF INSTITUTIONS OF HIGHER EDUCATIONS: FISCAL YEARS 1982–1990 at 14, Table 7 (1992) (38.9% from tuition and fees; 22.9% from sales and services). *See also*, HODGKINSON ET AL., NONPROFIT ALMANAC, *supra* note 23, at 167, Table 4.13 (about 62% of total revenues of educational sector constituted "program revenue").

50. LESTER A. SALAMON, AMERICA'S NONPROFIT SECTOR: A PRIMER 77 (1992).

51. *See* Mark Bendict, Jr., *Education as a Three Sector Industry, in* BURTON A. WEISBROD, THE VOLUNTARY NONPROFIT SECTOR 101, 110, 129 (1977) (tables showing size of for-profit sector in comparison to government and nonprofit sector); Levy, *supra* note 48, at 6–8.

52. Kentucky Bar Foundation, Inc. v. Comm'r, 78 T.C. 921 (1982) (continuing legal education); Rev. Rul. 74-16, 1974-1 C.B. 126 (managing credit unions); Rev. Rul. 68-504, 1968-2 C.B. 211 (banking); Rev. Rul. 65-298, 1965-2 C.B. 163 (update seminars for physicians). *See* HOPKINS, *supra* note 5, at 183.

53. *E.g.*, Daniel Shaviro, *From Big Mama Rag to National Geographic: The Controversy Regarding Exemptions for Educational Publications*, 41 TAX L. REV. 693, 736 (1986) (full and fair exposition text "ideologically biased"; should be replaced with neutral standards judging educational content); Thompson, *supra* note 35, at 487 (criticizing both the full and fair exposition and methodology test as unadministrable, leaving too much discretion in IRS and unnecessary; advocating exemption for all propaganda organizations unless they advocate illegal activities); Comment, *Tax Exemptions for Educational Institutions: Discretion and Discrimination*, 128 U. PA. L. REV. 849 (1980) (full and fair exposition test invites "unfair administration").

54. *See* Shaviro, *supra* note 53, at 729 n. 181; Thompson, *supra* note 35, at 511–32.

55. Thompson, *supra* note 35, at 511–12.

56. *Id.* at 519–24.

57. *See id.* at 514–16. Education scholars, in fact, have noted that one of the primary reasons for the existence of private schools is parental disenchantment with the values or educational methods used in public schools. *See* Donald A. Erikson, *Choice in Private Schools: Dynamics of Supply and Demand, in* PRIVATE EDUCATION: STUDIES IN CHOICE AND PUBLIC POLICY, *supra* note 48, at 82, 86–92 (describing Catholic, Fundamentalist and Jewish private elementary schools); Mary-Michelle Upson Hirschoff, *Public Policy Toward Private Schools: A Focus on Parental Choice, in id.* 33, 33–35 (parental choice in education is a fundamental goal of mixed educational system). In a sense, therefore, traditional private schools have existed precisely because of parental desires to indoctrinate their children with specific viewpoints.

58. *See* Thompson, *supra* note 35, at 524–532. One Treasury Department's General Counsel's Memorandum actually went so far as to state that the IRS had a "legitimate" concern that the activities of certain organizations advocating homosexual rights could harm society by encouraging or facilitating homosexual practices. GCM 37173 (June 21, 1977).

59. *E.g.*, Rob Atkinson, *Altruism in Nonprofit Organizations*, 31 B.C.L. REV. 501, 539–40 (1990) (discussing donations to higher education institutions as a form of altruism); Boris I. Bittker & George K. Rahdert, *The Exemption of Nonprofit Organizations from Federal Income Taxation*, 85 YALE L.J. 299, 333–35 (1976) (educational institutions are "public service" organizations that receive significant donations); Henry B. Hansmann, *The Role of Nonprofit Enterprise*, 89 YALE L.J.

835, 860 (1980) ("Institutions of higher education commonly depend heavily on voluntary private contributions . . . ").

60. Hansmann, *supra* note 59, at 860–61.

61. COUNCIL FOR AID TO EDUCATION, VOLUNTARY SUPPORT OF EDUCATION 1987–88 at 12, Table 10 (1989).

62. COUNCIL FOR AID TO EDUCATION, VOLUNTARY SUPPORT OF EDUCATION 1985–86, 1986–87, 1987–88 (1987, 1988, 1989 respectively). The data in these reports is extensively summarized and set in tabular form in John D. Colombo, *Why is Harvard Tax-Exempt? (And Other Mysteries of Tax Exemption for Private Educational Institutions)*, 35 ARIZ. L. REV. 841, 889–903 (1993).

63. The tuition and government grant percentages are based on 1988 data only. Samuel F. Barbett et al., STATE HIGHER EDUCATION PROFILES FOURTH EDITION 17, Table 5 (1992). Barbett lists private donations as accounting for only approximately 12.7% of education and general (E&G) revenues; the discrepancy between this number and that reported in the text is due to the fact that the Barbett report does not take into account donations to endowment or other capital funds, which we would include in the donative base for purposes of the donative theory of exemption.

64. The categorization of colleges and universities in this study was based upon the Carnegie Foundation for the Advancement of Teaching's college classifications. COUNCIL FOR AID TO EDUCATION, *supra* note 61, at 5. The "Research/Doctoral" group in the study combined Carnegie classifications Research I, Research II, Doctoral Granting I and Doctoral Granting II. The "Comprehensive" group included four-year institutions offering bachelor's degrees, at least half of which were granted in professional or occupational fields. The "Liberal Arts" classification consisted primarily of undergraduate colleges that award more than half their degrees in the arts and sciences fields. A complete listing of the surveyed institutions is included at *id.* at 16–58.

65. Colombo, *supra* note 62, at 903, Table 5.

66. The differences between the liberal arts colleges and the general comprehensive institutions can be accounted for by the simple fact that the liberal arts category contains prominent colleges such as Amherst, Bowdoin, Mount Holyoke, Radcliffe, Smith, Swarthmore, Vassar, Wellesley and Williams that have more established, and wealthier, alumni. *See* Roger L. Geiger, *Finance and Function: Voluntary Support and Diversity in American Private Higher Education, in* PRIVATE EDUCATION: STUDIES IN CHOICE AND PUBLIC POLICY, *supra* note 48, at 214, 226–229. These institutions tend to also have much higher expenditures than their counterparts, and hence private market failure (in this case, the inability to charge tuition that would fully cover the educational costs) places a greater economic demand on these institutions than the comprehensive institutions. In 1988, for example, these colleges accounted for total E&G expenditures of $396 million, 9% of the total expenditures of the liberal arts group, even though they are only 3% of the number of institutions in the sample. COUNCIL FOR AID TO EDUCATION, *supra* note 61, at 35–48. Their overall donative percentage for this year, not including

donated labor or adjustments for government grants, was 32% (donations of $126.5 million and estimated revenues of $396 million).

67. The data in this and succeeding paragraphs is taken from COUNCIL FOR AID TO EDUCATION, *supra* note 62. A tabular summary of the data relevant to this paragraph is available in Colombo, *supra* note 62, at 889, Table 1.

68. Colombo, *supra* note 62, at 893, Table 3.

69. *Id.* at 897, Table 4.

70. *Id.* at 903, Table 5.

71. VIRGINIA A. HODGKINSON & MURRAY S. WEITZMAN, DIMENSIONS OF THE INDEPENDENT SECTOR: A STATISTICAL PROFILE 169, Table 7.6 (1989). The estimate in the text was derived by taking the full-time equivalent employees reported in Hodgkinson & Weitzman for the educational sector, multiplying this number by 1700 hours per volunteer, and multiplying this result by $10.06, the hourly wage figure used by Hodgkinson & Weitzman to value donated labor. We disregarded the value of labor donated for fundraising purposes, since as we explain in Chapter 11, we would subtract the cost of fundraising from the donative base.

72. FRANK W. BREDEWEG, UNITED STATES CATHOLIC ELEMENTARY SCHOOLS AND THEIR FINANCES 1988, at 10, Table 6 (1988) (showing tuition and fees accounting for 45.3% of total revenues for Catholic elementary schools); DANIEL J. SULLIVAN, PUBLIC AID TO NONPUBLIC SCHOOLS 24 (1974) (tuition and fees account for 28.3% of Lutheran school revenues).

73. BREDEWEG, *supra* note 72, at 10.

74. SULLIVAN, *supra* note 72, at *id.* (summarizing in a table statistics taking from 1971–73 surveys of Lutheran schools).

75. COUNCIL FOR AID TO EDUCATION, VOLUNTARY SUPPORT OF EDUCATION 1986–87 at 86 (1988) and COUNCIL FOR AID TO EDUCATION, VOLUNTARY SUPPORT OF EDUCATION 1987–88 at 88 (1989). As with the tables above, the revenue numbers were estimated by taking the reported education and general expenditures for the period (amounting to $5.221 billion) and multiplying this figure by a factor of 1.02. This factor was derived from data reported by the National Association of Independent Schools, showing that in 1988, independent primary and secondary schools spent about 98% of their operating revenues. NATIONAL ASSOCIATION OF INDEPENDENT SCHOOLS, NAIS STATISTICS 1989–90, at 37, Table 26 (1990).

76. To arrive at this number, we took the estimated number of full-time equivalents for the educational sector as a whole as reported in HODGKINSON & WEITZMAN, *supra* note 71, at 169, Table 7.6, multiplied this number by 1700 hours per full time equivalent, and then multiplied this result by $10.06, the wage rate used by Hodgkinson & Weitzman to value labor. We disregarded labor value attributable to religious institutions or to fundraising. The resulting number was $4.6 billion (obtained by multiplying the 271,000 number in column five of Table 7.6 by 1700 and then by $10.06). Since this was a 1987 figure, the midpoint of our three-year data base, we multiplied the 4.6 billion number by 3 to obtain a donated labor estimate for the three-year period under review. We then apportioned this number to the private primary/secondary school sector based upon the ratio of cash

donations to these institutions to cash donations to the educational sector as a whole as reported by Hodgkinson & Weitzman at Table 8.1.

This methodology obviously assumes that donated labor will "track" cash and property donations. There is some indirect evidence that supports this proposition. Data on giving and volunteering habits, for example, show that those people who give more cash or property also donate more labor. HODGKINSON & WEITZMAN, *supra*, at 19, 37. One would assume that those inclined to donate their time would do so to those institutions to which they give money. Also, the amount of donated labor to each subsector of nonprofit activity appears to roughly correlate to donations. In 1987, for example, religious institutions accounted for roughly 49% of total donations to private nonprofit organizations and also accounted for 40% of the total donated labor. Education accounted for 9% of total donations and 9% of the donated labor; arts and cultural organizations accounted for 7% of total donations and 5% of total donated labor. *Id.* at 169, Table 7.6 and 177, Table 8.1.

77. HODGKINSON ET AL., NONPROFIT ALMANAC, *supra* note 23, at 147, Table 4.2.

78. This is not to minimize the government's role in providing direct government subsidies for cultural organizations, such as the National Endowment for the Arts.

79. While IRS Form 990 collects data on contributions and revenues, the IRS does not code these forms for the type of institution reporting. Thus while IRS 990 data can be used to get an overview of the finances of nonprofit organizations, categorical information does not exist. Telephone conversation with Ms. Cecilia Hilgert, IRS Statitics of Income Office, July 21, 1993.

80. Big Mama Rag, Inc. v. United States, 631 F.2d 1030, 1032 (D.C. Cir. 1980).

81. For example, a recent mailing to one of the authors by the Practising Law Institute, "a nonprofit organization," advertised seminars on tax strategies for corporate acquisitions, dispositions, spin-offs and corporate financing techniques. These seminars are to be held in the Waldorf-Astoria hotel in New York City and the Bel Age hotel in Los Angeles. One can participate for only $950 (not including, of course, hotel accommodations). We do not see advertised in this mailing anything like a subsidized dues program for corporate tax lawyers too poor to afford the fee.

82. *See also*, James Bennett & Gabriel Rudney, *A Commerciality Test to Resolve the Commercial Nonprofit Issue*, 36 TAX NOTES 1095 (1987) (proposing taxing receipts of any sale of product or service unless (1) more than 50% of the cost of production is financed by gifts or grants as opposed to sales receipts or investment income, and (2) the subsidized product is "directed at a specific recipient group or purpose deemed charitable.").

83. This does not eliminate the restriction on legislative lobbying, however, which is not aimed at gaining wider general circulation for a viewpoint, but rather at negating government failure. *See* Chapter 10, *supra*, at 173–75.

84. Treas. Reg. 1.501(c)(3)-1(d)(5).

85. Treas. Reg. 1.501(c)(3)-1(d)(5)(iii). *See generally*, Julie Noel Gilbert, *Research, Technology Transfers and the Unrelated Business Income Tax*, 9 EXEMPT ORG. TAX REV. 1277 (1994).

86. Rev. Rul. 68-373, 1968-2 C.B. 206 (drug testing not exempt); PLR 9316052 (Jan. 29, 1993) (approving biotechnology product research).

87. HODGKINSON ET AL., NONPROFIT ALMANAC, *supra* note 23, at 100, Table 2.38.

88. OFFICE OF MANAGEMENT AND BUDGET, SPECIAL ANALYSES FOR FISCAL YEAR 1990 at J-1 (1990).

89. Note that our test requires a tracing of donations to the ultimate source, so that the numerosity test could not be met simply by a single or a few firms dispersing gifts through many nominal donors.

90. Mark A. Hall & John D. Colombo, *The Charitable Status of Nonprofit Hospitals: Toward a Donative Theory of Tax Exemption*, 66 WASH L. REV. 307, 323–24 (1990).

91. *See, e.g.*, Board of Review v. Provident Hosp. & Training School Ass'n, 233 Ill. 243, 84 N.E. 216, 217 (1908); Sisters of Third Order of St. Francis v. Board of Review, 231 Ill. 317, 83 N.E. 272, 273 (1907).

92. The history of the hospital industry is recounted in a number of sources, including CHARLES E. ROSENBERG, THE CARE OF STRANGERS (1987); PAUL STARR, THE SOCIAL TRANSFORMATION OF AMERICAN MEDICINE 146–76, 430–38 (1982); ROSEMARY STEVENS, IN SICKNESS AND IN WEALTH: AMERICAN HOSPITALS IN THE TWENTIETH CENTURY (1989).

93. Donald Light, *Corporate Medicine for Profit*, SCI. AM., Dec. 1986, at 38, 42; Stanley Jones et al., *Competition or Conscience? Mixed-Mission Dilemmas of the Voluntary Hospital*, 24 Inquiry 110, 113 (1987).

94. The following sources extensively discuss the history of the IRS rulings and their relationship to the history of the nonprofit hospital sector: Robert S. Bromberg, *Financing Health Care and the Effect of the Tax Law*, 39 LAW & CONTEMP. PROBS. 156 (1975); Robert S. Bromberg, *The Charitable Hospital*, 20 CATH. U.L. REV. 237 (1970); John D. Colombo, *Are Associations of Doctors Tax-Exempt? Analyzing Inconsistencies in the Tax Exemption of Health Care Providers*, 9 VA. TAX REV. 469, 473–82 (1990); Douglas M. Mancino, *Income Tax Exemption of the Contemporary Nonprofit Hospital*, 32 ST. LOUIS U.L.J. 1015 (1988).

95. Rev. Rul. 56-185, 1956-1 C.B. 202, 203. *See generally* Colombo, *supra* note 94.

96. *Tax Reform, 1969: Hearings Before the Committee on Ways and Means*, 91st Cong., 1st Sess. 1427 (1969) (statement of Julius M. Griesman, attorney, AHA). *See* ANNE R. SOMERS, HOSPITAL REGULATION: THE DILEMMA OF PUBLIC POLICY 41 (1969) ("Thanks to Medicare, Medicaid, and numerous other public and private mechanisms for financing care for the indigent and medically indigent, in a few years free hospital care will approach the vanishing point."); Comment, *Federal Income Tax Exemption For Private Hospitals*, 36 FORDHAM L. REV. 747, 764 (1968) ("[P]ublic programs for mandatory hospitalization insurance, as well as the

ever increasing coverage of private insurance plans, threaten to leave hospitals without patients who require free or below-cost care.").

97. 1969-2 C.B. 117.

98. Rev. Rul. 83-157, 1983-2 C.B. 94. For a more detailed discussion of the 1956, 1969, and 1983 rulings, see the sources listed in note 94, *supra*.

99. 506 F.2d 1278 (1974), *vacated on other grounds*, 426 U.S. 26 (1976).

100. *Eastern Kentucky*, 506 F.2d at 1288–89. *See also* Medical Center Hosp. v. City of Burlington, 152 Vt. 611, 566 A.2d 1352, 1356 (Vt. 1989) ("[W]e do not believe that we are . . . required to ignore the immense sociological and economic changes that have taken place in the health care profession . . . ."); SHARE v. Commissioner of Revenue, 363 N.W.2d 47, 52 (Minn. 1985) ("[M]ajor changes in the area of health care . . . have necessitated changes as well in definitional predicates . . . ."). *Cf.* Utah County v. Intermountain Health Care, Inc., 709 P.2d 265 (Utah 1985) (changes in health care result in revoking charitable status).

101. *Eastern Kentucky*, 506 F.2d at 1288.

102. This unanalytic, question-begging approach characterizes much of the argument in favor of granting the exemption to hospitals. *See* Phelon S. Rammel & Robert S. Parsons, *Utah County & Intermountain Health Care: Utah's Unique Method for Determining Charitable Property Tax Exemption—A Review of its Mandate and Impact*, 22 J. HEALTH & HOSP. L. 73, 77 (1989) (arguing for revised definition of charity because "the *Utah County* court has articulated a standard for which compliance [by hospitals] is virtually impossible"); Mancino, *supra* note 94, at 1019–20 (maintaining that definition of charity must change to keep up with changes in hospital industry).

103. Utah County v. Intermountain Health Care, Inc., 709 P.2d 265, 274 (Utah 1985). *See also* David Hyman, *The Conundrum of Charitability: Reassessing Tax Exemption for Hospitals*, 16 AM. J. L. & MED. 327, 379–80 (1990) ("The right question to ask is whether the exemption itself makes sense, and not whether the old beliefs about exemption are anachronistic.").

104. Health Security Act §7601, H.R. 3600, 103d Cong. 1st Sess. (1993). This would have enacted the proposals of David Seay, with the United Hospital Fund. *See* J. David Seay, *Tax Exemption for Hospitals: Towards an Understanding of Community Benefit*, 2 HEALTH MATRIX 35, 45–48 (1992); J. David Seay & Robert M. Sigmund, *Community Benefit Standards for Hospitals: Perceptions and Performance*, FRONTIERS HEALTH SERVICES MGMT., Spr. 1989, at 3; J. David Seay & Bruce Vladeck, *Mission Matters, in* IN SICKNESS AND IN HEALTH: THE MISSION OF VOLUNTARY HEALTH CARE INSTITUTIONS 1 (1988).

105. *E.g.*, Geisinger Health Plan v. Comm'r, 985 F.2d 1210 (3d Cir. 1993) (HMO exemption denied); Federation Pharmacy Services v. Comm'r, 625 F.2d 804 (8th Cir. 1980) (nonprofit pharmacy exemption denied); University of Mass. Medical School Group Practice v. Comm'r, 74 T.C. 1299 (1980) (exemption for group practice of doctors associated with medical school upheld); Sound Health Ass'n v. Comm'r, 71 T.C. 158 (1978) (HMO claim of exemption upheld); Rev. Rul. 72-124, 1972-1 C.B. 145 (nursing home must offer services at "lowest feasible

cost" and maintain in residence anyone who becomes unable to pay in order to be exempt).

106. Federation Pharmacy Services v. Comm'r, 625 F.2d 804 (8th Cir. 1980) (nonprofit pharmacy selling prescription drugs at cost to elderly and handicapped not exempt); Rev. Rul. 85-110, 1985-2 C.B. 166 (laboratory testing and pharmaceutical sales subject to UBIT).

107. Geisinger Health Plan v. Comm'r, 985 F.2d 1210 (3d Cir. 1993).

108. For a summary of current IRS practice with respect to HMO exemption, see Philip S. Neal & Suzanne M. Papiewski, *Taxation of HMOs Now and Under Health Care Reform—Separating Fact From Fiction*, 9 EXEMPT ORG. TAX REV. 577 (1994).

109. BURTON A. WEISBROD, THE VOLUNTARY NONPROFIT SECTOR 3, 80–81, 93–98 (1977).

110. Hall & Colombo, *supra* note 90 at 406, n. 350 and sources cited therein.

111. J. ROGERS HOLLINGSWORTH & ELLEN J. HOLLINGSWORTH, CONTROVERSY ABOUT AMERICAN HOSPITALS: FUNDING, OWNERSHIP AND PERFORMANCE 29 (1987) (in 1904, voluntary hospitals received 36% of revenues from gifts); *id.* at 92 ("During the late 1920s almost three-quarters of capital for hospital construction came from philanthropy . . . .").

112. David Rosner, *Heterogeneity and Uniformity: Historical Perspectives on the Voluntary Hospital, in* IN SICKNESS AND IN HEALTH: THE MISSION OF VOLUNTARY HEALTH CARE INSTITUTIONS 87, 93 (1988). Strong confirmation of the role of religious and ethnic ideology and the influence of societal heterogeneity on the pattern of hospital development comes from a cross-national study that found that "in all countries with one prevalent religion, hospitals were run by the government, . . . but where competition existed among religious groups, they retained control of hospitals to protect and extend their sphere of influence." STARR, *supra* note 92, at 176.

113. STARR, *supra* note 92, at 169–70, 173; Robert C. Clark, *Does the Nonprofit Form Fit the Hospital Industry*, 93 Harv. L. Rev. 1417, 1458 (1980).

114. HOLLINGSWORTH & HOLLINGSWORTH, *supra* note 111, at 5–6, 24–25, 37.

115. DONALD R. COHODES & BRIAN M. KINKEAD, HOSPITAL CAPITAL FORMATION IN THE 1980s 23 (1984). *See generally* Joseph V. Terenzio, *A Survey of the History and Current Outlook of Philanthropy as a Source of Capital for the Needs of the Health Care Field, in* HEALTH CARE CAPITAL: COMPETITION AND CONTROL 238 (Gordon H. McLeod & Mark Perlman eds., 1978).

116. HOLLINGSWORTH & HOLLINGSWORTH, *supra* note 111, at 37.

117. GERARD ANDERSON ET AL., PROVIDING HOSPITAL SERVICES: THE CHANGING FINANCIAL ENVIORNOMENT 147–48 (1989) ("[B]y 1985, philanthropy represented less than 1.3 percent of funds used for hospital care . . . ."); INSTITUTE OF MEDICINE, FOR PROFIT ENTERPRISE IN HEALTH CARE 100, Table 5.2 (Bradford H. Gray ed., 1986) (in 1983, nonprofit hospitals received 0.4% of revenues from contributions—$370.9 million in all); Regina Herzlinger & William Krasker, *Who Profits from Nonprofits?* 65 HARV. BUS. REV. 93, 95 (1987) (donations amounted

to only 1% of total hospital expenses in 1983, from a selected sample of nonprofit chain hospitals); *Unrelated Business Income Tax: Hearings Before the Subcomm. on Oversight of the House Comm. on Ways and Means*, 100th Cong., 1st Sess. 183 (statement of Marion R. Fremont-Smith, Independent Sector) (2% of 1982 hospital revenue came from private contributions); *id.* at 996 (statement of Bradford H. Gray, Institute of Medicine) ("Charitable contributions used to be an important source of funds for hospitals, but they have now declined to less than one-half of 1 percent of hospital revenues . . . .").

118. *See* FRANK SLOAN ET AL., THE DEMISE OF HOSPITAL PHILANTHROPY (1989) (developing and documenting this "crowding out" thesis). See also the discussion in Chapter 7, *supra*, at 99–100.

119. Rosner, *supra* note 112, at 122.

120. *See* Richard W. Foster, *Hospitals and the Choice of Organizational Form*, 3 FIN. ACCOUNTABILITY & MGMT. 343, 351, Table 1 (1987).

121. The 1983 reform of the Medicare payment system for hospitals (known as the "DRG" reimbursement system, for "diagnosis-related groups") might greatly facilitate such an accounting process because it forms the basis for measuring precise revenues and costs on a service-specific basis. Bruce Vladeck, *Medicare Hospital Payment by Diagnosis-Related Groups*, 100 ANN. INT. MED. 576 (1984). Thus, a hospital might be able to exempt a portion of its patient care revenue by demonstrating that it receives substantial donative support for a burn unit and a neonatal intensive care unit, without having to separately incorporate these integral parts of its operation.

Index

About the Book and Authors

The tradition of tax-exempt status for nonprofit "charitable" organizations is well established, and few would argue with the principle. But the tax-exempt sector of the economy is vast and rapidly growing, resulting in the loss of billions of dollars of tax revenue. At the same time, we have no consensus on what purpose the charitable tax exemption serves, let alone agreement on what constitutes a charity.

In this important addition to the theory of tax law, Colombo and Hall develop an original "donative" theory that links the charitable tax exemption to the ability of an organization to derive donative support from the community. Their theory not only makes intuitive sense but also receives support from economic, political, and moral theory. Its implications would rationalize the charitable tax exemption, comport with legal precedent, and simplify the administration of the law.

The Charitable Tax Exemption is a major contribution to the theory of tax law and should be essential reading for a wide range of lawyers dealing with taxes. It will also be enlightening for anyone involved in the operation of a nonprofit organization.

John D. Colombo is professor of law at the University of Illinois at Champaign. He specializes in tax law and has written widely on tax exemption. **Mark A. Hall** is professor of law and public health at Wake Forest University. He has published many books and articles on the law and public policy of health care organizations.